MASTERS OF THEIR

CRAFT

TRADITION AND INNOVATION
IN THE AUSTRALIAN CONTEMPORARY DECORATIVE ARTS

MASTERS OF THEIR
CRAFT

TRADITION AND INNOVATION
IN THE AUSTRALIAN CONTEMPORARY DECORATIVE ARTS

NORIS IOANNOU

CRAFTSMAN HOUSE
G+B ARTS INTERNATIONAL

to Robert Lyons

Distributed in Australia by Craftsman House,
Tower A, 112 Talavera Road,
North Ryde, Sydney, NSW 2113
in association with G+B Arts International:
Australia, Canada, China, France, Germany, India,
Japan, Luxembourg, Malaysia, The Netherlands,
Russia, Singapore, Switzerland, United Kingdom,
United States of America

Cataloguing-in-publication data National Library of
Australia: Masters of Their Craft: Tradition and Innovation
in the Australian Contemporary Decorative Arts

Bibliography.
Includes index.
ISBN 90 5703 28 13

Noris Ioannou, 1947–

1. Decorative arts — Australia — late 20th century.
2. Decorative arts — History. 3. Crafts — Australia —
late 20th century.

Design   Craig Peterson
Printer   Kyodo Printing Co., Singapore

PLATE 1 (frontispiece)
Stephen Bowers (b. 1952)
Decorated Vase, 1994
Underglaze decoration, on-glaze lustres, Ht: 65 cm
(In collaboration with Mark Heidenreich)
Photo: Michal Kluvanek

CONTENTS

Eve and Adam

PREFACE:
THE ESPRIT OF CRAFT

This book had its genesis in early 1995 when, immediately after the launch of one of my earlier books *Australian Studio Glass*, a friend suggested that it was time I surveyed and wrote on the full gamut of the contemporary crafts. I readily agreed, perhaps a little too hastily, and a subsequent letter to my publisher received the immediate response to go ahead. It was not until June that I could begin any sustained work on the project which began immediately after a visit to Melbourne to attend the Second National Crafts Conference. This was timely in so far as it gave me the opportunity to run the idea of the book past practitioners, lecturers, curators and other professionals associated with the crafts, hence providing valuable feedback.

While the idea of the project was seen as exciting and worthy by all I spoke to, some considered the hierarchical and patriarchal connotations in the title *Masters of Their Craft*, as somewhat problematic. Certainly, from the perspective of the current post-modernist era's ethos of deconstruction and anything goes, modernism's underlying principle of mastery, that is, a defined vision of order and control, would suggest the use of such a title as a retrograde step. But if post-modernism offers an alternative view of the world as a collection of fragments and episodes, this book could be considered one of the many shards that go to make up the 'total' picture.

Certainly, I and my publisher saw no reason to jettison a word which has always been inextricably linked with craft. I emphasise that the present title utilises 'masters' in a neutral manner, one which evokes the outstanding skills, sensitivity, understanding, knowledge and technical control necessary to creating exceptional forms or images from any medium. From this point of view, mastery in a chosen field is a term which may be applied broadly: to those practitioners who are well-established, or to those who are mid-career or even newly-emerged, for surely, all are constantly striving for a particular level of achievement in their lifelong journey in the crafts.

Another area of concern was the fact that the term 'craft' in the late 1990s is still not used consistently — even within the fraternity of practitioners, educators, critics, students and curators. In addition, because of the overlap between professional and amateur craft activity, and because the wider public is still relatively ignorant of the development of the professional crafts since the 1960s, the term 'decorative arts' was selected for the subtitle. However, craft is craft, whether we prefix it with 'professional' or not, and it is defined in this book as a set of related though diverse

PLATE 2 (opposite)
Pat Davidson (b. 1950)
Eve and Adam, 1992
Dyed calico, white lawn,
commercial threads,
machine-stitched image (after Dürer),
appliqué stitched caption
50 x 36 cm
Photo: Michael Van Ewijk
(see also Plate 105)

practices which reaffirm tradition-based handskills and techniques, yet embrace new technologies and tools; focus on particular categories of materials, yet are responsive to new media; result in functional and/or decorative or expressive items; retain an awareness of the traditional and historical, yet pursue the innovative; and always, celebrate the creativity of the individual.

This text also aims to highlight the traditional aspects and values of fine crafting, that is, skills, medium-specificity, process, ornament, ritual, expression and function. Yet, on the other hand, the broadening of craft practices in the past three decades has gone hand-in-hand with the embracement of the visual arts, resulting in much innovative work which combines skill with individual expression, idea or meaning. Similarly, folk and outsider art practices, where ingenuity and materials recycling play a prominent role, and which are increasingly coming to influence contemporary craft, suggest a reassessment of the priority which we tend to give to the preceding values. In addition, the use of computers, lasers, new materials and other hi-tech applications and processes, are important aspects of craft practice which must also be accommodated in any such survey.

A word or two is necessary concerning the manner in which the selection of practitioners represented in this book was made, as it is inevitable that this will raise a few eyebrows. Quite simply it would have been impossible to satisfy all suggestions or points of view, given the ambit of such a text, in the same way that it has not been possible to include all craft practitioners of note working today. This point alone could have stopped the project dead in its tracks: there were even a number of people who considered that the process of selection was simply too daunting to tackle! I did not think so, and I applied my eighteen years of observation and experience in the world of craft in the matter of this choice and in the writing of the book.

Let me indulge briefly in sketching out this background as it strongly informed my approach. My active interest in craft began in 1971 with four years in London and on the Continent where I had the opportunity to view collections and exhibitions of historic and contemporary decorative arts. Back in Adelaide, and after a spell of teaching, I turned to full-time research and, to date, have written four books (not including this text) on the historic and contemporary decorative and applied arts in Australia, specifically in the fields of ceramics, glass and furniture. I have also acted as an editor for an anthology of craft, and, for seven years, have been the crafts critic and features writer for the South Australian daily paper, the *Adelaide Advertiser*. Over this time I observed and critically reviewed over two hundred exhibitions, a large proportion of which were travelling shows from interstate. In 1993 I returned to Europe to study the latest developments in the contemporary crafts, and in 1995, I attended and participated in a major contemporary studio glass seminar at the Creative Glass Center of America. A 1996 Churchill Fellowship which involved a study tour of North American folk art and contemporary craft, further influenced my outlook. Finally, I have written numerous articles on the contemporary crafts in Australia, judged craft awards, and have attended and spoken at craft conferences here and overseas.

In other words, my own life journey has very much been one in the crafts and it is this background which informed my selection of practitioners. Although my exhibition reviews and magazine articles on contemporary craft constitute a regular activity, my predominant work continues to be original research and writing in the field of historical Australian material culture. I have found it useful to shuttle between historical and contemporary crafts as the former provide models of crafting as a useful touchstone for the interpretation of contemporary practice — whereas the latter can provide the kind of experiential insight for understanding the past. This is the approach I have used in writing this text which, I hope, has succeeded in throwing further light on contemporary craft, its trends and directions, as well as on its historical origins and contemporary settings.

In writing the present text, I had both practitioners and a more general readership in mind, hence my decision to depart from the academic style of my past books to opt for a freer, more journalistic approach. If some readers bemoan the fact that footnotes are not included, they may turn to my previous texts which form the basis of the contextual material in this book. The descriptions, evaluation and analysis of the works in this text are based entirely on my experience and personal responses to the material.

Given this background and approach, my choice has been based on a number of criteria: for both mature and emergent practitioners, the key indicators included both traditional and skilful approaches to the manipulation of the medium, combined with a demonstrated ability to extend the genre in a contemporary context. I also took note of my personal responses to particular works — I did not feel that I had to necessarily like the works (although I mostly did), more cogently, there had to be an emotional or intellectual response, a resonance of some kind. I also aimed to achieve a selection which could be considered to be representative of the variety and diversity of approaches and forms to be found in contemporary Australian craft, and therefore I was mindful to cast my net as widely as possible, without entirely losing sight of the 'centre'.

I had in my mind the idea of providing a 'snapshot' of current craft practices, not only with some focus on those practitioners who are considered to have attained a level of mastery through long experience, but also including others who have revealed attributes of mastery, as well as initiative and a willingness to explore and push processes and boundaries. Practitioners were therefore first selected on the basis of their leadership and achievements in their various fields to comprise a core of established, mature masters. Added to these is a selection of mid-career and younger, more recent practitioners, who are opening up new directions of investigation, finding alternative ways of treating traditional materials and, generally, who demonstrate sensitivity and inventiveness in their medium.

A total of some one hundred and fifty-two practitioners working in the five principal craft media of wood, glass, clay, fibre and metal have been selected on the basis of craftsmanship and sensitivity to traditional materials, concern for function and ornament, as well as generally the ability to apply skills in effecting what often appears to be an alchemical transformation of medium, embodying aspects of the functional, aesthetic, conceptual or metaphorical.

For those interested in a statistical breakdown, the book illustrates the work of some thirty-four ceramists and potters, thirty-one glass artists, thirty-one fibre and textile artists, thirty jewellers and metal workers, and twenty-six furniture makers, turners and other wood-craft practitioners. This distribution approximates the overall level of activity within each medium, while the state-by-state breakdown is roughly proportional to population levels — although this was not an overriding concern. Anyone scanning the biographical listing will, however, note a strong multicultural diversity which also resulted inadvertently and which, I believe, reflects something of Australia's ethnic diversity. On another note, although I sought to achieve a strong Aboriginal representation in the various media categories, this proved difficult to achieve, despite prolonged approaches to various groups and national organisations.

The first chapter examines the origins of the crafts, their pre-industrial role and how they are perceived today, sketching out the range of approaches to contemporary making in the craft mode. Because my emphasis is on creativity within the conventional craft media — indeed, the intimate directness of the maker's relationship to the material — the remainder of the text has been structured accordingly. Five further chapters therefore introduce and elaborate on each of the craft media: on their primary characteristics; their historical and cultural associations; the traditional and innovative technologies applied to explore form, function and meaning; the trends and issues central to each; and their long-term and more recent masters, their skills, ideas and work.

My decision to simply order the text and group illustrations according to medium, rather than say on concept-based themes or interpretive categories, may seem modernist influenced. However, media-based categories still dominate craft writing and form the starting point for the curation of the majority of exhibitions in Australia. On the other hand, an ordering through a post-modernist jumble of images based on, for example, the craft object as function, as statement, as personal adornment, as personal allegory or as narrative, may certainly seem valid in the sense that this approach highlights practitioner intent and the kinds of different practices craft encompasses but, on the other hand, it has the tendency to diminish the very qualities that differentiate craft from other visual arts practices. My preference has been to see craft as a vital contemporary cultural practice, and highlight its *esprit*, namely the enthusiasm which craft practitioners bring to their creative work; they master its idiosyncrasies and secrets in order to coax out the essential qualities of each medium, creating artefacts which may be useful and decorative, which are expressive of a personal vision, which tell stories or comment on a universal truth, or are simply objects of allure.

Desiring to champion the craftsmanship of each practitioner, my interest has focused on divulging something of their inspiration and philosophy, describing individual approaches to design and materials manipulation, and revealing something of the interplay and influences of perennial sources: the latter can be as diverse as contemporary art, the primitive, folk and popular culture, memory, gender, architecture, feminism, literature, multi-media communications, and any of a number of current social concerns.

In approaching this presentation I have quoted statements provided by the practitioners themselves and, although these are sometimes ambiguous, they provide an important means of communicating intent and meaning. Indeed, I have often encountered practitioners who, when asked what their work 'means', generally state the cliché: 'It speaks for itself.' This is not so surprising given that practitioners are generally more concerned with the manipulation of the craft medium itself, rather than with the ordering of the symbolic medium of language — although the interaction of the two is also an area of exploration of some craft work.

This book champions various fundamental qualities and values manifested in and by craft: humans as creative makers; the relationship between intellect, hand and medium; the corporeal, emotional and aesthetic pleasures derived from the presence and use of the crafted artefact; its symbolic expressions or resonances; the intellectual content embodied in a work; and the pleasures of craftsmanship. But not all is in the realm of the intellectual and, above all, this book celebrates the immediate sensual appeal of the fine crafts as manifested in the late 1990s. All of the preceding may be summed up by four words often used to describe craft objects — skill and idea, tradition and innovation.

In closing, I would like to thank those who assisted me, for I received help from numerous sources in regard to recommendations for practitioners, as well as enthusiastic encouragement regarding the worthiness of the project, especially from: Beth Hatton, Gail Fairlamb, Janet Mansfield, Doreen Mellor, Jennifer Isaacs, Patsy Hely, Pip Sawyer, David Williams, Margaret West, Janet De Boer, Greg Healey, Marion Hosking, Jim Logan, Sue Rosenthal, Daniel Jenkins, Robert Foster, Maureen Cahill, Don Fortescue, Alvena Hall, Ivana Jirasek, Terry Martin, and Jill Fanning. The various state craft councils also made useful suggestions, especially the Crafts Council of South Australia; Craft Victoria; Tandanya: National Aboriginal Cultural Institute; and the Crafts Council of Western Australia. My thanks also to the Literature Advisory Committee of the Department for the Arts and Cultural Development (South Australia), for funding assistance towards the writing of the manuscript.

Finally, I would like to extend my gratitude to the one hundred and fifty-two craft practitioners represented in this book who responded most heartily with photographs and information, and whose work I commend to you, the reader.

Noris Ioannou
Adelaide, Australia

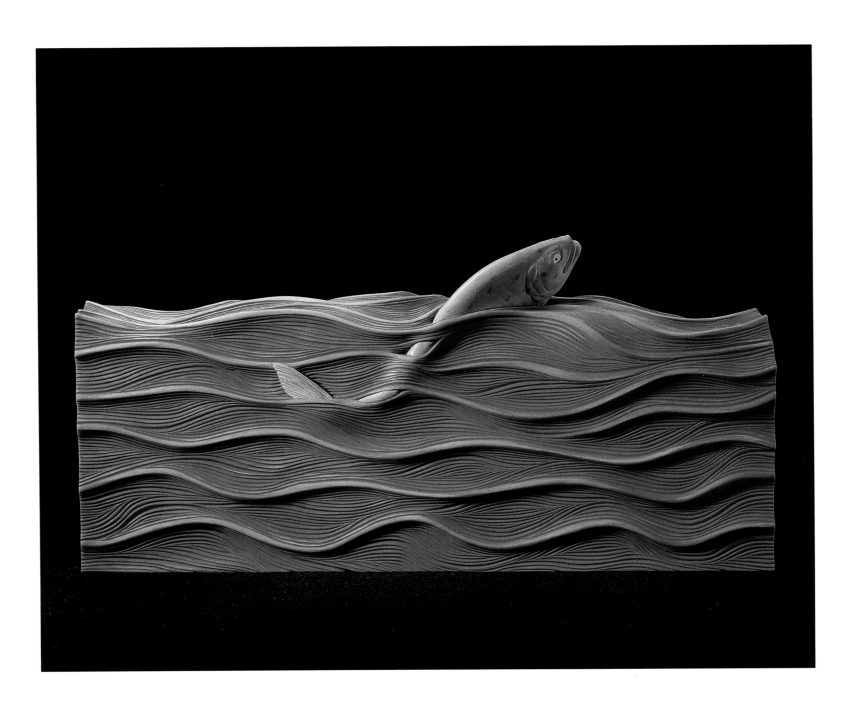

CHAPTER ONE: INTRODUCTION
A TABLEAU OF POSSIBILITIES

In the closing years of the twentieth century craft has become a personal journey of discovery, a tableau of possibilities, and a means of reaffirming enduring values. For both maker and user, the handmade realm of craft sustains the need to be creative, to construct identity and meaning, and to produce and interact with objects of beauty and usefulness.

The post-1960s professionalism and flowering of Australian craft has seen its key manifestations in pottery, ceramics, glass, jewellery, metalwork, textiles and fibrework, challenge our perceptions, delight our senses, and generally enrich our culture. In an age of relentless technological strides, the role of contemporary craft has been reassessed as a cultural activity which asserts and sustains particular values. With the end of the millennium in sight, the vitality, colour, form, sensation and metaphorically rich realm of the crafts becomes even more salient in the need to reaffirm the human element in everyday life.

And the touch of the hand is nowhere more evident than in the manual virtuosity of the finely handcrafted object: it attests to the pleasure of applying skills in the making of objects which, in turn, are useful, evocative and enriching of human life.

This book presents a survey and a celebration of the achievements and directions in the decorative and applied arts, often called the professional contemporary crafts, in Australia in the late 1990s. It exposes the works of one hundred and fifty-two professional practitioners specialising in the five traditional craft media of wood, glass, clay, fibre and metal. They include experienced craftspeople who are already recognised as leaders in their various fields, as well as mid-term and younger practitioners demonstrating verve and skill: the common denominator is that both groups are uncompromising in their efforts to express the particular essence of their craft — to 'master the medium'.

What is Craft?

Over the past two hundred years, the concept of craft has shifted and changed, but no more rapidly than in the past three decades; today, it embraces a variety of meanings and definitions. This is evident in the number of names assigned to those who practice the professional crafts: craftsworker, craftsperson, crafts practitioner, craft artist, designer-maker, medium or fibre/clay or glass artist, potter, ceramist, textile worker, art embroiderer, quilt-maker, weaver, fibre artist,

PLATE 3 (opposite)
Catherine Truman (b. 1957)
A Fish For The Fight, 1993
(Architectural Commission for South Australian Aquatic Sciences Centre)
Carved English lime wood,
Shu Niku ink, coloured pencil
15 x 49 x 6 cm
Photo: Grant Hancock
(see also Plate 158)

artist-in-wood, metalworker, metalsmith, jeweller, art blacksmith, turner, wood sculptor, and artist-in-wood, to name some of the more common appellations.

Similarly, the role or value of craft, that is, our perspective of what it means and contributes to society, has also shifted and broadened. Although industry now provides the vast proportion of our essential goods, contemporary craft activity has, paradoxically, increased in activity and still aims to provide functional items for daily life — tableware, furniture, clothing, lighting, jewellery and so on. But the professional crafts are recognised as fulfilling other roles beyond the primary intention of making useful articles; makers may choose to focus on decorative work which enriches the sensual and symbolic qualities of public and domestic settings; or they may choose to focus on making one-off objects which are primarily intended to be conceptually explorative or make personal statements, be socially or politically commentative, embody narrative, be allegorical or otherwise simply be sculptural.

The manner in which the crafting activity is pursued also varies: craft practitioners may work on their own; with a group of others sharing resources in cooperatives; or else they increasingly interface with other professionals, architects, industrialists and interior designers in a variety of approaches.

Today, the crafts are not simply something that can be defined by a narrow definition based on the functional and decorative: we require a more thoughtful, material culture perspective if we are to examine the present-day permutations of craft practice. Given its evident complexity, any exploration of the social meaning or cultural role of contemporary craft must begin by defining its cultural context and that, in turn, suggests an investigation of its historic origins. From there, having circumscribed the cornerstone characteristics of craft, it is easier to delve deeper into its core or take forays to its boundaries where we may examine its spirited divergences and shifting manifestations.

Pre-industrial, Traditional Craft

What we see as contemporary craft today is the direct result of the six thousand years or so of humanity's past. In Australia, within our relatively short history of just over two hundred years, craft has altered from its pre-industrial manifestation, to evolve through what may be conveniently distinguished as five phases, each with their own recognisable characteristics: folk or pre-industrial craft; making-do or bush traditions; the Arts and Crafts Movement; Bauhaus-Modernism; 1960s counter-culture revival; and the present phase of the contemporary crafts, sometimes referred to as post-modernism.

It was during this gradual development, essentially a series of revivals with each phase emphasising features of craft according to the social values and fashions of the period, that craft accumulated the cultural baggage which characterises and explains its present-day diversity and role.

What exactly defines craft? First, we may consider a broad perspective which sees craft as occupying a particular zone within the broad band of creative processes which result in our material culture — literally anything that is made by people. But we need to be more specific.

If we look at the pre-industrial, that is historical, appearance of craft, we are provided with a touchstone from which our present attempts at definition may emerge. In the pre-industrial past, the crafted artefact was intricately linked to individual and community identity, and to social life generally. Given the post-industrial setting of modern life we tend to overlook the once critical role craft played in providing virtually all of the articles necessary for daily life, the totality of our material culture.

The social and political upheavals of the late eighteenth and nineteenth centuries, which led to migration of people from Britain and central Europe to Australia, were in part caused by the Industrial Revolution. This in turn had led to a decline in need for traditional trades or crafts; in Australia, migrant craftsmen found an environment where they could once more flourish — that is, until the Industrial Revolution and its effects also extended to our shores.

The village-crafts economy, which once flourished in Australia during the nineteenth century, was exemplified by one of the ethnic groups which made Australia their home — the Prussian Protestants, later known as the Germans. The transfer and practice of age-old Germanic crafts in Australia in an unbroken lineage for a period of some sixty years, demonstrates how traditional craftsmen could successfully re-establish themselves in a pre-industrial, colonial setting. The critical role played by these migrant craftsmen within regions such as the Barossa Valley and elsewhere in Australia, is underscored by the community support that was clearly evident for their craftwork: cabinetmakers, potters, basket weavers, blacksmiths, masons and other craftsmen were to be found in most of the larger village settlements. They established a thriving system of craft workshops providing a range of basic requirements which allowed the village folk to be self-sufficient and relatively independent of the larger migrant British population.

Within their community, these craftsmen commanded the cultural blueprints and specialist manual skills necessary to fashion natural resources into culturally familiar forms. In the rural, pre-industrial setting of early colonisation, homes, churches, schools, agricultural implements, tools, furniture, waggons, clothing and cooking implements — the framework of a community — could not exist without the craftsman. With timber cut from the forests, and clay dug from the hills, the furniture maker and potter applied their knowledge of design and an experience of handskills formulated and honed over centuries of tradition. It was the craftsman who created the Barossa Valley's essential character, the distinctive ethnic appearance of its churches and homes, and the myriad parts that made up the domestic setting itself: the chairs and tables, the dresser and wardrobe, the linen press and blanket box; the religious and family celebratory wall embroideries and tapestries; the carved wooden kitchen implements and earthenware cooking pots — in short, its entire material culture.

Craftwork had its benefits for the individual craftsman himself: being able to reinstate himself in his original calling was important for his sense of self-esteem; and his work not only provided economic and psychological security through his role within the community, but also gave him a sense of stability through the familiarity of routine tasks, and through the ordering of materials into culturally familiar artefacts. Aside from their practical uses, these traditional crafts also had additional benefits for the community. Uprooted from their homeland and having journeyed to a distant and unfamiliar country, these people suffered the loss of their traditional supports, and faced the arduous tasks of physical, emotional and social survival in a new land. The re-establishment of their Old World communities, customs and traditions was one means by which the sense of alienation and discontinuity could be dispelled. Traditional, handcrafted objects provided familiar and tangible links with the past and, through their presence and use, engendered a sense of cultural continuity.

In pre-industrial Australia, the sustained replication of the craft artefact underlay cultural values which favoured a sense of permanence and tradition. The replication of a form with distinctive cultural traits also had the effect of highlighting and propagating its symbolic content. Time-honoured folk crafting traditions were therefore an unstated means of propagating familiar cultural forms: as such, the practice and replication of folk craft traditions in the Barossa Valley, for example, not only resulted in furnishings and other articles of necessity, but, from a wider perspective, these were also symbolic and assertive of the values of the central-European culture in which they were created and used. For settlers in a new land, their presence contributed towards a perception of cultural continuity, mitigating the alienating effects of migration. Specifically, for the Barossa Germans, traditional folk crafts also expressed the essence of Germanic material culture, one intricately linked to its religious and ethnic basis.

What can we draw from this sketch of the pre-industrial context of craft? That craft knowledge and its associated handskills were highly valued, and fulfilled economic, cultural and psycho-logical roles; that the continuity of tradition was an essential aspect of daily life, one which could be maintained and expressed through repetition of familiar forms; that craftwork engendered a sense of personal and community identity; and that there were intimate links between the craftsman's activity and the making and using of crafted artefacts. In summary, craft activity was a dynamic practice, then equivalent to the making of cultural meaning.

Within this historic setting we surmise that craft is characterised by four key qualities. First, it is chiefly made by hand, and hence the mark of the maker implies an intimacy in its origins. Second, it is linked to specific mediums and particular techniques and processes which transform the raw material into form: namely, wood and woodworking, clay and pottery throwing, metal and forging, and fibre and weaving. Third, craft artefacts are designed with specific uses in mind, as is evident with furniture, clothing, pottery and various agricultural or domestic implements. There is also a symbolic or ritualistic function beyond 'practical' use: hence the forms and decorative motifs of furniture, pottery and jewellery, for example, embody certain ritual or other meanings specific to the community for which they were made.

The fourth quality of craft is its sense of tradition, that is the handing down from generation to generation of a set of customs, beliefs, and more specifically in relation to craft, set ways of making things. As such, craft becomes a signifier of links to the past and, therefore, of cultural continuity. This characteristic emerges from the actual practice of particular crafts, as well as being implied or expressed in the presence and use of craft artefacts. Tradition, as derived from historic settings, evokes specific associations as they relate to the medium itself, to familiar, time-honoured forms, decorative motifs or styles, as well as the set ways in which artefacts are made and used.

The preceding reveals how the crafted artefact once signified skill, dignity, independence, identity, craftsmanship, utility and cultural continuity, as well as various social values in relation to cohesive and homogenised community settings — essentially pre-industrial folklife. Craft's intricate links to social life in the nineteenth century cannot be over-emphasised. We tend to overlook these essential historically determined attributes of craft in the present setting of contemporary society given the post-industrial make up of modern life where machines and industrialised processes have taken over most production systems.

With its original social role of utility and tradition no longer in the forefront, professional craft is now practised for a variety of reasons other than the preceding. In particular, certain aspects of traditional craft are still seen as relevant — if not more so — and it is these which have come to the fore. Today, the emphasis has shifted to highlight the following facets: nostalgic or romantic associations with pre-industrial life; the construction and reinforcement of personal identity and self-esteem; alternative employment choice or independence; a source of rich sensuality; its use for social critique; and the rediscovery of its considerable potential for metaphorical, symbolic and ritualistic meanings.

These craft basics — the processes, history, traditions and other folk approaches to making — are directly and indirectly influencing craft practitioners today. But before examining these features or qualities in detail, other developments occurred between the 'end' of the pre-industrial age of craft and the contemporary craft revival of the 1960s which had their effects on present-day expression and practice.

Making Do

In the late nineteenth century, as the frontier receded and colonialism gradually gave way to Federation, harsh necessity and even poverty brought about by widespread drought and economic recession, extended the practice of the traditional pioneer crafts into a genre of crafting which is now referred to as 'making do'.

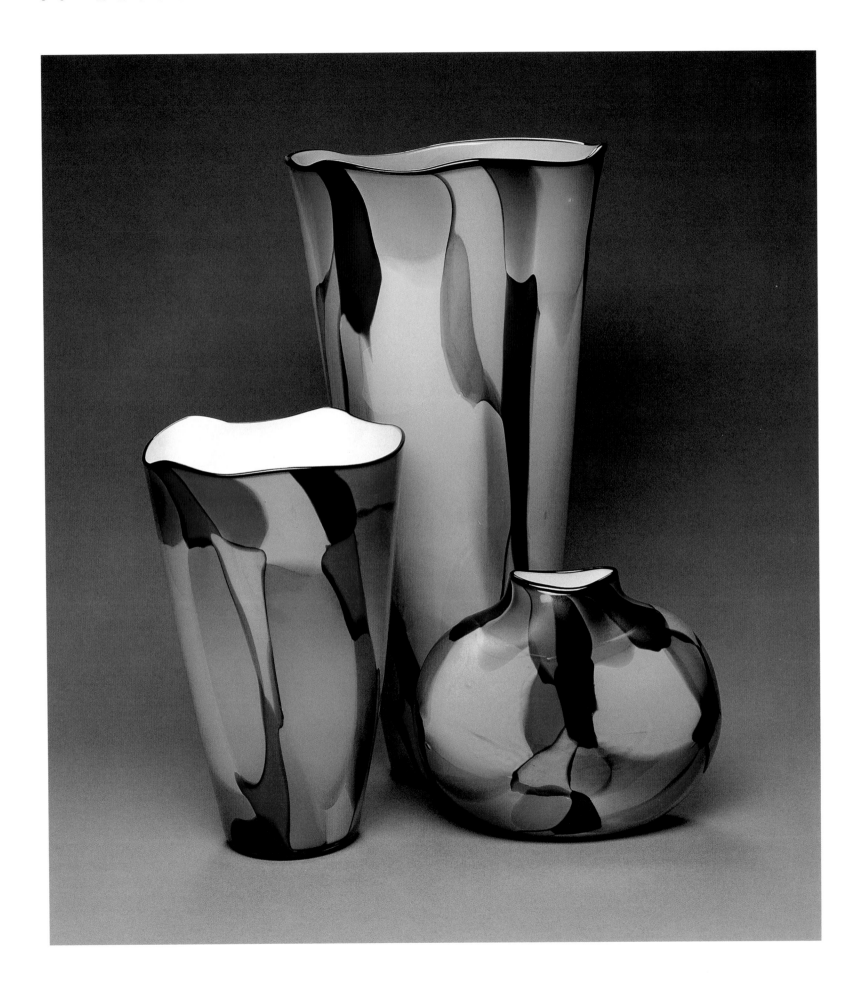

The years of the Great Depression in the 1930s provided the setting for a further stimulation of making-do activity, and the prudence of farmers and city dwellers alike, coupled with their bent towards improvisation, led to the salvaging of materials from the jettisoned products of the industrial age, to be recycled into particular classes of domestic furniture, textiles or other household articles.

The rural custom of improvisation using natural resources at hand, combined with the use of recycled materials, resulted in a tradition of making do activity which, especially lately, has influenced the contemporary crafts. Making do and its basis in the recycling of materials has informed and invigorated most of the conventional craft media, especially wood, jewellery and fibre, and is a theme examined in those respective chapters.

The Arts and Crafts Movement

By the early nineteenth century, the split between art and industry, which had emerged along with the Industrial Revolution in England, had led to the impoverished design and quality of its products. One response was the establishment of schools of design in the 1850s as a means to revitalise the industrial applied arts. Others saw the remedy to the 'soulless technique' of industrial manufacture and its uninhibited embracement of historical styles, in a return to more fundamental values as once embodied by the medieval artisan. The subsequent rise of a handicrafts philosophy, and the establishment of arts and crafts guilds and societies, saw the birth of what came to be known as the British Arts and Crafts Movement.

In particular, the influential writings of the critic and moralist John Ruskin, as well as the prominent socialist and craft practitioner William Morris, took a 'backward-looking perspective' and emphasised the dignity of hand labour, as well as the integrity and viability of the pre-industrial, or folk, craftsman who was both maker and designer, labourer and artist.

Although based on the British Arts and Crafts Movement, the Australian version was mostly centred about a number of middle-class based arts and crafts societies (established in most of the states) which, although fostering the value of handwork, were more interested in emulating European styles: as such it was essentially divorced from the former's underlying political and social sentiments.

Certainly, the perception of the worth of crafting for the sake of the enjoyment of creative activity and the aesthetic benefits of handicrafts in the home, saw the gradual rise of the crafts as a leisure-time activity from the late 1880s. In particular, the object was made by hand, and hence gained a special attribute perceived as lacking in the factory-made product. Whereas the colonial craftsman minimised any decorative elements in his or her work, seeing this as secondary and simply 'applied' to its practical function, this early twentieth-century crafts revival now tended to privilege, or at least accentuate, the former decorative aspect over that of function, and attempt its integration with form and medium.

PLATE 4 (opposite)
Maureen Williams (b. 1995)
Coloured series, 1996
Free-blown
55.5 x 28 cm (largest)
Photo: Robert Colvin
(see also Plate 49)

The arts and crafts movement was the first in a series of revivals of craft, espousing a return to craft's original qualities, in this case based on a Victorian, romanticised model of the pre-industrial craftsman. Although the handicraft and rustic ethics of the movement revitalised much of the decorative art of the period, its main contribution was, perhaps, its strengthening of craft with a new tradition of social and political protest.

Today, the nineteenth-century arts and crafts movement is still the subject of sporadic debate, as well as being an area for sourcing innovative historical styles, principles and ideas which emerged as a product of the philosophical influences of the movement.

Bauhaus-Modernism

That events in the crafts arena seem to be following particular cycles of renewal and decay become even more apparent when one compares the parallel developments of the crafts revival of the late nineteenth century — itself born of the social reaction to industrial production — to those of the present revival which originated in the 1960s. In both cases, a handicraft ethic underpinned the philosophy and nature of the products that emerged, and in both cases, industrialisation and machine production was seen as antithetical to the movement. However, in both periods, the handicraft ideal subsequently became the subordinate component in the new workshop systems of production which followed the re-unification of designer with industry.

While the British Arts and Crafts Movement sought to invigorate the decorative arts through a reassessment of the idealised pre-industrial craftsman, influential groups such as the Bauhaus and Werkbund schools in Germany were 'forward looking' in so far as they attempted to reconcile design ideals with mechanisation, originating a new machine aesthetic, and establishing workshop systems which combined the efforts of craft practitioners, designers and industry in a new relationship.

Unfortunately, the original craft-based ideals of the Bauhaus eventually gave way to theory and practice which stripped away craft elements from its design approach. Add to this an obsession with functionalism and an abhorrence of ornament, and it is clear why the results were eventually viewed as sterile and dehumanising.

Nevertheless, the influences of the early twentieth-century Bauhaus School is evident today, not only through the modernist ethic which it promoted, and which is still expressed in a proportion of craftwork, but also in the various design and craft courses around the country. It is especially evident, for example, in the workshop-centred structuring of the Canberra School of Art. Included among this institution's eleven, medium-based workshops, are those specialising in the traditional craft media including textiles, gold and silversmithing, ceramics, wood and glass. Within each of these, students vigorously pursue a program with strong individual impetus and freedom, exploring medium, structure, traditions, aesthetics, concepts and techniques. A number of practitioners represented in this book are graduates or teachers of this institution.

From 1960s Revival to 1990s Post-Modernism

The extraordinary growth and diversification of the crafts from the 1960s has been well documented through a profuse literature which emerged alongside and parallel to the activities of the crafts practitioners themselves. Since the late 1960s, this craft studies movement has sought to generate research, critical writing and debate on the activity of the crafts, leading to a plethora of specialist journals and books. Out of the widespread debates focusing on craft's diversity, meaning and role, as aired in these sources as well as in the regular craft seminars and conferences conducted around the country each year, certain themes surfaced and took precedence according to the fashions and biases of the day. Can craft be art? This was the question which predominated during the late postwar crafts movement.

Diversification from original mainstream modernist traditions of studio practice (which had their origins in ceramics) had led many practitioners to embrace the conceptual preoccupations of the fine arts. In particular the perennial 'art versus craft debate' saw crafts practitioners tussle with the rigid value system which privileges particular areas of the visual practices, while marginalising others — especially craft.

From the beginning, the debate was founded on a polarised perspective of hand-versus-intellectual skills: whereas fine art was defined as concerned with the avant-garde or concept, the emphasis of craft was deemed to be on technique, medium, tactile elements and function. From the late 1970s, because craft practitioners and their organisations were keen to improve their economic well-being, as well as the aspiration to simulate and be evaluated on the same terms as fine art, the tendency to devalue craft's traditional qualities soon become entrenched. Even the language and values of modernism were used to further this perception which devalued craft's essential aesthetic and ethic nature, its unique blending of medium, technique, function, skill, ornament, tradition, sensuality and mastery.

It was not until the emergence of a climate of post-modernism in the late 1980s in Australia that this tendency was critically questioned. Post-modernism favoured a deconstructionist and inter-textual approach. With identity, language and status in the crafts in flux, the art/craft debate was widely recognised as having failed to provide the means to resolve these and other key issues. Nor could it accommodate the variety of craft practices which had emerged and which had become well established during the 1990s.

These ever divergent trends in craft practice were accompanied by an increased activity in writing, and an increased willingness to investigate any number of alternative models and to formulate alternative questions: a new phase in the quest to comprehend and relocate craft was instituted. The rise and acceptance of interdisciplinary perspectives for investigating craft have begun to redress previously distorted views, and have led to a considerably more invigorating and open debate and writing in the area. Among the more interesting and scholarly approaches to craft discourse writing and criticism are literary theory, anthropological models, material culture approaches, analytical, descriptive and narrative strategies.

As a result, texts range from subjective narratives which explore the links between memory, making and the craft artefact, to semiotic analyses of the meaning of craft in urban settings; ethnographic accounts of contemporary makers and their contexts, to comparative exhibition commentaries; art historical analyses or descriptive, technical discourses on craft production; studies of the social setting of the contemporary crafts, to historical narratives and cross-cultural studies.

This interdisciplinary phase is gradually clarifying our understanding and accommodating the plurality seen in contemporary craft practices.

Craft and Design

The late 1980s saw a particularly strong design culture pervade industry, technology, fashion, architecture — and craft. Design has always been an integral aspect of craft, but its responsibility has shifted according to particular periods, groups and countries. The present-day emphasis on design in craft practice had its origins in the schools of design established by the British in the early nineteenth century. These institutions were very much a response to the crisis of conscience caused by the ills of industrialisation, and were intended as a means of training artisans and artists in the service of mechanised production.

In Australia, similar schools of design were founded on the same principles, many of which are the forerunners of today's tertiary design or art and craft schools. Today, craft students in these schools are instilled with a strong ethos of design, so much so that the term design-maker has emerged as a preferred title by many crafts practitioners as it highlights the design component. There is some irony in the fact that the 'hands on' processes and media-specificity of the crafts have led their practices to themselves become a focus for the revitalisation of design, and to act as a source for texture, ornament, process and symbol.

This process was instigated in an even earlier period: whereas in early nineteenth-century England design became a separate activity from the handwork of artisans employed in factories and workshops, this was not the case in Prussia where the Biedermeier furniture style came to be developed principally through the design efforts of individual craftsmen.

The Biedermeier style, popular in the period between 1820 and about 1835, was essentially a neo-classical one whose formal vocabulary was derived from the values of truth-to-materials and functionalism, as well as from classicism itself. An important element which characterised Biedermeier was the design process: prior to this furniture movement, Empire and earlier periods of furniture making were guided by architects and artists who were also the predominant originators of furniture design. The Biedermeier period saw a break in the dominance of these groups, with the responsibility for design, as well as the making, becoming the domain of the cabinetmaker. As a consequence of this change, whereby the design and making became the responsibility of one person, the potential for a more intimate sense of craftsmanship to emerge and influence the outcome of the overall design became underscored. Henceforth, an emphasis on the natural qualities and appearance of timber and the exposure of construction techniques became integral to the aesthetics of any piece of furniture.

In addition, as 'designer-makers' in their own right, the assessment of apprenticeship cabinet-makers now included their ability as artists, as well as craftsmen. Aside from the technical aspects of craftsmanship, the apprentice's drawing and design skills emerged as an equally important part of his training. Because the craftsman came to develop the style, rather than the architect or designer as in previous stylistic movements, craft values were seminal to its construction.

As we have seen, in the late nineteenth century this unification of craft and design was also attempted by the pioneers of the British Arts and Crafts Movement, although their model was an idealisation of the pre-industrial craftsman. Others, notably the Bauhaus School, sought to unify design, machine production with craft skills. Unfortunately, the Modernist ideals which emerged from such places became overly concerned with the rational and the uniform, and somehow, the values of craft were lost.

It was not until the mid- to late 1980s that design was once more self-consciously unified with craft, although as mentioned earlier, this more recent phase has, with some irony, seen the latter revitalise the former. Today, the greater proportion of craft practitioners are graduating from courses which are structured around design, and as a consequence, they tend to demonstrate a lateral problem-solving approach to materials, form, function and ornament, one which differs to previous linear, solely technical approaches.

In the late 1990s, design and making approaches to the crafts have manifested a split so that two broad types of handmade article may be distinguished. These are referred to here as 'Designer Chic' and 'Feral Craft'. Both types are handmade objects of desire which seem to be imbued with 'attitude', but especially so for the latter. There are differences: Designer Chic is contemporary craft as it has developed from the models discussed just above. It is represented by the more conventional path of international design in finely-crafted, usually hi-tech materials, sophisticated sleek lines, innovative design, and links with industry. Designer-Chic exemplifies craftsmanship and industrial design, leaning towards the allure of consummate craft finishes, adhering to a limited edition mentality, emphasising the intellectual and the functional.

Feral craft, on the other hand is, as its name suggests, more likely to be off-beat and folksy, and less concerned with attention to detail having a funky, quirky and even 'emotional' quality. This is one of the more vibrant advancing edges of the crafts and is informed, in part, by contemporary interpretations of making do traditions, as well as an infusion from folk approaches to creativity. As an approach, Feral Craft is therefore freely joyful in its celebration of the decorative, in the use of any materials that come to hand, and in its irreverence of the conventional; it represents an alternative cutting-edge of craft and design, one which has eschewed the perfection of craftsmanship and the industrial, Italian dominated, design sensibility, taking instead a path which revels in fun, folksy naivety and an ecosense ideology as seen in the recycling of materials.

Craft and Industry

The design boom has occurred in tandem with a relinking of craft with industry. Consumer scepticism in a product-saturated society, has led to a resistance to goods produced by innovative technology, and the hi-tech look with its non-decorative and minimalist features has seen a return to the natural and individual qualities offered by craft.

Although industry and its processes were once seen as antithetical to the contemporary crafts movement, the 1980s and 1990s have seen a strong trend whereby many crafts practitioners have reconciled craft philosophy with design and large-scale production, establishing links with industry. Numerous projects, many assisted through government funding schemes, have successfully brought craft practitioners and manufacturers together, restoring creativity and 'democratising' design in economic production; there are even agencies whose aim is to catalyse this process of collaboration between artisan and manufacturer. This may occur in a number of ways: industry may engage crafts practitioners to design and prototype models which are then put into production; practitioners may establish their own industrial base, melding craft, design and limited or larger production runs; or practitioners may simply appropriate industrial processes and techniques, applying them on a studio-based scale.

The 'inherent uniqueness' of craft, its potential for metaphor and sensuality, its ornate traditions, coupled with the evident mark of the maker, imbues the handcrafted article with highly valued qualities that manufacturers wish to reinstate as a means of countering the dulling uniformity of series production. They seek the fusion of craft attitudes and 'hands-on' approaches to making with industrial methodology.

It is generally recognised that the individual who combines both design and hands-on making activities develops insight and skills in materials manipulation and expression which may be more fecund than those who specialise in one or the other. After all, the crafts practitioner is not only intimately involved in the conceptual stages of design, but also in the sensual, manual process of making whereby feedback generated from shuttling between the two stages can stimulate considerable creativity.

Today, craft practitioners have the opportunity to select from one of a number of approaches to creative making, with a proportion preferring to keep their options open and, being multi-skilled, shift readily from studio work to industrial prototyping. Readers will note a considerable number of practitioners in this book who follow such a pattern. This fluidity, and the trend for a transition from studio-based crafts practitioner to designer-maker, has considerably broadened both the role and defining boundaries of the crafts.

Craft and Architecture

As we have seen, at the beginning of the century, modernism originally sought to rediscover ornament, to re-unify architecture, craftsmanship and art. Instead, the movement led to the monotony of the 'international style', and its accompanying dehumanised urban environment. Yet, unlike much fine art, craft has considerable potential to be intimately integrated into the fabric of a building. Today, public planners, developers and architects no longer need to be convinced of the perceived need to add character and identity to the built environment, to develop a sense of place through the integration of craft and architecture.

From the early to mid-1980s, efforts to re-establish the original unity which once existed between artisan and architect have been widespread. The aim of a successful collaboration between architect and crafts practitioner is to create an holistic expression, a structure that has identity, creative animation, and sense of place. Through collaboration, a symbolic program is established as an underlying directive drawing together the approaches of both architect and artisan. In this manner, structure, ornament, texture and motif are articulated into an integral statement.

Crafts practitioners and other artists are engaged to apply their understanding of materials, their skills and 'crafting' sensitivity to integrate into the architectural structure ornament, texture and form to engage, evoke moods and tell stories.

The collaborative process also highlights the differing attitudes to materials and approaches between architect and craft practitioner. From the functionalist/technological perspective, the architect determines the necessary manipulation and control of the pragmatic functions of the building — movement, use, space and light. On the other hand the practitioner, through his or her craft skills and medium-specific approach, can introduce aesthetic, narrative, symbolic and sensual elements frequently overlooked by economic and technological solutions.

For architects and artisans, collaboration can be a fulfilling and challenging activity which combines social skills with an exploratory process; it is motivated by work which stems from a genuine need rather than simply economic or decorative motives; synthesis towards the common theme must always predominate over personal motivations.

Models of Making

In the setting of post-industrial Australian society there is a diversity of approaches in the professional crafts, constituting what we may refer to as an ecology of craft production systems, one which reflects the developmental stages craft has passed through over the past two hundred years or so.

Other areas of creativity — such as the fine arts, design, architecture and fashion — to which contemporary craft practice is linked, are all affected by the influences of the marketplace, audience make up, politics and technology. As these broader social forces change, so do the various roles of craft production. It is pertinent too, to realise that, as craft is no longer just about making objects of use or ornamentation as in the past, although this reason is still relevant — be they pots, textiles, furniture, glassware, jewellery — plurality of choice in the current labour and consumer market, and the sensual, commentative and symbolic pleasure, handmade objects can confer to daily life and contemporary culture generally.

The making of artefacts by crafts practitioners, designer-makers, artisans or artists — whatever they term themselves — now occupies a number of niches: they may be independent, marginally linked to mainstream manufacturing, or perhaps working with architects or designers. Since the mid-1980s, the coming together of practitioners to form a craft collective or cooperative workshop, has especially been a growing trend.

Some eight models of crafting practice may be distinguished, each with its own set of identifying features. It is not a fixed picture, and in the context of a shifting scenario it is useful to define the main models of practice, including a brief outline of their historical origins.

The making of artefacts by craft practitioners, designer-makers, artisans or artists who are either independent, or are more or less marginally associated with mainstream manufacturing, occupies numerous niches. Current approaches to making objects may be categorised into various types or models of creative activity and which describe the variety of contemporary professional craft practices active today. These are intricately linked to other areas of creativity including the fine arts, design, architecture and fashion. A complex network further links craft to the vicissitudes of the marketplace, audiences, consumers, politics and technology.

The simplest — and some would say — traditional, model for contemporary craft production is the 'studio model'. Historically, the studio model evolved from a fusion of modern notions of the folk potter of rural, pre-industrial communities — in both England and Japan. From these early beginnings emerged the ideal of the artist-craftsman as embodied by the late nineteenth century, middle-class arts and crafts revival. The studio model was articulated and practiced by adherents of the Anglo-Oriental ceramic ethos which emerged in the 1920s (see Chapter Two). In its basic expression, the studio craftsworker linked late nineteenth-century handicraft notions of social protest and value, to a personalised system of production which embraced all aspects of the process — materials, handskills, processing, designing, making and marketing.

The studio potter of the late 1940s through to the 1980s exemplifies the model, and one may list Harold Hughan, Les Blakeborough, Milton Moon, Eileen Keys, Col Levy, and Peter Rushforth among those master potters in Australia who have remained faithful to this original studio model. Another distinguishing characteristic of this model was an underlying philosophy which sought integrity and engagement at all levels of the making process, as well as adherence to a functionalist and 'truth-to-materials' aesthetic.

Over the past three decades, the studio system has undergone much modification. It is still applicable in explaining the practices of a considerable proportion of contemporary crafts

practitioners, although few would admit to working within its original philosophical and aesthetic guidelines: modesty, truth to materials, tradition, utility, domestic links and a relational marketing style, are features that have become modified or relegated to a lower priority over the 1980s, although the mid-1990s have seen a re-evaluation and reaffirmation of their worthiness. During the 1960s and 1970s phase of diversification of the crafts, they became replaced by other values such as individualism, non-traditional materials, exploration, innovation, unique rather than production work, and the institutionalisation of marketing.

One particularly dynamic area of craft practice is the 'collectivism' of craftworkers into a cooperative or collective workshop. This is a model for craft making which may be closely compared to the artisan workshops which once flourished in urban centres in nineteenth-century Australia, particularly during the phase which preceded full industrialisation. Similarities between the contemporary and historical expressions of the collective workshop include the involvement of a handful of craftspeople, and a sharing of infrastructure and marketing skills. However, there are important differences: in the historical model, craftworkers were dominated by a patriarch family while a specialisation of skills between the members was typical.

The cooperative workshop can vary in its make up, but it usually consists of a handful of craftspeople, from as few as two or three sharing a studio, to as many as twenty or more. It is readily apparent that the economics of making and competition from local and overseas industrialised manufacturers is one of the chief forces driving this trend. By sharing resources such as studio space, kilns and other equipment, the economics of making by hand becomes more effectively competitive with industrial production.

However, there are other, social, reasons which are affecting this trend, although these are less readily defined. Traditionally, craft was responsible for all of our utilitarian and decorative domestic needs. Made in the setting of the village or small town, craftsman and consumer dealt with one another directly. Industry not only replaced the goods traditional handcrafts once supplied, it also destroyed the intimate community setting of their making. Today, craft satisfies our craving for the human touch, for a richer cultural setting, for self-expression, for symbolic purposes — and for community links. The latter, as we shall see, is being steadily reinstated by the craft cooperative.

By working in a common space, there is much peer support and interaction, with the sharing of ideas and information, as well as encouragement and feedback on work in progress. Additionally, the potential for closer contact between practitioner and community is facilitated by the craft cooperative which extends its benefits through the promotion of the values of self-realisation, closer community relations, integrity, and in short, a celebration of individual enterprise. It democratises manufacture, needs less capital to employ a group of individuals, permits individual enterprise, and returns craft to its community base, an important source of its vigour and values. In this manner, hand creativity can, in turn, invigorate the urban setting with a sense of cultural value beyond the provision of mere commodity.

In the contemporary collective-workshop, the 'overseer' is replaced by consensual group management and cooperative members only occasionally share or specialise their skills base — although multi-skilling is usual. Their work also remains their own, from design to conception, with stylistic and other influences often originating from within the cooperative. The commonly held ideals and aims which lead to groups of individuals to coalesce and work collectively in this manner, appears to be an increasingly popular trend for graduates of art schools or trainees leaving craft organisations. Examples of this collective-workshop model include The Gray Street Workshop, Jamboree Clay Workshop, Ipso Facto, Roar 2, and Whitehall Enterprises, to name a few.

Another relatively recent emergent system of craft practice is the collaborative model. This occurs when two areas of creative activity interact with one another, a prime example being the interaction of craft and architecture as described above. Briefly, the original unity between artisan and architect has been reinterpreted as a 'collaborative effort'. Underlying the collaborative model is a desire to reinstate human values into the built environment. The model embraces group and individual social interactions centred about discussion, design, research and prototyping to effect an integration of craft, architectural and engineering skills. Group activity towards a common theme dominates individual motivation.

Another model aims to build links between craft and industry. This may occur in two ways: the designer-maker model involves individuals modifying their studio practice to emphasise design and the making of prototypes, these are then produced in small batch or limited edition runs by themselves or through contract with existing industrial manufacturers. This system, where the design and prototype stages of the creative process do not need to be repeated, is seen as more efficient than 'one-off' commission, exhibition, or 'conventional' studio practices.

There are two variations to this studio designer-maker approach which warrant their own categories. The first, designer-maker employed, applies when a manufacturing firm contracts crafts practitioners or designer-makers to design special edition runs of a particular product. Here, industry initiates contact and organises a collaborative effort. On the other hand, the studio designer-maker is based on self-initiated effort with industry as simply an adjunct to production needs.

The second variant of the preceding studio designer-maker model is a group-organised version, distinguished here as the designer-maker cooperative. This involves specialist teams consisting of industrial and interior designers, crafts practitioners and artists working together either as a freelance cooperative, or under institutionalised control. Individuals within the group pool skills to design and develop prototypes of a range of articles which are then put into batch production through their own workshops or through existing manufacturing industries. The latter may be implemented in any number of variations including the subcontracting of only selected components of the articles with final assembly effected by the designer-maker members.

Yet another variant of this model operates at the Jam Factory Craft and Design Centre in Adelaide, where a training-through-production approach involves small groups of apprenticeships, each led by a master craftsman in the operation of specialty workshops. Through hands-on experience and team work, workshops in ceramics, wood, metal and glass, design and make various lines of craft articles. As an approach it is a hybridisation of the studio-craftsman and collective-workshop models, although one which is maintained chiefly through annual government subsidy.

Summarising the eight main models of approach for craft practices currently co-existing in Australia we have: the studio, collective-workshop, collaboration, studio designer-maker, designer-maker employed, the designer-maker cooperative, the designer-maker institution, and the trainee-in-production model. The distinguishing feature of the latter four models, compared to the first four, is the gradual progression in a making process where design and handskills are integrated, to one where the design process is split and then reintegrated with industrialised production skills.

Today, it is not uncommon to find practitioners who are working in a style which combines two or more of these approaches: they may produce one-off exhibition work on a studio basis; design and prototype models for industrialised application; or collaborate with architects and others. Often cited as an additional attraction of contemporary professional craft practice, the versatility to shift from one mode to another has acted to further diffuse the conventional definitions of craft.

Craft Knowledge

As the quest to define and comprehend the relevance of craft became intensified during the early 1990s, various alternative perspectives have come to the fore which shift the emphasis from the conventional criteria to more esoteric notions. They include the view of craft as a 'way of behaving', as 'an attitude to making', or even simply, as a particular 'value system'. The latter is perhaps a maturation or renewal of the alternative philosophy of the 1960s counter-culture movement, one which sees craft as a repository of essential values, even a new ethics of care for humanity and nature.

The latter raises the query: are we placing too much responsibility on craft? Possibly, but the intimate relationship craft practitioners have with their chosen medium teaches them to respect and value it, to use it carefully, and of course, to make articles which, on the opposite pole of modern industrialised goods, are intended to outlast their owners. Certainly it is arguable that the sensitively crafted article, as opposed to the mass produced, has the ability to raise the awareness of concern in its owner-user, perhaps to even instil a sense of reverence for materials, to raise public consciousness of rapidly depleting natural resources, endangered species and other environmental issues — all are dealt with in the work by practitioners within this text.

At the time of writing, the most fashionable perspective under debate is the evident yet vital realisation of craft as a system embodying unique knowledge. This refers not so much to knowledge as acquired facts that may be passed from one person to another or through textbooks, but rather the kind of practical knowledge which derives through the direct experience of making artefacts. Promulgated mainly by the British craft writer Peter Dormer, who refers to this concept as 'tacit knowledge', it shifts our focus from attitudinal or 'way of making' notions, to the idea of craft as the unique integration of perception, experience and handskills as possessed by individual practitioners. On the one hand this practical craft knowledge is personal, specific to the individual; on the other hand it is universal in so far as it is based on an accumulation of centuries of human experience, skills, tradition and culture.

Paradoxically, when craft is defined as a genre of knowledge in participation and in skills acquisition, that is, as a 'doing' discipline, in a very real sense it returns us to the realm of the crafts as practiced in the colonial or pre-industrial age. Then, as now, practical craft knowledge or experience empowered individuals and the guilds which they set up to restrict the knowledge within the initiated of their tribe. In the past, such empowering was generated from the practitioner's ability to be able to make particular, valuable articles from base materials; industrial technology was not then available as an alternative means of production, as it is today, to make similar articles. And while contemporary technology relies on the complex organisation of many individuals and systems, craft knowledge on the other hand frees the individual practitioner from mainstream, organisational patterns of thought and integrated making processes, allowing them to pursue personal ideas and approaches to creating articles of practical use or symbolic meaning.

While the idea of practical craft knowledge is as old as craft itself, over the past century in particular, this notion was overlooked and the individual practitioner's knowledge became devalued as the scale, economy and speed of industrialised and hi-tech processes took over, and indeed, seduced society.

Just what was the nature of craft knowledge in the pre-industrial age, and how was it transmitted and passed on from individual to individual? One of the key factors which played a part in the successful transfer of European homeland craft traditions and styles to Australia as described above, was the master-apprentice system of training of professional craftsmen. This system was strategic in the manner that skills, techniques, traditions and styles — in other words craft knowledge — were faithfully transmitted from generation to generation. It would appear to be still relevant today.

The master-apprentice system of training in the crafts in Europe was a time-honoured one, well-established by the Middle Ages when trade guilds had emerged to set standards and protect craftsmen. The guild system regulated the formal organisation of the apprenticeship method of training men in the crafts, the degree of competition, quality of work and prices of crafted articles. An hierarchical structure evolved whereby the European guild system decreed that, in order to earn his status as a master cabinetmaker, boys should pass through the stages of training as apprentices and journeymen. They first became apprenticed at the age of fourteen to serve a term of seven years — although by the early nineteenth century, this term appears to have been reduced to three or four years, depending on the city or region. They would then be released from their formal indenture of apprenticeship when aged twenty-one. Each stage, apprentice, journeyman and master craftsman, had its particular social requirements, rituals and dress code, all directed at inculcating through mimicry and practice, craft knowledge.

Today, this medieval, master-apprentice system appears to have been unconsciously modified to fit today's socio-cultural setting, and elements of the system are to be seen in most places of learning and making. The essential component of the system, that of a master instructing a junior or apprentice in the arts of his or her craft, remains a very efficient method for providing the setting for the acquisition of practical skills, one which relies on experiential, tactile and conceptual processes.

One of the most evident modifications of the current master-apprentice system has been the considerable emphasis and encouragement given to developing individual creativity and innovation. Whatever the emphasis, the late twentieth century is still surely dealing with the key elements or essentials of craft, that is, the 'masterly' integration of the conceptual and cultural with manual, practical skills. It is intriguing that this so-called craft knowledge has become the focus of discussion and is, once more, recognised as the cornerstone of craft's being or core strength. Certainly, it is a form of knowledge which has been passed on, for many generations, through its own innate structures, to survive and thrive in its own right in this post-industrial age of technological expansion.

Towards Mastery: Strategies and Journeys

When the diversity and eclectic nature of the contemporary crafts is examined closely, it is possible to discern a number of patterns in the approach practitioners take in constructing and interpreting meaning through their personal experience or perspective of life. They may choose to focus on making crafted artefacts which have practical use, are decorative, or are expressive through bricolage, deconstruction, ambiguity, abstract or representational strategies. These and other approaches are employed by crafts practitioners to make visual statements which challenge and question our relationship with the material world, or to illustrate universal truths about the human condition.

In the period of rapid expansion of craft movement between the 1970s and late 1980s, we have seen how the mainstream thrust included a gradual moving away from an emphasis on medium, technique, function, and tradition, to steadily embrace the conceptual, and generally more complex and avant-garde or seemingly sophisticated forms of expression.

In some media, this progression eventually led to the prevailing notion that concept or artistic intent should prevail over medium. While it was the influences of the fine arts which pushed craft towards painterly or sculptural concerns over the 1980s, there was a tendency for visual arts practitioners to turn their attentions to technique, process and medium. The notion that craft has its own inherent qualities worth exploring for their own sake, or as a means to highlight other conceptual concerns, was a perspective which finally began to influence mainstream crafts practitioners themselves. As a result, the view that the manipulation of the various craft media purely for their own inherent qualities, for a time anathema to the crafts movement, was no longer deemed problematic, so that skill, function and decorative appeal were once more accepted as valid as concept and idea.

The difficulty in striking a balance between the inherent, physical beauty of the medium and its metaphorical potential is another issue which has preoccupied practitioners. The visual properties and sensory attractiveness specific to each of the media are acknowledged as having the power to seduce the practitioner: should he or she simply work within the realm of these aesthetics, or does a successful piece transcend the characteristics of the material so that the artist's spirit or idea takes precedence?

This ambiguity was in part a consequence of the debates during the art/crafts ascendancy in the 1970s and 1980s, when fine arts values resulted in a perceived marginalisation of craft's inherent qualities. The present view prefers a plurality of approaches and attitudes rather than a hierarchy of values and accepts that, on the one hand there are practitioners exploring the physical and historical qualities of the medium, whereas on the other hand, others are exploiting selected properties, manipulating these to primarily achieve conceptual aims. In the latter, as long as the end result does not entirely jettison the qualities of the material, or make some reference to the techniques and processes employed, then we remain in a realm recognisable as craft.

Each craft medium has its own unique, inherent language made up of a vocabulary derived from its unique properties: its textures, colours, forms, aesthetics, traditions, and its particular set of historical and cultural associations: that is why they are recognised as craft media. If the medium is the message, how and what is the potential vocabulary and language of each specific craft as manipulated and interpreted by contemporary practitioners?

The potential for expression of each medium may also be described as its potential metaphorical power, or even, its 'inner being'. Each of the conventional media come with a set of specific emotive, symbolic and ritualistic associations and responses that have accumulated over the period of humanity's exploitation of them. With glass, for example, this response derives from its unique light-influencing properties in combination with deep-seated culturally and historically determined meanings — its beauty, fragility, and its coldness; wood is organic, suffused with mythology and texture; clay instantly responsive to our touch, powerfully gestural and symbolic of earth; fibre envelops our bodies, softens our walls or floors and speaks of many stories; metal may be precious or strong, primitive or sophisticated.

The heart of any craft practice is the expression of the essences of that craft — its physical,

PLATE 6 (following page)
Mark Douglass (b. 1964)
Chaise Lounge, 1990
Forged, welded and painted mild steel, cast glass, upholstered leather
2700 x 500 cm
(see also Plate 93)

historical and cultural being — through skills and processes intrinsic to it. Understanding and exploiting a medium's potential for metaphorical expression, why each elicits particular psychological, emotional or sensual responses is of vital relevance if the crafts practitioner is to gain mastery of the medium.

While these approaches are variously explained and illustrated in the following chapters, it is instructive to examine some of these in some detail at this point.

That curious but common expression found in the realm of the professional crafts, 'the resistance of the material', reveals something of the attitude and approach contemporary practitioners have to their medium. To effect desired changes in form and appearance, the medium is treated in a variety of ways, with the hands, with tools, with machines, with heat, and with chemicals. But the medium is described as having an intrinsic 'resistance' to being changed: in one sense this perceived resistance is real and is a consequence of the molecular structure of the medium in question. Transformation of any medium from its base state to an artefact embodying desired characteristics, therefore requires an understanding — or knowledge — of the medium's properties and its reaction and response to certain treatments. Of course, it also necessitates a hands on, that is technical, exploration and experimentation in manipulating the medium so that its properties become known, and its responses predictable.

So in a sense, resistance could be seen as referring to the level of knowledge, or the degree of 'know-how', a practitioner has achieved: it is his or her personal level of understanding of the medium's inherent characteristics and the skills attained in its manipulation, and hence the degree of control the practitioner has over the medium. This necessitates an understanding of its historical uses and manifestations, its cultural and social significations.

Technical skills and knowledge aside, how is intent and idea translated into form? Every craft involves an integration of what may be termed 'poesis' and 'praxis'. The former refers to the content and meaning of art, while the latter relates to the means of technical realisation. Craft knowledge melds these into theory and applied practice — a process of technology or 'know-how'. Practitioners frequently grapple with the comprehension of that special nexus: the interaction of medium with technical process and idea, and it is at this point that mastery emerges.

However, technical processes are not simply ways of getting things done, but are inextricably part of the practitioner's aesthetic or artistic intent. We realise this when we consider how the manipulation of any craft media engenders a form of direct feedback through hands and visual perception, and hence, through the actual technique which is directed from the underlying motivation and idea for the work. The actual process of making therefore suggests the progression of form and expression, permitting the practitioner to develop his or her idea through technique.

The process of making further highlights the intimate relationship that the craft practitioner has with the medium. In particular, it clarifies the way intended form gradually materialises, modified through the realities of the medium's inherent properties, and the processes and degree of control available to effect changes. The practitioner somehow balances his or her critical and intuitive faculties to arrive at a perception of what might be, subsequently translating personal vision into the medium, through the step-by-step routine of feedback and technique; it is at this point that a dialogue between poesis and praxis, between the physical and the spiritual, or the interaction between art and technique leads to a creative, masterly work. From this perspective we see that craft becomes a journey, and the means for exploration and greater understanding: exploration of the maker's understanding of him or herself, and understanding of the qualities of the medium and the know-how to manipulate this into an embodiment of inner vision.

A perspective which is helpful in understanding creative processes is that of the bricoleur. It was first articulated by the anthropologist Claude Lévi-Strauss, who saw the concept of the bricoleur or bricolage as a means of explaining the condition of contemporary culture and culture-makers. He likens the bricoleur to junk collectors who search about and reclaim bits and pieces of abandoned culture, then reassembling these discards into new, useful representations. The successful application of bricolage leads to the re-representation of familiar images or symbols, into unfamiliar ones which project an alternate or new meaning; it is a strategy by which symbolic representations of reality are selected and integrated to produce a work which can have a recognisable element of originality. Used effectively, it can therefore be a potent tool in the exploration of ideas, in the projection of inner vision — and as a critique for contemporary society. Within this text, readers will note a number of practitioners who take this or similar approaches, either consciously or otherwise, and include Rod Bamford, Wendy Wood, Stephen Bowers, Susan Cohn, Greg Leong, Richard Doheny, Pierre Cavalan, Gay Hawkes, Shaelene Murray, Inga Hunter and Peter Hart.

But the creation or selection of symbolic representations of reality is no simple task if originality is sought, and it requires the practitioner to take a psychological perspective or stance in order to perceive the final appearance of the intended object. To be successful, bricolage and other creative strategies necessitate the interplay between the practitioner's intuitive and critical faculties because, unless they have sourced their intellectual and emotional experience and effectively linked and expressed these through their craftsmanship, there is a risk of producing superficial or mannerist works, rather than masterworks.

Indeed, the issue of what is original or not has been a preoccupation within the crafts movement, especially during the mid- to late 1980s. Driven by a mix of economic, institutional and cultural influences, there was a tendency for practitioners to investigate various techniques and conceptual approaches in a somewhat superficial manner. The results were generally formal appropriations with little content, craft which simulated fashionable decorative pastiches, or followed a formula for ironic eclecticism or popular allusion.

There is a considerable difficulty in making what may be recognised as an original masterwork: how does the practitioner achieve a balance between the influences of traditional models and the pressures of innovation, hence avoiding outmoded fashion or self-conscious pastiches? To be original it is generally agreed that the work must provide the viewer with a new perception, a new way of looking at the world which reveals the maker's private vision of the world. New visions or perceptions may be achieved if elements from pre-existing or historic models of representation are reworked within a new configuration. But a reworking of the ordinary into the extraordinary first requires the clarity of personal insight: work may be deemed original if it is not too esoteric, if it is adaptive, if it somehow takes into account previous models; and further, if it challenges, if it is accessible, and if it permits a glimpse into the maker's private vision.

Ultimately, the practitioner who has mastered his or her craft has created a successful work if it expresses a sense of the maker's experience and self, and which permits the viewer to enter into a relationship with the work which may in turn, modify their own view and place within the world. In this there is connection between self and universe, between self and others.

The process of trial and error, of experimentation and risk, of art and its means of realisation (of poesis and praxis) are among the steps which lead to the mastering of craft. Craft today is often viewed as a practical means of cultural transcription whose processes may be compared to those of writing: just as the writer attempts to order symbols, words and phrases to compose narratives and meanings, so too, the crafts practitioner uses various processes and techniques to develop a vocabulary of expression, transcribing meaning into the medium of his or her choice.

Marketable Commodity or Humanitarian Values?

If advancing technology was once, erroneously, considered the greatest menace to the survival of crafts, their commodification and institutionalisation over the past decade is emerging as possibly one of its greatest present-day threats. The tendency by the various state and national craft organisations to seek to expand markets and mediocritise craft articles solely as commodity in a world saturated with goods, is surely but steadily diminishing its inherent difference and values. Fashion, market forces, and commercial advertising have become the means to sell the myth of the handmade, its nostalgic associations or its fine art edge.

In addition, the extensive bureaucracy which has come to overlay the professional crafts in Australia, more so than in the United Kingdom or in the United States, has created a polarity between those who are at the coalface of crafting, the makers, and those who have come to be a part of an organisational structure which has proliferated in the past two decades. The latter promotes, markets and 'directs' the so-called 'craft industry', as it has unfortunately come to be called in Australia.

In the push for professionalism, economic gains and heightened status, craft today is visible predominantly as institutionalised 'fine craft as commodity'. Reduced to an economic and decorative function, its potential expressiveness as a dynamic, socio-political and cultural activity has been diminished within this setting. While the reality of survival means that craft practitioners need to earn a living by selling their products, a single-minded focus on the crafts as a marketable commodity is the antithesis of its enduring qualities — its creativity, its humanitarian values, its cultural and social significations. Can craft be marketed without devaluing its intrinsic values, or is the pragmatic marketing of craft a materialistic philosophy which continues to limit human potential and individuality, inevitable in reality?

Perhaps craft's ethos of value and care, of knowledge and integrity might infuse the Western economic model to create a more sustainable system, one which melds pragmatism with its humanistic values. It takes little imagination to see that the cycle of decline and revival is bound to be repeated in the not too distant future: in this pivotal period of the 1990s, the following decade will be critical to the wider perspective and role craft assumes in the early years of the new millennium.

Taken from another perspective, this phase of redefinition of the notion of craft is but one of the many expressions of post-modernism's deconstructionist agenda, one which seeks to reconfigure the Western tradition. So we may view craft as a cornerstone for the evaluation of the industrialist-consumer value system; as a pathway leading to a return to the values, even ethics, the handmade embodies — personal skills, self-worth, care, integrity, tradition, connectedness, and so on. Ultimately, we may simply see craft as a creative impulse which seeks the integration of handskills, perception, mind and meaning.

In this dawning age of virtual reality and the ever pervasive technological environment, the fusion of body, perception and the natural world through the processes of craft, and our subsequent practical, ritualistic and sensual interactions with the crafted artefact, have a role in the expression and exaltation of our humanity. If I were to point to one aspect of the crafted artefact which especially identifies it, I would suggest that it is its potential for sharing and linking. We see this in the many stages which lead to the creation of the crafted artefact, in the exchange of gifts, in the way a treasured item is passed down through the generations or triggers specific memories, and in the way the crafts can act as a focus for human ritual, celebration and pleasure, on both practical and symbolic levels.

Summary

No doubt it is the peculiar quality of each medium which attracts each practitioner to intimately engage with his or her choice: the potter slaps and squeezes clay, the woodworker planes and carves wood, the glass artist blows into the molten mass, the textile artist intertwines fibres, the jeweller taps and twists the metal. There are probably other reasons, as varied as the personalities and motivations of the makers, but there are common grounds — such as the love of tactile work, the pleasure of seeing form emerge from chaos, and the eventual transfer of the work into its place of display or use.

The examples in this text serve to portray the manner in which craft practitioners in Australia explore, refine and combine techniques and processes, making artefacts of practical and decorative use; or objects which communicate through metaphoric, emotional, allegorical or aesthetic moods, or comment on political or social issues.

Readers will discover that themes are wide ranging and may include — across the gamut of the media — investigations of the figure and its psyche; myth and allegory; landscape as metaphor, or perhaps the interest may be to investigate the notion of decoration or function; while others explore the metaphoric expressions of the vessel; the ritualistic functioning of objects, other practitioners may concentrate on expressing ecological concerns, feminism, gender, memory, or various aspects of the human condition; yet others may have an interest in the actual making process itself; or perhaps it may be the personal realm involving particular psychological states, or else telling personal or family stories. And while I have endeavoured to indicate the parallels, connections and links which commonly occur between the differing media, it is up to each reader to scrutinise and search for these according to their curiosity and interests.

Whatever is selected or attracts the practitioner, their task is centred on opening up new directions of investigation, finding alternative ways of treating traditional materials, developing skills and techniques, honing their craftsmanship and generally, aiming for mastery in their medium. Some work within traditional techniques and media boundaries and aesthetics to reassert past values and ideals, to produce lyrical works which satisfy our practical demands or stimulate our sensual and corporeal appreciation. Others are inclined to stretch our notions of the role of craft, challenging our perceptions and intellect, or evoking and interpreting in a new light the rich layers of mystery, and the ritual of timeless processes and forms.

They demonstrate that the contemporary crafts are an area of creativity which contribute significantly to our cultural richness; this is especially acknowledged when we are reminded of that part of our material culture which is held closest to our emotions: consider the pleasure and significance of a piece of jewellery, a ring or brooch given as a gift or to celebrate an anniversary; try to visualise your favourite cafe without its crafted decorative architectural fittings and furnishings, its handcrafted tables, plates and bowls; feel the pleasure of the well-crafted armchair; luxuriate in the textural richness of your clothes.

The characteristics of each craft medium, its patina, peculiar sheen, its colour, and historical or cultural associations, are juxtaposed with other elements: it can emphasise historical processes and unlock personal memories; it may explore the notion of function as an aesthetic rather than as practical use; it may unravel the history of a technology; it may embody myth, or memory; it may tell a story, or play out a ritual — the possible expressions are limitless.

Craft is no longer just about making objects of use or ornamentation: today, craft satisfies our craving for the human touch, for a richer cultural experience, for our symbolic yearnings, and as a celebration of individual enterprise. Whimsical, romantic, sensual, sophisticated, intellectual, modernist or punky, but rarely simply functional, their common denominator is the use of familiar materials and the presence of the human touch, the essential core of craft — qualities, themes and ideas which are explored in the following chapters and embodied in the illustrated works.

In viewing the following illustrations of craft works, it may be salient to raise a few points. As one would expect, the fecundity (intellectual fruitfulness) of the displayed works varies, from those which elicit an immediate response, to those which require longer contemplation, and those which possibly leave the viewer cold. In part, this is due to each person's social conditioning and the life experiences and preconceptions they bring to bear on their observations. Whatever each person's cultural baggage, I would urge the reader to scrutinise each piece with some consideration, and perhaps to consider questions such as: does the work embody elements of originality, or does it relate or make references to past models? Does it elicit a strong emotional response from the viewer, or is it the intellectual faculties which are stimulated or challenged? In other words, how does the work connect? The discerning viewer may look for evidence of a proficiency of handskills, intuitive responsiveness to the inherent qualities of the medium, the embodiment of interesting ideas or personal vision, an awareness and expression of knowledge of the cultural associations that accompany each medium and its craft practice and the tensions or balances between tradition and innovation.

Finally, the viewer may simply take pleasure from the various attributes and qualities to which he or she is especially drawn, and perhaps muse on the crafts and their renewed role as a dynamic source of human creativity and contemporary material culture.

CHAPTER TWO
CLAY – METAMORPHOSIS IN FIRE

Clay's directness and sensitivity of response is unique. Of the earth, clay returns us to the basics of existence: there is no other material that begins its life as a pliable product of erosion from primary rock, to be beaten, squeezed, poked and otherwise smoothed and coaxed from chaos into coherent form. Clay is a metaphor of the elemental, for we arise from and return to clay: 'We are the clay, Oh Lord, and, Thou, our potter,' proclaimed the Biblical Isaiah. Add to this its charged cultural and historical associations and it is clear why clay cannot be manipulated without paying homage to its long and intimate links to humanity.

Clay does not lifelessly offer itself: it responds with a yielding sensitivity to the practitioner's actions, setting up a two-way flow of influences. In this way, clay and its craft of pottery or ceramics is a dynamic, lively process, a physical and mental dialogue between practitioner and medium. As a consequence, fingerprints, grooves, thumb-impressions, cuts, indentations and other signs of the gestures of the maker are fixed in fired clay; and more often than not, these are clearly visible in the form or on the surface of the finished product. Then there is the transforming and cathartic chemistry of fire which takes over, simultaneously and mysteriously conferring its own unpredictable imprint: flame flashes, colours and glaze changes, fire converts the elemental and malleable clay into solid, enduring form to become virtually indestructible, carrying the signs and aspirations of its maker into an unknown future.

The practitioner can manipulate changes consummated by fire, to reinforce or complement his own intended finishes, so that the fired clay proclaims its origins, covertly in subtle means or expressly through its earthy palette, cracked and larval textures or other signs of its nature. Whatever path of engagement in hands and through fire the ceramic shape eventually assumes, it cannot be devoid of meaning, whether intentional or not on the part of the practitioner; the language of clay is inherent in its substance, in its identification: simply choosing to work in clay makes the initial statement.

On the other hand, clay is also a medium which can, with cunning and skill, be made to look like anything but the earth from which it emerges. *Trompe l'oeil* effects can suggest the surface of any other material, be it velvet or chamois, or the highly reflecting surface of a mirror, the grey glint of steel, the grainy texture of wood, or the suggestion of skin. In this way, ceramic work can evoke anything from a quietly satisfying feeling of domesticity, a mood of reflection and meditation,

PLATE 8
Owen Rye (b. 1944)
Winged Form, 1995
Anagama firing, fly ash glaze
22 cm
Photo: The Visual Resource

or a startling tactile and visual sensation. Ceramic work can also be unsettling through the ideas it can be made to embody or express, challenging our complacency, stimulating intellectual or artistic yearnings, triggering long-lost memories, or rousing subconscious desires or dreams.

Aside from the signs imbedded by hand, clay as a medium suggests and projects its own inherent messages or meanings. The techniques and processes used to manipulate clay are also similarly linked to a variety of traditional associations and hence, carry their own meanings and indications of artistic intent. Indeed, its rich history and cultural content seemingly oozes from its enticing pliability. These are the reasons clay is such a favourite with practitioners, and these are the properties which may be exploited for creative expression, so that clay manipulated by skilled hands through a tuned mind can become almost anything.

The Clay Rush

Emulating the trail-blazing lead studio-ceramics practice enjoyed from the 1960s to 1980s, today's practitioners are transforming clay into an extraordinary range of expressive forms, either

exploring the timeless aesthetics of the vessel, or realising its sculptural qualities, or else working the medium for its narrative or allegorical potential.

Australia has a long history of ceramics which extends from the early years of settlement in the late eighteenth century, beginning with the introduction of production throwing by migrant Staffordshire potters, and including age-old folk pottery traditions as introduced and practiced over much of the nineteenth century by migrant German and Cornish potters. The Arts and Crafts Movement saw the emergence of studio and artist potters from about 1919, with the expansion of studio pottery from the immediate postwar period. But it is the decades of the 1960s and early 1970s which are recognised as the formative years of ceramics as a modern movement in Australia.

PLATE 9
Gwyn Hanssen Pigott (b. 1935)
Still Life with White Cup, 1995
Wood-fired porcelain
28 cm
Photo: Tim Marshall

PLATE 10
Sandy Lockwood (b. 1953)
Slab Dish, 1995
Salt-glaze (woodfired) with slips
41 x 17 cm
Photo: John Lascelles

Indeed, it was ceramics which spearheaded the crafts movement in this country, with the latter part of the 1970s through to the mid-1980s experiencing a 'clay rush', as would-be adherents flooded into this area of studio craftwork. Until the early to mid-1980s, clay remained the pre-eminent medium of expression for the crafts movement in this country, although since the late 1980s, its leading edge has given way somewhat, to the advancing wave of activity in the other craft media, notably glass.

Charting the ceramic movement's energetic progression, beginning with its revival in the early 1960s, reveals that this area took off from a base of hybridised pottery principles derived from traditional British and Asian sources. These sought to re-evaluate folk and pre-industrial pottery aesthetics through the exploration of medium, function and craftsmanship. In this genesis we see the reasons for the split in the two mainstream areas still somewhat discernible in studio practice in clay today: vessel aesthetics, and alternative or eclectic practices.

The Vessel

Today, confronted as we are by the bewildering manifestations of form, colours and expressions that ceramics assume, it is sometimes somewhat of a relief to walk into a gallery and see its most fundamental expression — the vessel. The handmade vessel as a vehicle of expression is a powerful one. It is an elemental form which harkens back to the origins of humankind's tentative forays into altering nature and initiating our long journey of material culture. Clay was first hand-formed into simple, crude vessels; then the discovery that this earthy material hardened when exposed to fire led to the use of the wheel to throw rounded vessels, and finally, that glazes could seal porous earthenware walls.

Any vessel made today, no matter how simple or complex, evokes these early beginnings, and embodies the knowledge of a long path: it has been a seven thousand-year-old ceramic adventure.

The vessel may be generated through the discipline of the wheel, or else constructed through the greater freedom of handbuilding. It may be consciously linked to any of a number of cultures, historical and contemporary, or it may stand alone as an expression of the identity of the maker, or more widely, as a metaphor for various aspects of our humanity. The clay vessel is eminently accessible, we are all surrounded by vessels of one kind or another, and our responses to this enduring form has been conditioned since birth. Its function, to hold or contain food, liquid or other substances, has a directness and essential quality intimately linked to life: the vessel as life-giver. Or else we may view it as simply creating a volume, articulating surface and decoration; foot and lip, body and neck — comparisons with the human body are inevitable.

The endless replication of the clay vessel into a multitude of forms and guises, not only represents an essential aspect of craftsmanship, but also embodies the sense of tradition, of set ways of making forms determined over a very long period of time through community consensus.

The vessel tradition in ceramics is a well-established one which continues to attract its followers. They variously choose to develop a line of work centred about the vessel, this may be domestic production work of little pretension but affordable and useful in the home; or else it may be quite unfit for actual use yet focus on the idea of function; or perhaps the form of the teapot is of interest in relation to its ritual or historical links; or it may be simply an exploration of aesthetics, of decoration or glaze effects. On the other hand, the vessel may assume a strictly metaphorical function and represent psychological aspects of self, make ironic statements, or parody an art movement.

There is no doubt that the affinity for the vessel will never wane. Aside from its rich historical continuity and ever-present challenge, one of the reasons for the allure of the pot is the primacy of its origins on the wheel, or from slab and other hand-building techniques. Where and when did this attraction begin? Most ceramists today are aware of the pioneering work of the early studio potters, but it was the influence of the British potter Bernard Leach which determined the course. Leach's study of Japanese and other Asian cultures' folk pottery traditions, were fused with his revival of elements derived from the British folk pottery to derive a singular philosophy of clay. Published in *A Potter's Book* in 1940, the particular blend of Anglo-Oriental principles he espoused have influenced contemporary ceramics world-wide to this day.

Leach's teachings were strongly defined and included an espousal of Oriental concepts of aesthetic sensibility, such as restraint, humility, simplicity, and truth-to-materials, aimed at making pots 'with soul'. Although, within its teachings, the Anglo-Oriental school promoted the integrity and respect of the potter, the personal expression of the maker was considered secondary to the aesthetic qualities sought for in the pot; indeed, the negation of self was essential if the essence of the pot was to be revealed through its natural ceramic, traditional and functional, qualities.

Today, these principles still provide the framework for the work of a number of potters in Australia. Within this group there are a number of specialist branches of practice including raku, stoneware, salt-glaze and wood-fire, all of which attract a strong following.

Ceramic work can take us back to the origins, to the simple ingredients of clay, form, colour and texture. But it is the vessel which is the quintessential form, for it reduces the ceramic process to its primary relationship, melding hands, clay, fire, function and surface.

However, in returning to the historical analysis underlying the present-day ceramics scene, it is important to take note of developments in the early 1970s. It was in this decade that the innovative directions sparked by Peter Voulkos in the United States began to spread and influence ceramic practice in Australia. The influence of Japanese Zen Buddhism as expressed in the natural, spontaneous and traditional qualities of Bizen, raku and other Japanese folk pottery types, as well as the energetics of the American art movement of Abstract Expressionism, were reinterpreted by Peter Voulkos and his contemporaries. They rejected the strict tenets of Leach's teachings in favour of an innovative, irreverent and ideas-oriented approach to clay. The result

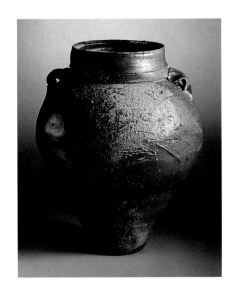

PLATE 11
Janet Mansfield (b. 1934)
Jar, 1994
Anagama firing
45 cm
Photo: Roger Deckker

was the 'artistic' liberation of the medium, and through the influence of popular trends in the fine arts, ceramics branched into two mainstreams, one represented by the former, traditional approach, and the other an 'anything goes' movement with few, if any, rules or restraints.

As a result, ceramics practice over the past two decades has come to be characterised by its plurality, by a multiplicity of approaches which grade from traditional, vessel-centred work exploring historical, natural and decorative qualities, through to the highly experimental, sculptural, abstract and innovative pathways of expression.

In part, it is this bewildering kaleidoscope of approaches which has, over the latter part of the 1980s, led to a slowing down of the original momentum of the clay rush, for much of the treatment of clay as a medium for social commentary, or for sculptural or conceptual expression, had become mannerist, formal and superficial. The emulation of art trends, the repetition of visual imagery, the specious use of post-modernist strategies, and the endless parodying of function can only go so far. Not unexpectedly, for a time, a sense of impotence and confusion underlay the ceramics movement.

Since the early 1990s, a re-evaluation of the medium and a return to origins — in a traditional, artistic and personal sense — has seen a renewed explorative attitude and a stronger sense of values which have reinvigorated contemporary ceramics. The strongly identifiable genres of clay practice in the late 1990s each have their band of followers determined to extend the creativity and identity of their particular ceramic idiom.

As in the past, ceramics practice today is once more an enlivened journey of discovery, not only for the practitioner in a personal sense, but also one which seeks to express a reality of tradition, culture and aesthetics, with an intensity of idea in this medium — not to mention handskills.

Because of the numerous directions and constant flux in contemporary ceramic practice, any attempt to form a comprehensive perspective would require more space than is available. The following therefore simply overviews the more predominant genres; perhaps, post-modernist plurality and its accompanying eclecticism may be comprehended more effectively if we view ceramic practice from its fundamentals of form, medium and meaning. Within this purview we may consider the making of three-dimensional objects, be they pots, sculptural, architectural or figurative works in fired clay. The following examines some of these broader genres, their attendant skills, underlying principles, concepts and/or themes.

A word on what appears to be a distinctive split in the contemporary ceramics field, the choice practitioners make, or agonise over: whether to create pots or ceramic works which are essentially functional, or essentially expressive or sculptural. Frequently, the ambiguity between these two distinctive approaches is itself an area of exploration, hence blurring the boundary to create intriguing, and often quite engaging, tensions and dialogues.

PLATE 12 (opposite)
Peter Rushforth (b. 1920)
Stoneware Blossom Jar, 1996
Jun glaze over iron glaze,
wax resist decorations
32 x 25 cm

Fire, Form and Texture

Ceramic art today still revels in the primordial qualities of the most basic processes known when clay and fire are brought together. The magical transformations wrought in this action are the basis of the attractions that certain genres of ceramics retain to this day, notably raku and wood firing. Of the latter, there are a number of variations or sub-genres, including the Japanese anagama, raku, Shino, Bizen, and the world-wide, salt-glaze firing. Each has its own set of aesthetics and historical or traditional associations, and each makes its own demands on the practitioner, although natural qualities, firing uncertainties, the medium and an intuitive capacity on the part of the practitioner, comprise a common set of characteristics.

Wood firing has especially attracted what may be considered a cult following within the world of ceramics, with regular wood fire seminars and conferences attracting numerous adherents in Australia. The wood fire aesthetic is bound to Oriental, and notably, long Japanese cultural traditions. We especially see this in regard to raku, although the subtleties, colours, and textures of wood-fired ceramics are a part of an ethic related to Zen Buddhist philosophy, one which favours meditative, simple, humble, and natural guidelines. The infinite varieties of earthy hues, of browns and ochres, the flashes of red, the glaze drips, the creamy mottled surfaces, and poolings, these and other qualities form the understated but sensual, wood-firing palette.

Fire and its effects on clay is the primary focus, and the 'gifts of the gods' unpredictability of the process is especially sought — when does the influence of the maker give over to that of nature? It is a kind of self-effacing relationship which relinquishes the tight control usually seen in other areas of ceramic practice. But it is not a simple matter of throwing a pot and firing it in a wood-fuelled kiln: there are considerations of clay types, of form, of decorative intent, of traditional treatment or innovative twist, of which timber to use for fuel, and the length of firing. In this manner, the process of wood firing returns the maker to fundamentals, to considerations of form and texture, surface and colour to the interaction between clay, fire and maker.

Perhaps more than any other area of contemporary ceramics, wood firing retains the lifestyle connotations which once formed such an integral part of the task of being a potter or ceramist in the 1960s and 1970s. The lengthy firing periods, the exchange of knowledge and the sharing of skills, also demand a cooperative spirit which infuses this area of practice.

More often than not, wood-fire pottery tends to be wheel-thrown and functional. Jars, bowls, vases, cups, teapots and other domestic wares comprise much of the output, although vessels as contemplative or aesthetic objects which may be linked to historical antecedents are also common. Sculptural, non-functional objects are also produced, although the cultural content associated with wood firing would seem to inhibit these as a principal area of activity.

Bizen ware is Japan's most ancient form of pottery, and is still being produced after more than one thousand years. It requires long wood-firing periods of eight to ten days, the pots being made from clay which can withstand the long and high-temperature firing in a climbing kiln of four or more chambers. The favoured qualities of Bizen are its simplicity of form combined with the creative subtlety of its ethereal ash glazes, formed from natural ash deposits on the pot's surface during the extraordinary — and unpredictable — firing process. One such adherent of this specialty is Heja Chong (b. 1950), who was born in Japan of Korean parents. She studied Bizen ware firing under the master Yu Fujiwara before migrating to Australia in 1983, where she has since practised this ancient ceramic process.

> For a long wood-firing potter such as myself, the 'process' of creating is absolutely integral to the artistic expression that is often only seen in the finished product. The endeavour of firing the kiln over an eight to ten day period is a 'rite' that demands total commitment. It is this commitment and adherence to ritual itself that forms a vital part of the artistic endeavour. I perceive my own development as an artist not only in terms of output, but through the success with which I maintain the momentum of creativity and obey my chosen flame, ideally seeing that flame more and more clearly, and hopefully perhaps revealing that flame to others.

The simple, understated forms and subtle wood-fired surfaces of Chong's work are very much those kinds of pots which reveal an aesthetic essence which requires little more than quiet observation for the appreciation of their marriage of unique surfaces and consummate forms.

The magic of the flame has also long been Owen Rye's (b. 1944) realm; he has worked continuously for fifteen years developing wood-fired ceramics, especially using the ancient Oriental anagama or tunnel kiln firing technique. Once more, as in the related Bizen style, wood ash deposited over a long firing period confers a patina which evokes the centuries-old tradition on which this genre is based. Piled on top of one another in the traditional climbing kiln, the pots are thrown with this in mind, their walls thickened, their forms are usually squat, although some deformation is acceptable as a part of the desired and subdued surface/form aesthetic.

Rye aims for a contemporary interpretation of the ancient qualities desired in these pots; originally these were spontaneous, simple, functional, earthy, flame-touched. Rye sometimes first dips his pots in feldspar glazes, or simply relies on fly ash; whatever the approach, he always endows them with the maker's hand, gestural, slight, bold, then allows the kiln firing to take them through a rite of passage. He may then enhance glaze effects by sandblasting, etching or other abrasive acts, creating a surface which simulates the meteor-blasted surface of the moon: cratered, silver-grey, and very, very old.

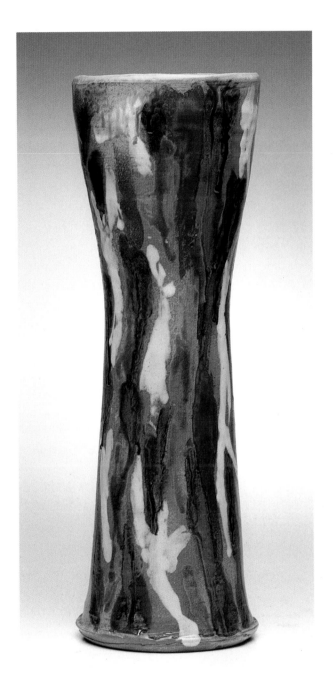

PLATE 13
Milton Moon (b. 1926)
Landscape Image, 1996
Stoneware with ash glaze,
oxide decoration
55 cm
Photo: Clayton Glen

Critics relate my work to Japanese ceramics but I see only a distant or unconscious influence. I attempt to develop forms and especially surfaces with a feel of 'antiquity'. Until recently, all my work has been wheel thrown vessels, but I am now playing with larger forms (sculpture). My work derives from firing technique, not from contemporary trends in the crafts, although I admire and study the work of others, especially Chester Nealie and Alan Peascod, and various painters and sculptors.

As a process-directed practice, Rye's anagama-style, wood-fired pots display the very subtle, regional qualities of the local clay and wood, while the potter's mark rests deep within the pot, expressing a state of quiet being.

The gentle seduction and sophistication of Gwyn Hanssen Pigott's (b. 1935) wood-fired porcelain pots appear in direct contrast to the aged, rustic and dramatic patinas of the anagama wood-firing approach. Combining porcelain with wood-firing is itself an intriguing idea, not necessarily a new one, but one which combines the subtle effects that wood-firing may confer with the delicate, almost paper-thin walls of the pots. Always working with minimal forms, Hanssen Pigott covers these with soft celadon, iron and gold-lustre glazes.

Hanssen Pigott likes to group her pots into still-life tableaus so that the characteristic curvaceous forms and gentle colour palette produce pleasing visual effects comparable to the still life canvases of the Italian painter Giorgio Morandi, one of her influencing sources. Others include the work and philosophies of British potters Lucie Rie and Bernard Leach as well as Hans Coper. Since her venture into ceramics in the early 1950s, Hanssen Pigott has continued to refine her idiom. Volume, glaze, function, and colour, and the spatial relationships between various forms have been gradually evolving towards ever more delicate and harmonious interpretations. Today, the dignified calmness, indeed, the serenity of her wood-fired ceramics, expresses an aesthetic that is at once timeless as it is personal.

Beauty. I don't understand it; but hope for it and sometimes feel it. Often, in the most menial, everyday objects, it begs a stillness and offers kindness. It is essential; absolutely necessary. It could be an Italian coffee bowl, or the space between two bottles. Whatever it is, I want to be open to it. To be part of it. For now, I am intrigued by the fine line between the monotonous and the lively; the dull and the subtle. I use porcelain for its strength when fine, and the way the rims absorb light; I fire with wood to add a bloom of fine ash to the glazes — but not too much!
I want nothing inessential in the work.

Salt-glazing is another specialised, traditional category of wood-fired ceramics. From the moment any potter or collector picks up a well-thrown salt-glazed pot and examines its organic-like, skin texture and distinctive sheen and feels its sensuous surface, they will be hooked to the genre.

PLATE 14 (opposite)
Jeff Mincham (b. 1950)
Masked Man, 1995
Raku, copper matt finish, stone base
32 x 23 cm
Photo: Grant Hancock

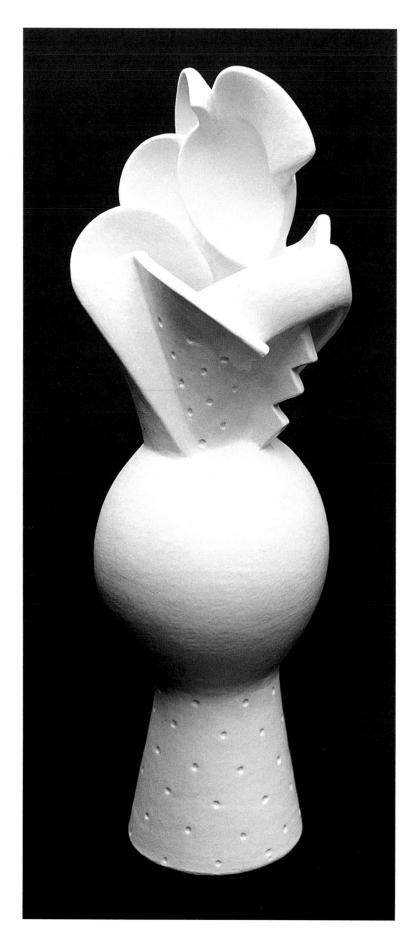

The technique and art of salt-glazing is a world unto itself: unlike most ceramic areas, salt-glaze is a once-fire process, described as an atmospheric glaze; it's also a demanding genre, not suitable for the wimpish ceramist, as it requires dedication and physical endurance. In Australia, salt-glazing is an important sub-genre of wood firing as most of these potters also use a wood firing kiln.

Salt-glazed pottery has a long history which, in this case, tends to be connected to European rather than Oriental origins, and which infuses and informs the genre. Australia has a considerable history of salt-glazing, it being introduced by convict and free potters within the first few years of settlement in 1788. From that time, to the third quarter of the nineteenth century, salt-glaze pottery was one of the more popular means of making stoneware vessels for a variety of commercial and domestic uses, until Bristol, majolica and other Victorian glaze types rendered it obsolete.

Historically, it was especially developed in South Australia where, in the Barossa Valley and the Adelaide Hills, German migrant folk potters together with their Cornish counterparts, maintained the tradition into the 1890s. Functional production-work comprising domestic and commercial vessels for the storage of oils, wines, acids, beers and other substances, has bequeathed an extraordinary salt-glazed heritage. Yet, to date, this has yet to inspire or be a source of influence for contemporary salt-glazing in this country. Indeed, it is an irony that Australian potters are more aware of European traditions directly in their source country, rather than in the distant cultural shores of their own homeland where they survived long after their demise in the Old World.

Nevertheless, energetic work with all the hallmarks of salt-glazing — its orange-skin textures, the pooling, glaze drips, textured surfaces, strong forms, and functional vessels — is emerging from a dedicated group of enthusiasts.

Sandy Lockwood (b. 1953) is one of those few potters who have decided to master this difficult medium over the past fifteen years. Her pots, generally vases, jars, bowls and trays, are unified in their seemingly casual forms; few would actually be used, most would simply exist as objects for aesthetic appreciation. It's an appreciation of their direct communication of a ceramic sensuality: salt-glaze can

PLATE 16
Andrea Hylands (b. 1952)
Origami Bowl, 1995
Bone china, cast and handbuilt
27 x 31 cm
Photo: Andrew Barcham

do that, and Lockwood's pots would reward anyone who loves ceramic art for its natural physicality: they are exemplary in their organic thrusting, they are luscious in their display of the marriage of salt and its consummate relationship with clay.

> The medium of clay fascinates me because of its fluid responsiveness. This unique potential can be carried through the entire making process into the finished object. The fluidity of the material enlivened by salt glazing facilitates expression of the human gestural vocabulary which forms a significant aspect of my work. I believe that the best contemporary craft exhibits expertise with materials and creative talent bound together by a passion for the medium. The jigsaw is quite complex and most of the pieces are invisible. There is no short cut, and the maker's journey is not always easy. Sometimes however, it is glorious.

Janet Mansfield (b. 1934) has worked in the field of salt-glazed and wood-fired ceramics for some thirty years. She brings to the genre a long and very broad experience, based as it is on her practical expertise and considerable contact with many of the world's master potters.

Today, although the colour range and qualities of salt-glazing may be extended through the use of both traditional or innovative techniques such as cobalt oxide slips, engobes and metallic lustres, Australian potters appear to prefer work which enhances the fundamental characteristics and expressiveness of this genre: its inherent drama, spontaneity, and the unique effects achieved

PLATE 15 (opposite)
Fiona Murphy (b. 1958)
Hybrid Figure, 1995
White clay, slips, mid-fire glaze,
hand-formed from slabs
61 x 22 x 19 cm

from the unpredictability of the firing process. Mansfield certainly follows these precepts with her work centring about functional forms, jars, tea bowls, platters and cylindrical vessels, the emphasis being on wood-fire surface and glaze aesthetics.

> I find this medium involving and challenging. All the forms of human expression and endeavour are required by the potter: physical activity in preparing and researching the materials and processes; thought is needed to make shapes appropriate for purposes of aesthetics and function; and spirit and wholeheartedness are needed if the work is to be inspirational.

Peter Rushforth (b. 1920) is one of Australia's pioneer studio master potters, having begun his career in ceramics as early as 1946. Rushforth adheres to the postwar, Anglo-Oriental tradition in this country, his wood-fired anagama, Shino and other stoneware forms embodying its humanistic philosophy and expressing its principles of aesthetic excellence.

> The materials and processes of pottery can be used to express the beauty of the natural qualities inherent to fire on clay and earth materials. Each pot form can be a journey of discovery and a personal expression of beauty; it can express human as opposed to the mechanical qualities of the machine.

Rushforth's Chun-glazed pots, with their nebulous-like, wax-resist decoration, have a particularly strong feel of Oriental tradition: their pure forms accentuate intriguing irregularities conferred by the wood-fired kiln, while their glorious blue glazes are seemingly radiant. Working within these guidelines, this master potter has brought the beauty of Australian clays and glaze materials to a sophisticated, ever fresh, level of expression.

Wood-firing produces pots — salt-glazed, or based on ancient Oriental ceramic traditions, or otherwise — which can be unaffected and restrained, embodying qualities of naturalness, yet powerful in the manner which their simple forms and subtle surfaces evoke a depth of feeling in the viewer — often one of tradition, satisfaction, comfort and warmth in everyday life. In this respect they may be extraordinarily exuberant and humanistic objects.

Zen, Landscape and Expression

Aside from the wood-fire approach and its distinctive manifestations, there are potters who, although they have been influenced by Oriental traditions or by Anglo-Oriental practices as derived from the Leach school, have used these as a basis, departing somewhat to develop their own aesthetic sensibility, one which vigorously reflects their individual approaches and ideas, often within an Australian setting.

Milton Moon (b. 1926) is one such potter who has, over a forty-five year career, drawn together the threads of his work to create his own Australian idiom in clay. Moon has unceasingly searched for such a nexus, beginning with a mastery of the traditional folk pottery of Japan, immersing himself into its Zen culture, and emerging to apply its philosophy of restraint, contemplation and

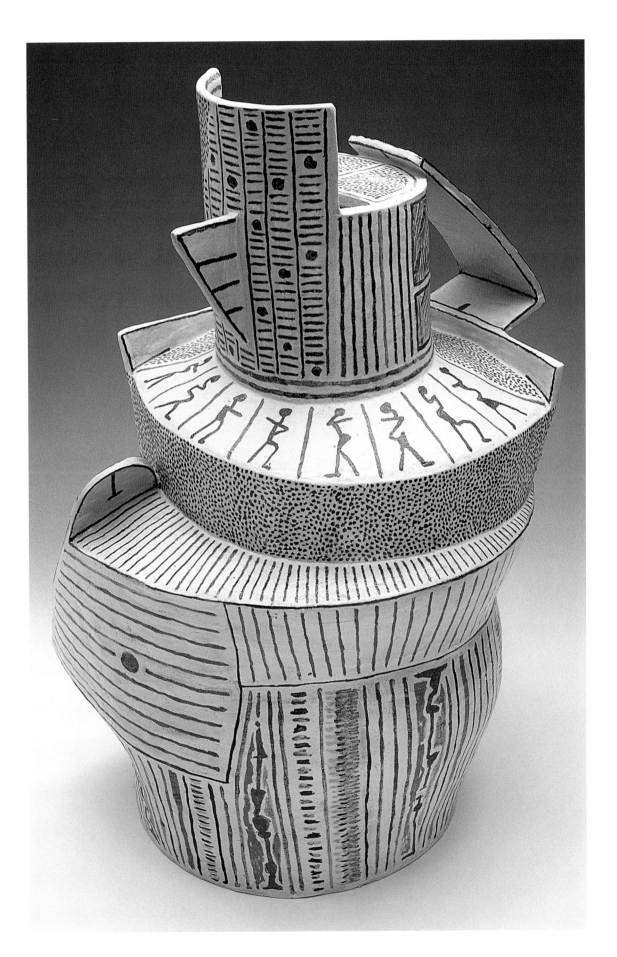

PLATE 17
Stephen Benwell (b. 1953)
Vessel, 1991
Stoneware, handbuilt,
underglaze painting
45 cm
Photo: Terence Bogue

PLATE 18
Beverley Gallop (b. 1951)
Vessel: Sirens on the Rocks series, 1995
Earthenware, copper and iron slats
and slip,
handbuilt and plaster moulding
26 x 16 cm
Photo: Hans Versluis

PLATE 19 (opposite)
Wendy Wood (b. 1970)
*Red Figure Volute — Krater:
Alison Looking Down at Bob and Cyan*, 1993
Wheelthrown, earthenware,
terra sigillata,
photo-screen image
45 x 30 cm
Photo: Matt Kelso

simplicity, to express the essences of clay and the Australian landscape. The Flinders Ranges, that rugged, ancient mountain range north of Adelaide, provide a source for developing his palette of colours, textures and forms. His ceramic works boldly capture impressions of stony, dry river beds, or the textures and tonal gradations of the ancient river red gums; the sense of vitality and place is palpable. Zen has directed his hand in the spontaneity of the brushwork, in the slashes and daubs of ochres, deep reds and pure white and black.

Moon's pots are an intersection of Zen philosophy, a clay discipline drawn from the European tradition, and a personal directness of vision, as well as an identification with the sense of place that is the arid Australian landscape.

> For the remainder of my creative life I am concerned only with a response to the land of my birth. The trace elements that have nurtured life in this land will, I hope, provide me with similar sustenance. Others may be inspired by an Internationalist approach to Art but these concerns are not mine. The highest mountains or the arid flatness of this land contain an essence both beautiful and haunting. It is this spirit that prompts my vision and it is a privilege to listen and respond.

The influence of Zen culture in ceramic art has been especially pervasive through the traditional Japanese pottery called raku. Once originally restricted to the making of bowls for the traditional tea ceremony — hence its Zen basis — the appropriation and development of raku as a genre of ceramics in the 1960s extended its potential expressiveness for Western ceramists. Especially appealing was the all-important post-fire reduction stage of raku which gave a range of subtle glaze effects, and which shifted the emphasis from Western rationality to an eastern philosophy exalting nature and spontaneity. In raku, the play of fire creates extraordinary shades, flashes and smoked iridescent effects which are readily married to free-handling, asymmetry and fortuitous imperfections in the clay — attributes which are all encouraged by the 'nowness' of Zen.

Although the consummate raku potter can manipulate and control the 'gift of the gods' post-fired smoking and reduction stage to produce an ever increasingly spectacular range of effects, this alone is not sufficient to produce a work of ceramic art: there are considerations of form, surface texture, colour and glaze, qualities which, when combined artfully, lead to an outcome which distinguishes the mediocre from the professional and which extends well beyond the component 'parts'.

Jeff Mincham (b. 1950) is one of this country's masters of the genre, at once pushing the medium to its most subtle and lavish limits of aesthetic and sculptural expression. Mincham's mastery of these qualities is immediately evident in the singular visual and emotive effects generated by his twenty-year long affair with raku.

If the soul or personality of a pot is taken as the mark of its essence — as it often is in this genre of ceramics which retains links to the Leach school of pottery — Mincham's works are profuse with this quality. The exploration of the vessel from this perspective is Mincham's singular achievement thus far. He often works with striking, though minimal, large-scale forms which have references to early Oriental bronze vessels, adding lugs, handles or indentations to create stunning textural effects and to evoke past ritualistic uses. These eloquent forms are integrated with a surface patination which often glows with a rich palette of rusty oranges, burnt sienna, garnet, claret reds and a hint of lustre. Among his more recent past works, his aptly titled *Othello* jar, for example, is a large vessel which exploits the black-fired aspects of raku, effectively embodying the dark, mysterious, sensual but menacing qualities of the Shakespearian character.

This self-assured quality is especially seen in the tactile, coiled-surface work of other vessels, or in the shape and attachment of handles and lugs, in the proportions of body, lip and foot. Although unlike his earlier, more gestural, works, Mincham has more recently reduced these additions and honed his techniques to the point that the work is often a gestalt of clay, fire and hands.

> The principle motivation of my work has always been aesthetics, even though I have until recently, confined myself to the vessel format. This is due in no small part to my exposure to Japanese ceramic ideas early in my training. These ideas have seemed to offer limitless possibilities in their expressive range, however, I have now arrived at a point where I want to say something quite different from these former preoccupations; after so many years I find I tend to think in 'clay' terms. It is now a question of turning my potter's knowledge and experience towards a new expressive genre that seems to call me.

Lately, in line with this change in direction Mincham has departed from his powerful vessel series to produce figurative work. *Masked Man* combines raku firing with a copper matt finish to enhance the expressions of strength and impregnability of the chunky, chain-mesh surface; and although the human features are concealed, the mouth and eye openings of the mask reveal an agonised cry suggesting psychological entrapment.

PLATE 20
Prue Venables (b. 1954)
Black Teapot and Cup, 1995
Porcelain, handthrown
19 x 14 x 8.5; cup: 9.5 x 9 x 6 cm
Photo: Terence Bogue

Reconfiguring the Vessel

The vessel need not remain the territory of traditionalists: there are many clay practitioners who take great delight in expressing its decorative or sculptural potential, or simply using it as a starting point to explore various concepts, make personal statements or for social critique. Such explorations of the sculptural qualities of the vessel, often in relation to function and surface qualities, result in a wide variety of expressions. These can be difficult to categorise as they often have features which overlap, but where the vessel is the starting point for the explorative journey, they have been grouped as follows.

Fiona Murphy's (b. 1958) ceramics are intensive sculptural investigations into the convolutions of surface, texture and decoration as elements which constitute the vessel. Most of her *Biomorphic* forms are curvaceous and are waisted once or twice, or else are based on a standard baluster form which is used as the starting point for various modifications. The rims of her pots undergo various metamorphoses, either rounding off into minimal neat edges, or else unfolding into crenellated, cubist ensembles and other elaborate profiles. Surfaces are generally left in the unglazed, porous appearance, with throwing rings visible, or else, partly smoothed and further textured with delicate chatter work. Others are given regular dimples or gestural 'scratches', eye-like dot patterns or coloured patches of cross-thatching — these are always sparingly added.

The forms are at once elegant and seductive, and often strongly suggestive of female essence. But the final effect is a heightening of the idea of an organic form and its enveloping of space, and even a sense of unfolding, of deconstruction and reconstruction.

> My biomorphic vessel forms convey aspects of human experience — my particular focus. Slowly modelled then shaped, the complexity of ideas is reduced until the form's essence remains. As sculptural forms they suggest natural processes; when placed in groups they express another layer of meaning through their spatial relationships.

Surreal, alien, extra-terrestrial, Andrea Hylands's (b. 1952) abstract vessels lift our perception of ceramic art to a new level of perception. Working with the absolute white purity porcelain and bone china, Hylands creates bizarre variations of the vessel; often, these seem to be derived from organic sources, perhaps microscopic diatoms or some other little-seen life form. The white and smooth surfaces porcelain provides are an effective 'canvas' for the application of brilliant colours, her designs centring around the simulation of alien skin membranes or skins.

Her focus is one of design, as well as on virtuoso technique and skill, assembling and marrying abstract porcelain forms with a perfectionist's approach to graphic decoration. Yet, despite their novel forms, their tactile spines, rich skin venations and overall strange imagery, these creations retain their identity as ceramic vessels, and in this way, establish a dialogue of paradoxes.

The latest series of work is about reinterpreting the pot in an abstract way. These complex vessels are a product of intricate processes, and have been enriched with decoration and embellishment. These pots use distortion and deception, they lie somewhere between the ordinary and the extraordinary, suggesting an ambiguity of purpose. In this way, the familiar becomes a surprise, exaggerating the surreal aspect of a pot as opposed to a pot as an everyday object.

The sculptural and painted iconography of Stephen Benwell's (b. 1953) ceramics is emphatically characteristic of this potter's work. The deconstruction of the vessel into sculptural components and its reintegration into new configurations is his preferred approach, simultaneously working the surface as a carrier for idiosyncratic, symbolic and ornamental qualities. There is a suggestion of cubist exploration in the way he cuts the vessel into planes which are then reassembled to produce a sculptural object, one which retains strong references to its origins, yet which now carries a figurative striving. This imagery is enhanced by complex designs painted on the surface, often seemingly casual and looking much like doodles animating and unifying the form.

PLATE 21
Kevin White (b. 1954)
Vessel, 1995
Slip-cast with Limoges porcelain,
underglaze blue
and red-enamel pigment
16.5 x 13.8 cm

PLATE 22
Patsy Hely (b. 1946)
Jug with Two Spouts, 1994
Porcelain, slipcast and assembled
10.5 x 9.5 cm
Photo: David Young

PLATE 23
Alan Peascod (b. 1943)
Ego and the Art of Self Inflation, 1995
Vitreous terracotta, gas reduction fired,
hand finished
34 cm

These crisp sculptural forms, with their rich patterning, are imbued with a refreshing sense of the naive, but this belies the complex intellectual basis of their construction and the personal meaning Benwell wishes to communicate — one which invites the viewer to ponder their enigmatic qualities.

Similarly, deconstruction and reconstruction, and the relationship of form, surface and texture is Beverley Gallop's (b. 1951) interest, although she is also concerned with figurative explorations. Her reference point is also the vessel, its inner and outer surfaces, and its potential for sculptural explorations a particular focus. Her unique forms seem to be caught in the act of a secret unfolding, a seemingly instinctual metamorphosis from static, inorganic clay into mobile organic shapes, and even chameleon creatures, half human and half vessel.

I seek to create complex surfaces, allowing the methods of construction to suggest
their own conjunctions. The point at which the inner and outer surfaces meet, and
the fugitive nature of texture and colouration.

In an entirely contrasting approach, Wendy Wood (b. 1970) creates vessels as a contemporary material expression she refers to as 'alternative culture'. She is exploring this broad theme through a series of ceramic vessels based on Greek Attic Black Figure Pottery (c. 550 B.C.). Sometimes making complete forms, other times large fragments or shards, Wendy authentically simulates the character of this archaic genre of pottery, yet subverts its original use by combining the traditional ancient forms with contemporary images. Wood utilises a technique which photo-screen-prints the surfaces. However, instead of scenes of Classical Greek mythology, Wendy's vessels and shards have images from everyday life: a mum pushing a pram; a man watching television; a couple in modern dress conversing. The works evoke the idea of mythologies and legends, but specifically, Wood wishes to create an illusion, one which acts as a shock, or to trick people into 'thinking they are looking at authentic ancient pottery, but seeing contemporary life instead…'

Wood's work is usually shown in museum settings within display cabinets, complete with shards and labels which have text styled in the manner with which archaeological displays would be identified. In this manner, she contextualises the work in a setting which further enhances the deception of their authenticity. As a result, visitors receive a gentle shock on realising the true nature of the work. Hence Wood is a ceramic illusionist, creating cultural tableaus seemingly of an ancient past, but in reality of a very immediate present: the effect is powerful, and intellectually refreshing.

> The ceramic medium has enabled us to view the past through its immortalising characteristics. Traditionally, the ancient Greek form was a means of conveying stories, everyday events and narratives through its imagery. I too wish to document my generation and culture, but through contemporary methods such as photography and mechanical type. Lately, I have begun to further the incorporation of technology into my work by using images that have been generated by computer from home video movies.

Ancient Greek Krater vessels carried their surface decoration as part of the function, telling stories or teaching moral values. For the latter, just think of the those elaborate classical vases with their friezes of gods and humans, reliving myths, legends, parables or historical events. Wood's work similarly relies on the storytelling functions of the traditional component of her vessels as the 'carrier' for her contemporary parables. Hence, predominant design elements in common with all examples of Wood's work include recognisable ancient forms in combination with contemporary images of day-to-day life. Replacing Greek mythology with mundane scenes represents a process of bricolage in which image substitution is used to imbue the imagery of everyday life with the mystery and power of what it replaces — in this case mythology.

In Wood's ceramics, a materialised 'present as past', recontexualises contemporary culture, or reclaims it through a type of creative archaeology; it's a strategy which effects a reversal of our scrutiny onto ourselves. This 'neo-archaic' genre is also seen in the work of Rod Bamford, Richard Doheny, Brian Hirst and Paul Sanders.

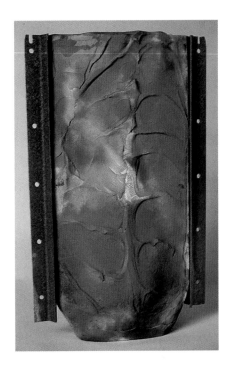

PLATE 24
Paul Counsel (b. 1953)
The Stamp of European Possession, 1994
Clay with patinated copper surface and corroded steel
60 x 28 cm

PLATE 25
Brigitte Enders (b. 1949)
Guardian, 1993
Slab-built stoneware, blackslip,
stencil, oxidation firing
32 x 34 x 9 cm
Photo: Klaus Moje

Wood's post-modernist, neo-classical jars are ambiguous, evocative, engaging and intertextual — they are replete with layered meanings. Her simulation of ancient ceramic textures and surfaces creates patinations which evoke conditioned responses, and hence, the illusion of age and meaning; unlike authentic relics which offer paths to the past, contemporary craftworks of this genre such as Wood's work, offer an affective re-experience of the present, hence possibly aiding in our adaptive mental constructs for order.

Utility as an Aesthetic

Using the notion of function as a starting point for developing an approach to ceramics remains an attractive one for contemporary practitioners. Function is not necessarily restricted to practical utility such as pouring tea or holding liquids: it may also refer to ritual, ceremonial and symbolic uses. Usually, it is difficult to separate one from the other. Exploring these aspects of the functional in pottery results in engaging, familiar and satisfying work. It may not challenge in a conceptual sense, but it is often pleasing to the eye, sensuous to the touch, and comforting for its delivery of basic needs.

Prue Venables (b. 1954) is one such potter whose focus is on a direct expression of the functional qualities of domestic wares. Reduced to its essentials of shape, surface and design for use, Venables demonstrates sensitivity to her medium, bringing out the visual as well as the utilitarian elegance of the most minimal forms of traditional pottery, yet imbuing it with a modern sensibility. Working with the translucency and strength of porcelain allows her to achieve extraordinary delicacy in her thrown and altered forms: teapots and cups, bowls, jugs and dishes; these are finished with a clear calcium glaze, and sometimes with finely painted surface decoration. Earlier references to eighteenth- and nineteenth-century English industrial pottery styles linger, but more recent influences include simple metal and plastic vessels, such as oil cans and toffee tins, remembered from her childhood. With their unusual, slightly askew sides, the latter confer a gentle but alluring eccentricity, a hallmark of her work.

> My particular interest is in the making of functional pots — simple objects to be held and used and provide a lifetime of challenge and excitement. Recent pots are thrown, then altered when wet. New bases are added at the leather-hard stage. The thrown clay becomes a building material rather than a finishing point — completed pieces retaining the sprung tension of their thrown origin. I enjoy the contradictory nature of some of these pieces — where apparent simplicity conceals a laborious making process.

Kevin White (b. 1954) is similarly concerned with the qualities of the functional as an aesthetic of form, and which he expresses in combination with a fine sensibility in graphic design and brushwork. His elegant work is always made using Limoges porcelain, then decorated in underglaze blue with an on-glaze red enamel pigment. Teapots, bowls and other vessels fuse the distillation of his experiences in Japan and England: the former is evident in the spontaneous and elegant style of his brushwork combined with the application of traditional, red enamel pigment. As such, the decoration sometimes hints at Imari Ware, while the latter is suggested by the delicacy of his slip-casting techniques.

> My works stem from a preoccupation with functional aesthetics, and whilst the work is seldom prescriptively utilitarian, its character seeks to be revealed through use. Whilst at rest, the work may act as the custodian of ceremony, in use to celebrate it.

Patsy Hely (b. 1946) has reduced form to absolute essentials, whittled away surface decoration, and has left exposed the stages of the making process to construct very simple pots with surprisingly strong character for use about the home. Using an off-white porcelain, she slip casts then assembles forms with only the barest minimum of touch in dressing up the final clay surface. And while a strong industrial sensibility is evident, it is the touch of hand that is dominant.

> My attitude/philosophy toward contemporary craft is in a state of flux: is contemporary craft an artifice? Are contemporary and craft mutually exclusive terms? What's wrong with machines — are things made by hand *really* any better?

Her questioning approach leaves her open to many possibilities, themselves evident in the boldness of her work which poses riddles, and suggests new solutions to time-honoured pathways.

On the Edge: Sculptural and Figurative Expressions

At the other extreme of clay practice, practitioners may eschew the focus on the vessel, and for that matter, any traditional ceramic basis, to pursue an approach of innovative, free-expressionism, often allied to various art movements or notions current in the visual arts.

The sculptural or figurative genre of ceramics is a vibrant one: it is multi-thematic, eclectic in its sourcing of imagery and ideas, it may be ambiguous, it may be gestural, abstract, complex, folksy or academic, it may be closely representative of the external world, or symbolic of inner life. At its essence, clay becomes the starting point for realisation of a concept through the creation of a form which articulates surface and space, mass and volume. It may or may not be representative, it may embody symbols, it may or may not relate to historical or contemporary antecedents.

Strategies for consciously imbuing a visual imagery or language with various meanings varies according to the treatment and cultural location and signifiers utilised. For example, the scale the practitioner chooses to work in has its own connotations: large works make their emphatic statements compared to medium-sized works for everyday associations, or small to miniature for the intimate. Similarly, the finished surface has its phraseology: whether raw to suggest the primitive, or stone-like to indicate impregnability, or highly glazed for sophistication or perhaps

PLATE 26
Rod Bamford (b. 1958)
Rehabilitation and Retribution, 1992
Bone China
31 x 200 cm (large object)

PLATE 28
Mitsuo Shoji (b. 1946)
Ritual Plates, 1992
Terracotta
36.5 x 36.5 cm (each tile)

superficiality; and colour is powerful: monochrome focuses the eye on form, whilst varicoloured finishes can be lifting, joyful, red is obvious, blue is cool, sombre, distancing. Another tool is ambiguity: it puzzles and stimulates the intellect, questions convention and provides alternatives, demands attention and thought.

In this post-modernist setting, historical references or traditional elements or motifs similarly carry their own meanings, while the context of their use further extends the practitioner's vocabulary of expression. The latter may be drawn from any culture or period, the flotsam and jetsam of society selected and reordered to create new meanings, ironic references, to parody, to criticise, to explore, to mirror, to suggest, to tell stories, to evoke memories, to challenge, to shock, or to make familiar the unfamiliar.

In this way, the sculptural or figurative ceramist represents, investigates, questions, or simply celebrates aspects of the human condition through the medium of clay.

Alan Peascod (b. 1943) is an acknowledged authority on lustre technology and Islamic ceramic art, including its philosophical basis — and more widely, a 'ceramist's ceramist', as I have described him in the past. A master in his field, Peascod's recent work has seen the maturation of figurative work satirising the modern human condition. Whilst expanding this interest the artist

PLATE 27 (opposite)
Richard Doheny (b. 1966)
Ironic Paradox: Destruction of Cultures,
1995
Terracotta, coloured slips,
thrown and modelled
220 x 65 cm

PLATE 29
Jenny Orchard (b. 1951)
Australian Bunyip Teapot, 1995
Slipcast and handmade earthenware
30 cm

retains a special commitment to the container form in recognition of its unique creative powers and identity.

He has a singular, unrelenting approach to his ceramic practice, describing his work as coming into existence 'because of an independence and focused, observational studio experience that seeks to find inherently visual and tactile ceramic qualities in form and surface finish.'

Slumping, cracking, fusion, crawling, clinking, tonal modulation, texture and colour variances — these form the basis for a ceramic vocabulary that articulates complex ideas, investigates various issues, and challenges the status quo.

Peascod's sculptural ceramic work emerges as a consequence of this depth of experience, technical expertise, and strongly defined ideological stance. His strident approach to a relentless, self-critical intellectual assessment, is tempered by intuitive processes, and combined with the skilful manipulation of form and uniquely glazed surfaces to express an abrasive, forceful, satirical, and even acerbic, figurative imagery. This establishes dialogues around various themes, often complex and abstract, including hedonism, criticism, the meaning of aesthetics, opportunism, and creative discourse.

Peascod's philosophy includes the rejection of the use of industrial ceramic processes, choosing to focus on a personalised development of motifs and ceramic processes sourced from Middle Eastern traditions. Combined with his willingness to take risks, he has created an individual iconography within the realm of contemporary ceramic art.

Paul Counsel (b. 1953) combines clay and corroded steel to create works which represent, metaphorically, the interaction of Aboriginal and white societies respectively. He is especially interested in the impact colonisation had on our first Australians and, by juxtaposing these primary materials, he alludes to certain events and practices which have taken place since 1788.

> Controlling the way the past is remembered enhances the potential for controlling the way the present is viewed. A concern I hold is that our history has been prejudiced by ideals and assumptions which lie at the foundations of our ways of thinking. With regard to the Aboriginal experience, my work is a response to a need I perceive in white Australia to change the way we remember our past.

Counsel specifically looks at issues of alienation, identity, genocide, landscape, and cultural destruction. His challenges are presented in distinctive sculptural combinations of fired clay and corroded steel: the former with its patinated copper surfaces evokes the colours of the Australian landscape, and hence symbolises the Aboriginal people, while the latter, with its inherent technological stridency, represents white society. Both of these mediums carry various associations, and it is with their skilful juxtapositioning that he produces a visual language for projecting various meanings: significations of subjugation, cultural invasion, possession,

PLATE 30
Susan Jorgensen (b. 1951)
But the Bird Still Sings, 1994
Terracotta, fumed copper glaze,
wheelthrown and handbuilt
75 cm
Photo: Louis Nigro

PLATE 31
Fiona Hiscock (b. 1965)
Still life Urn, 1995
(Text: 'Inside, outside, upside down,
don't you feel like leaving town')
Earthenware
54 x 40 cm
Photo: Terence Bogue

assimilation and integration, are effectively communicated through these means. As a cultural bricoleur, Counsel's metaphoric reconstructions of an historic past provides an opportunity for reflection and perhaps, even atonement.

Brigitte Enders (b. 1949) explores an expressionist geometric aesthetic, juxtaposing formally structured planes and adding minimal decorative motifs to achieve abstract solutions in clay. These sculptural efflorescences explore volume and space, surface and frozen movement; they articulate mathematical equations through physical manifestations. In *Guardian*, edges are mechanically precise and keen, surfaces smooth, colours reduced to dot and line motifs of gold patterned over black. The predominant sculptural elements, the planes, are neatly calculated in their conjoining, emphasising a precision of technique and finish, and projecting a powerful sense of control which is certainly admirable, yet unnerving.

Less abstract is the use of historical narrative to order the present, a kind of 'lost civilisation' theme which has long been a popular one for exploration by clay practitioners. The idea of presenting an imaginary future fallen civilisation, a 'read the present as a future past' so to speak, is effective if there is a depth of content in the details and forms. If approached with imagination, this style can provide a realm of rich imagery and metaphor, acting as a critique of contemporary culture.

Rod Bamford (b. 1958) has been one such ceramist who has been particularly preoccupied with this theme, developing its potential for metaphoric expression for some years.

> Although I was taught craft skills, I reject romantic or nostalgic attachment to revivalist movements. Instead, I am concerned with the evolution of contemporary practice in a so-called post-industrial era. Here, technological, information and organisational factors associated with industrial development have radically altered our social understanding of the creative process and object. My recent work is concerned with issues connecting social history, technology and industry, an aesthetic informed by refined materials, processes, and aspects of redundancy which affect both objects and people.

Bamford is therefore especially interested in the use of ceramic shards, especially those made from industrial processes, to delve into past ceramic traditions. He creates his own shards which are then reconfigured into constructions, hence recontexualising technological history into new discourses. This creation and destruction, or assembly and fragmentation process, recalls the post-modernist, cultural bricolage strategy. *Rehabilitation and Retribution* demonstrates that this process can even result in forms that seem to have their own unique, cultural integrity and existence. Bamford's pseudo-archaeological artefacts or 'neo-antique' fragments set up intriguing dialogues, the glazed and unglazed surfaces and snatches of decorated ceramic fragments giving clues to the would-be investigator.

Richard Doheny (b. 1966) is similarly interested in the 'reconstructed past as future'. He creates ceramic works on a very large scale, using Classical and Gothic architectural imagery as his visual idioms, and fusing the gestural marks of the creative process with applied, overt symbolism centring about spiritual and materialist themes. In one series, church arches and cloisters are presented as haunting, romantic ruins, evoking a mix of mystical medievalism, Christianity, and lost beliefs. But it is Doheny's monolithic Grecian or Roman columns which are especially vigorous in their materialisations, the physical, handmade evidence of the ceramic process a metaphor for destruction, and of self-consuming societies.

> I am concerned with megalomaniac empire builders, diseased minds whose only desire is to possess. Self-esteem being judged on the ownership of things including other people, power and resources.

Doheny has honed his techniques to the point that the work appears raw and incomplete, but this is where the strength of his imagery emerges. Sometimes, as in *Ironic Paradox: Destruction of Cultures*, he leaves the work entirely unglazed so that the clay surface exhibits flame marks as an alternative sign. Deconstructed, the symbols of Western life have been reduced to their basic components: classical columns are fractured midway, their decaying surfaces, rapid painterly effects, dry-glazed finishes and other post-modernist references, linking historical and contemporary sensibilities — the present enhanced by the past.

PLATE 32
Lorraine Jenyns (b. 1945)
Dislocation 6: Archaic Smile, 1995
Ceramic, wood, glazes, acrylic paint
45 x 30 x 15 cm

Although Mitsuo Shoji (b. 1946) similarly produces ceramic sculptures, often as installations, the conceptual basis for his work derives from issues in the contemporary visual arts, combined with elements related to the essential qualities of clay. Although traditional Japanese ceramic practices are not his interest so much as innovative explorations, aspects of his past homeland culture are often revealed in his work, notably in the way he uses scale and texture, and in the directness of expression his work assumes.

His work departs from our usual ideas of ceramics, and is just as likely to combine glass shards with terracotta, or express concepts purely in fired or unfired clay: as such, Shoji's work is representative of the furthest edges that ceramic practice may extend without losing its identity within the visual arts spectrum.

Typical of Shoji's more recent work is a complex installation in six parts which he created as an exploration of 'human thought'. It included works produced in multiples or as multi-media constructions, or else as sets of fired ceramic objects, variously expressing or representing aspects of human emotions or intellectual processes. Particularly intriguing was his *Daily Ritual Objects*, a

PLATE 33
Gerry Wedd (b. 1957)
Tower and Pin set, 1995
Thrown, coloured slips
22 cm
Photo: Mark Kimber

PLATE 34 (opposite)
Peter Johnson (b. 1952)
From One Place To Another, 1995
Handbuilt, coiled, colloidal, coloured slips
160 x 22 cm
Photo: Michal Kluvanek

wall-mounted work consisting of twenty large terracotta tiles with carved low-relief images of a variety of tools and other objects including a screw, knife, comb, watch and spectacles. Another work in this installation recreates these objects in the round, transformed from two to three dimensions: this generates metaphoric references to our relationship with the material world.

Clay, in these and his other works, fired or unfired, confers its own set of associations, especially in the context of Shoji's use of this medium's ability to shift from plastic to solid form: as such, these transformations become representative of shifts in thought and emotion.

Narratives and Icons of Suburbia

In the past three or so years, memory and storytelling have been the big themes for ceramists and glass artists — as well as for practitioners of the other craft media. Each of these media carry their own set of cultural associations or historical links, and these, together with the sculptural and decorative imagery they are moulded into, convey the personal fantasies or dreams of each artist. But it's not all serious, and what could be depressing or otherwise serious themes, are often explored with humour or irony.

Jenny Orchard (b. 1951) works in slip-cast ceramics, creating eccentric figurative forms, often with zoomorphic or floral allusions. These are ingeniously developed from a set of basic geometric shapes which are finished in brightly decorated colours and patterns. Horny protuberances or tendricular handles often sprout from exotic figures, teapots, mugs and other forms, which dance about with an energetic vigour.

The distinction between functional and sculptural is often blurred in Orchard's work: her teapots often have an organic vitality which belies their utilitarian intentions; indeed, in some of

PLATE 35
Ben Booth (b. 1969)
Aviator, 1995
Press-moulded, handbuilt, stoneware,
ashglazes and mixed-media
60 x 60 cm
Photo: Dan Armstrong

these forms one must search hard to find the lid or spout, the teapot having taken the image of an imaginary mythological creature such as an Australian bunyip or some other fantastic hybrid. Her African background is undoubtedly one of her other sources of visual influence, as noted in the horns and surface patterning which often suggests animals of the plains, just as enlarged lips and head-dresses conjure the endemic peoples of the continent. Further influences have tempered these into contemporary forms. Also notable are the typical feminine shapes of her work, as seen in their rounded appendages and bodies which, in combination with their functions as objects such as teapots, emphasise domestic associations.

Orchard's sculptural forms derive their eclectic, yet unified, imagery from these diverse sources: industrial processes, various cultures and their myths, and her own personal urges to construct meaning.

> I am interested in the interplay between culture and form. My work emerges from
> my particular experience of English tradition, African and Aboriginal artistic
> expressions and mythologies, as well as from Australian contemporary culture.

Orchard's *Australian Bunyip Teapot* demonstrates this fusion of diversity as seen in its parodying of the English teapot, the portrayal of an Australian mythological creature, the bold patterns and colours which evoke a sense of Africa, and the sleek look of the contemporary slip-cast finish she utilises.

This kind of eclectic sourcing towards the creation of imagery in clay could easily lead to uncomfortable hybrids were it not for the application of rigorous intellectual and intuitive processes on the part of the practitioner. Susan Jorgensen (b. 1951) similarly applies these abilities, in this instance to search history and its cultural traditions for motifs and other elements for her large-scale figurative work. This ambitiously investigates the human form, its nature and its changing relationships with social mores over various periods and cultures.

Her allegorical female figures have a distinctive imagery which references early Chinese, medieval European or African sources. These female figures — usually crowned, helmeted or wearing medieval head-dresses — invariably shoulder small houses, castles, casks, books or baskets; they stand bowed under their weight, delicately poised on small primitive carts, as in *But the Bird Still Sings*. Terracotta and fumed copper surfaces which display textured patinas resembling rusted metal, are heightened by the addition of screws, bolts and lugs over their bodies, these qualities and elements further layering the metaphoric richness and timeless quality of the figures.

> The human form is the perfect vehicle for the expression of my experiences in life.
> The possibilities of line, gesture and meaning are at the same time limitless and
> very personal. Any unravelling of meaning behind my work is entirely personal
> and depends on the disposition of the viewer, as it is mostly created at a
> subconscious level rather than with intellectual preoccupations.

PLATE 36
Stephen Bowers (b. 1952)
Coffee Mugs, 1994
Underglaze decoration, on-glaze lustres
Ht: 11 cm
Photo: Michal Kluvanek

Fiona Hiscock (b. 1965) takes the familiar form of the vessel and imbues it with a personal narrative of ideas and imagery to similarly explore aspects of the human condition. Her stoneware forms depart somewhat from conventional appearance — handles have extra curls, spouts are exaggerated — while the decorative imagery and added text tell tales from the domestic setting. Having grown up in the countryside, Hiscock has retained an interest in pioneering values, carrying these with her into the urban setting where they have become interpreted and embodied in her work.

PLATE 37
Thancoupie (b. 1936)
One Flower Pot: Mosquito Man, 1992
Handbuilt, stoneware, iron and
manganese stains
22 x 21 cm

I love the way vessels bring people together and act as a witness of our celebratory and more humble moments. Harking back to a bygone era carries some inherent issues of nostalgia, yearning and idealisation which I attempt to convey in my work. I attempt to subvert this by adding various symbols from the natural, rural and urban settings.

This exploration of personal narratives in clay has attracted many ceramists, including Lorraine Jenyns (b. 1945) whose figurative sculptural works have developed over a long career in ceramics. These are always colourful and vibrant, varying in their expression and mix of the joyous, humorous, cynical, symbolic, primordial or poignant. In this way her work represents a personal journey whose overriding theme is one of festivity and a celebration of life.

Jenyns combines conceptual and expressive approaches of painting and sculpture with ceramics to concentrate on expressing her ideas, but without being especially obsessive about the medium and its finish. Through handbuilding, she imbues her work with an immediacy of execution, while her use of bright earthenware underglazes enhances the folksy, almost naive, imagery of her pieces; colour is an essential element.

Jenyns's fascination with Classical Greek, Egyptian, pre-Columbian and other ancient cultures is apparent. Her work takes elements from these sources and reconfigures them into new symbols. Hearts are a favourite motif, representing love, joy, mystery or yearning. Assembling motifs into engaging visual compositions of realism and fantasy, she also creates enigmatic meanings in her quest to make connections and to view life from an enlightened perspective — as evident in *Dislocation 6: Archaic Smile*: 'I am interested in developing new mythologies in a contemporary society which has lost that connection — not just as narrative which deals with the distant past'.

Gerry Wedd (b. 1957) packages his ceramics with stories of everyday life, and whether they are about relationships, personal aspirations or domesticity, they are often autobiographical. He is a master at communicating conflicting emotions with an energetic visual style — love and hate, violence and optimism, betrayal and honour, death and life. Using domestic wares or large urns as carriers of his restless, narrative iconography, and by applying rich underglaze graphics, semi-relief work and other techniques, he creates a characteristic, neo-baroque imagery. This often combines a set of favourite motifs such as hearts, dogs, scissors, skulls, and rolling pins which act as symbols of various emotional states. When applied to such ordinary items such as teapots and jugs, these are transformed from their daily routine functions into objects imbued with strong irreverence and wry humour, deriding our domestic myths.

I work in three or more areas, jewellery, ceramics, and drawing, but the greatest portion of my time is spent on production. Most of my work activity is concerned with a notion of 'the domestic', either in a practical (functional) sense or a dramatic one. I'm much more interested in Dennis Potter (the writer) and Leonard Cohen's work than that of any craft or art practitioner.

PLATE 38
Pippin Drysdale (b. 1943)
Constellation I, Pinnacle series, 1995
Porcelain, glazed and stained, platinum lustre;
three firings
24 x 23 cm
Photo: Victor France

Wedd's opulent ceramics present an imagery which is potent and touching as he explores suburban myths with a compelling mixture of cynicism and optimism, but tempered with a liberal sprinkling of irony and wit; *Tower and Pin* combines these issues in the quintessential domestic forms.

Figurative elements are also prevalent in Peter Johnson's (b. 1952) work which sets out to explore identity and its relationship to human behaviour in the everyday setting. His work varies from decorative vessels and small-scale figures through to quite impressive, almost life-size figures. The former focuses about a series of reliquary or Canopic-like jars which are decorated with underglaze panels depicting narrative vignettes of suburban life, the lids surmounted by small figures of boys in playful — though static — poses, toys in hand; they evoke narrative and biographical themes.

His striking large-scale figures of boys are presented as engrossed in play, always on their own, and sometimes with a toy aeroplane in hand, as in the piece *From One Place To Another*. These

PLATE 39
David Potter (b. 1955)
Network, 1995
Stoneware, thrown with decal
onglaze decoration
54 x 32 cm
Photo: Terence Bogue

figures have curious, frozen poses, their eyes lifeless and sad, suggesting an inner emptiness or sense of meaninglessness. Constructed by handbuilding and coiling, with colloidal, slip finishes coloured in soft, earthy tones, their presence evokes a surreal or dreamlike state, heightening the idea or a sense of memories condensed into fired clay. Johnson constructs his figures to invite our own projections, or else to trigger universal fears: has youth passed by? Who am I? Are we alone?

Ben Booth (b. 1969) is similarly drawing on biographical preoccupations, although his subject matter is seemingly less serious. He considers his interest in ceramics 'as an extension of a childhood consumed with model making and pyromania'. Reconfigured with a humorous facet, his work attempts to embody 'a possible past or future'. He takes two paths towards this quest. The first creates an imagery of the 'aviator', a puppet-like figure as the mad inventor cruising through the air. Conceived in matt stoneware and partly dressed in a bizarre apparel made up of found objects such as a tea strainer as an eyepiece and an old blow-torch base as a backpack rocket device, *Aviator* evokes the imaginary world of childhood — and perhaps that lingering urge to escape reality.

Booth's second path of exploration retains this playfulness and the theme of flying or escape, ostensibly from the gravity of earth, but more likely from the pressures of contemporary life. He constructs ceramic spaceships and asteroid objects, which he presents as an installation hung from the gallery ceiling. These funky, baby-like rocketships are cute, their ceramic bodies have *trompe l'oeil* surfaces simulating rivetted metal sheets, fins and goggle portholes, some carrying the passenger's baggage tied with rope on raised external platforms. Booth's figurative works invite us to journey back, to take delight in a gentle humour, to smile without any edge of cynicism or irony.

Ornamental Concerns

Once ceramic art was straightforward, there was no ambiguity: a pot was a container for holding substances or preparing and using foods; a sculpture decorated a space, signalled status or represented religious figures or spirituality. Vessels and other ceramic works carried their surface decoration as part of their overt function, indicating contents, adding variation to otherwise monotonous surfaces, celebrating skills, proclaiming wealth, revelling in visual richness, telling stories or teaching moral values.

So decoration was never simply decoration, but was inextricably linked to the overall design of the artefact, so that it functioned to express particular values or signs. Then along came the modern movement with its sterilising machine aesthetic and its emphasis on mechanical, repetitive and plain surfaces. This anti-craft ethic has been rejected and lately, with the liberalising philosophy of post-modernism, the richness and enduring qualities of the tradition, and narrative of ornament have been discovered and applied anew.

Contemporary craft practitioners invariably demonstrate a sensitivity to the histories and

traditions of ornament and decoration in the decorative and applied arts; these are being actively researched and re-evaluated, appropriated and quoted, reassembled and reiterated. From the pre-historical to the Celtic, from the Classical to the Gothic, from the Baroque to Rococo, from Art Nouveau to Art Deco, the choice is considerable. Within the long history of endeavour in ceramic art a cornucopia of technical and stylistic genres and decorative conventions has accumulated. The former includes terracotta, majolica, salt-glazed pottery, blue and white, lustre wares, raku pottery, Limoges Porcelain, and Imari Ware, to name but a handful: all are repositories or formulas for decorative adornment, its narratives, its textural gestures, its motifs, its evocations, and its conventions. The painted or decorated pot or fired clay artefact often acts as a canvas for painterly gestures or for figurative or abstract embellishments, for graphic representation or visual commentary — or else it simply enriches our sensual environment, adding colour, texture, exuberance and presence.

Among Australia's foremost ceramists, Stephen Bowers (b. 1952) is a designer and decorator noted for his extraordinarily refined and exuberant, underglaze brushwork. His decorated domestic wares and exhibition works reference the rich traditions of historical applied decoration to present as a marvel of rhythm, balance, colour and graphic design. Bowers's figurative underglaze work is often based on his interest in Australian fauna and flora which he embellishes with a humorous edge. They often incorporate elements or fragments of earlier pottery decorative traditions, sometimes derived from nineteenth-century Staffordshire, such as the Oriental blue-and-white. In this sense, Bowers is a decorative bricoleur rummaging through history to extract motifs and snatches of patterning and decoration which he reworks into virtuoso tableaus which delight and intrigue the viewer.

> The best pieces of functional domestic pottery can easily enjoy recognition as being stylish and beautiful; they can also be complex, charming and meaningful. My style of decoration is what I tend to be best known for — I give a lot of attention to detail and the possibilities for decorative surfaces, combining and juxtaposing images that interest me to create ironic or whimsical 'situations'. I consider my work to be self-reflective, quirky and amusingly decorative — a kind of personal antidote or oblique strategy for coping in this daunting age.

Decorated Vase and *Coffee Mugs* are works which reveal Bowers's ceramic mastery and graphic wit in an opulence rarely matched in the field, while simultaneously demonstrating how the fusion of decoration with function can imbue everyday articles with a renewed life.

Although an increasing number of Aboriginal Australians are taking up ceramics as a full-time career, they still remain in a minority in respect to those who practise traditional Aboriginal crafts, or in comparison to the non-indigenous population in this field. Of the small handful of Aboriginal people who took up ceramics during the early years of the crafts movement, Thancoupie (b. 1936) is without a doubt their foremost practitioner. Brought up in a tribal

PLATE 40 (opposite)
Ray Taylor (b. 1944)
Raku Pot, 1996
Raku, slips
14 cm

Aboriginal setting in Northern Queensland, since the early 1970s she has been hand-building and firing stoneware vessels and tiled murals. Her pot forms are invariably spherical and decorated in a style which is contemporary, yet recognisably Aboriginal in their subject matter.

Thancoupie's pots are frequently decorated with stylised Aboriginal figurative symbols, such as the circle motif which represents life. They are arranged as friezes which present narratives based on the indigenous Australian mythology. Although these stories have been translated into a non-traditional medium in respect to Aboriginal culture, they effectively capture and express the sense of place and meaning as encoded in the Aboriginal Dreamtime. Her figurative or abstracted imagery is usually incised into the pot surface and enhanced through the use of stains or glazes in earthy, matt stoneware colours.

Thancoupie's biographer, Jennifer Isaacs, describes her work as 'a combination of true traditional knowledge and religion of the land, and a contemporary sense of the history of art and the artist's place in the wider society'. Certainly, Thancoupie's vessels demonstrate how the decoration can transcend superficial surface gesturing to become a carrier of potent symbolism and meaning. Her *Mosquito Man* decorated pot, for example, refers to the Dreamtime story of the Knool tribe's corroboree where the participants 'danced days and days'. Thancoupie's round pot with its bold frieze of stylised, elongated figures effectively captures the exuberance and longevity of this Dreamtime dancing.

From another perspective, Pippin Drysdale (b. 1943) makes pots which celebrate their functions as containers and their surfaces as carriers of colour and pattern. Her highly refined recent works, all bowls, are quintessential metaphors of the female form as giver, while their decorated surfaces capture the open horizons and colours of the Australian landscape. These detailed painterly lines and stipples in oranges, ochres, yellows and gentle lustres may represent cracked dry soils, or else they could perhaps depict the striations of native tree trunks, or simply the abstracted impressions of long distant horizons. Drysdale's linear, gestural markings enhance the purity and warmth of the minimalist forms of the vessels which, in their presentation as groups, evoke central desert monoliths and landscapes.

> My *Pinnacle* series are formal objects which exploit the bowl's ability to convey
> dualities — to contain oppositions. The subtle shifts in colour in the groupings
> mirror the subtleties of hue to be found in the Western Australian interior.

These *Pinnacle* series are yet another successful departure from Drysdale's previously accomplished decorative work, demonstrating her ability to combine form with surface to produce ceramic work of considerable elegance.

David Potter (b. 1955) is a practitioner who has the ability to project an intensely individualised expressionism of ceramic tradition through the focus of the vessel and its decorative potential. Exploring the boundaries of clay, history and self, he has lately taken to developing his work using unique and innovative sources. His research has been centred around traditional forms and pattern-making lately discovering, in his investigations of new types of designs, interesting similarities between new technologies and the ancient craft of weaving. Combining these disjunctives he has produced vessels with complex yet lyrical surface imagery, one which communicates aspects of contemporary technological society, its paradoxes of art and destruction.

> Designers often describe the grid patterns produced by circuit boards in terms of the warp and weft structure of woven textiles. A narrative is set up between the history of classical pottery and the new patterns generated by circuit boards primarily designed by computers for the benefit of man. I believe that these and other forms of patterning can draw attention to a blend of old and new and in some way add to the history of cultural signifiers.

Pots as cultural message carriers has been a theme encountered with other ceramists' work in this text; Potter's intriguing and imaginative *Network* pot takes this theme to a new level of investigation, while confirming that there is inspiration to be found in technological progress.

More concerned with allure than with complex meaning, Ray Taylor (b. 1944) specialises in the exploration and expression of decorative effects within the genre and possibilities provided by raku. He has honed his command of raku firing, its technical oxidation and reduction intricacies to the point that he has considerable control over glaze effects, colours and their intensities. In particular, he has extended the colour palette of raku into a dazzling range of colours, using the surface of his almost exclusively spherical vessels as a canvas for applying painterly gestures.

Taylor's focus is the decorative, especially the relationship of colour, movement and pure form. Glazes are applied in a series of sweeping brushstrokes, usually using a broad brush, while the glaze thickness is varied to create areas of relief texture. Smaller areas of the surface are sometimes left unglazed in order to produce blackened backgrounds which act to intensify the applied colours. These skills result in surface patterns which evoke something of the effect of light through leadlight glass, or else the strokes and colours suggest impressionist oil painting.

> The reason for choosing raku as my primary means of expression is that it facilitates the rapid development of ideas and techniques. The daily and ongoing cycle of glazing a single ceramic form in approximately one hour provides constant feedback. This process encourages exploration, experimentation and refinement of technique; it is also an exciting process because each day I have the reward of new work.

As they swirl around the vessel, his bold and energetic brushstrokes, effectively his signature, define curves and suggest order emerging from an organic chaos: clay can be luscious.

CHAPTER THREE
GLASS – ALLEGORIES IN LIGHT

Fractious and dangerous, enduring yet fragile, alluring in its glittering reflections, a barrier which protects yet permits the passage of light, a material which extends humanity's endeavours — there is something about these paradoxical qualities of glass which engenders emotive responses, quite different to those of the other craft media: little wonder that, among the conventional craft media, its relationship with the practitioner verges on the idiosyncratic.

This testing relationship may be among the factors which lead glass practitioners to appear especially determined in their bonding as a group, and so relentless in their need to define themselves through this medium's vagaries. Indeed, it is the unique qualities of glass, especially its tension of opposites and its effects on light, which imposes this degree of introspective intensity on its practitioners.

Those who choose to interact with this medium discover, at their command, a substance which is reflective, refractive, dispersing, enhancing or diminishing of light. And in turn, these qualities are enhanced by strong emotions engendered by this medium's cultural associations. As a consequence of these unique properties, ideas expressed in glass may represent or signify particular concepts, cultural nuances or emotive states, more effectively or dramatically than those communicated by the other media. It is these qualities, contradictions and strengths which empower glass, and which entice its practitioners to enter into and master this realm of light and metaphor.

Today, studio glass is nothing short of astonishing: its range of expressions — be they sculptural, functional, decorative, metaphorical, narrative or commentative — is overwhelming, while the high level of skills evident in the various transforming techniques applied to the medium are impressive. While mastering the subtlety and complexity of glass takes technical skill, perseverance and experience, it also requires clear artistic intent if the end result is to be more than an exercise in showmanship. Content is also important, yet the inherent physical qualities of the medium must not be overlooked: studio glass practice therefore entails a subtle balance.

Given these qualities, it is not surprising that, while the 1980s were exemplified by ceramics and other areas of craft practice, the 1990s have emerged as the decade for studio glass. For more so than any other craft medium, glass seems to suit this decade with its frantic pace, its paradoxes, and in short, its millennial temperament. The reflective and brittle qualities of glass neatly

PLATE 41 (opposite)
Robert Wynne (b. 1959)
Untitled, 1995
Blown, iridised gold, sand-blasted
33 x 30 cm
Photo: Greg Piper

PLATE 42
Clare Belfrage (b. 1966)
The Party, 1996
Handformed and blown
35 cm
Photo: Suzi Wild

dovetail with the deconstructionist trends and multiplicity of possibilities that post-modernism encourages. Through contemporary studio glass we may spy a semblance of contemporary society as it seeks to comprehend and reinvent itself, not only through the substance itself, but also through the myriad metaphors and expressive forms glass can assume in the hands of its makers.

Today there is a general consensus that glass is experiencing its most dynamic renaissance since its early historical period; its numerous devotees are 'pushing the medium', blowing, casting, or otherwise trailblazing ideas and form into being. Given this vivacity, it is surprising to realise that hardly twenty-five years have passed since the ideology and practice of studio glass was initiated in Australia.

Over its brief history there have been many changes including: a progression of pioneers and latter generation practitioners; the expansion of glass techniques from a limited repertoire to multiple, hi-tech practices; a revival of historic techniques and processes; a considerable expansion in the number of key institutions which offer courses in glass; a broadening in the variety of personal approaches to glass expression; the emergence of a trend which sees the development of a personal idiom early in the career of practitioners; influence from the various art movements on glass art, especially pop art, surrealism, expressionism, historicism, painterly, figurative, satirical and decorative movements.

PLATE 43
Jane Cowie (b. 1962)
Muscipula, 1996
Blown and hot-formed
20 x 60 x 40 cm
Photo: Michael Haines

As a medium glass is, by its nature, not as familiar or as readily accessible as clay, fibre or wood. Consider how glass rapidly loses its fluidity and malleability when deprived of a source of heat. We may also point to our smaller population base as one obvious reason, as well as the complexity and cost of establishing studio-sized glass furnaces, and the difficulty of acquiring the initial specialist skills glass demands. It was therefore not until the mid-1970s, that the conditions necessary for the Australian glass movement's genesis were met and, over the following two decades as events unfolded, the glass movement grew gradually moving towards its present-day, centre stage position in the crafts scene.

Australian studio glass has passed through three phases not unlike those experienced by its counterpart movement in the United States. The first, the pioneering phase, unfolded throughout the decade of the 1970s. It included the establishment of a basic infrastructure of fundamental skills, suitable kilns and studios. Glass blowing and flat glass comprised practically the sole methods for making studio glass for most of this period. It was also an imitative phase, and the free-blown forms, colours and ideas of visiting American glass masters were emulated by the rising wave of glass makers in their struggle with this unfamiliar medium.

The second phase, evident from the close of the 1970s and which continued through to the mid-1980s, was one of technological innovation, diversification and sophistication. Its most

PLATE 44
Chris Pantano (b. 1948)
Tribal Mask, 1996
Sandcast, glass, metal, wood
44 x 24 x 11 cm
Photo: Errol Larkan

significant consequence included the spread of kilnforming, as well as the ideological split in functional production work and one-off, exhibition work, sometimes referred to as 'glass art'. The craft movement's embracement of fine arts values during this phase led to the rise of sculptural and idea-based work.

From the late 1980s through to the opening years of the 1990s, a third stage emerged whereby makers now began to focus on honing specific skills and developing personal, expressive niches. Technological innovation, once equated with artistic intention in the earlier years of this period, became recognised as an insufficient reason for studio glass; while the split between technique and idea which had occurred over the 1980s shifted into a process of reintegration.

Themes which emerged in the growth of contemporary studio glass practice, and which are still relevant today include: the process of skill and cultural transfer from overseas and between practitioners; the struggle between art historical and broader, cultural, perspectives of glass; the glass-clay cross-over; the peculiarities of the medium including its alleged 'seductive' property; concerns for originality; the shifts in balance between craft and fine arts values; the enduring attraction of certain areas of exploration and representation including the vessel and sculpture; and the nature of the crucial interaction between medium, technique and idea — that is, its poesis and praxis.

It is necessary too, that the links which exist between clay and glass not be overlooked: besides the similarity between the two media in respect to the requirement of heat to effect change, a surprisingly large proportion of glass practitioners have also been educated in ceramics, or made the switch to glass later in their careers. However, unlike the contemporary practice of ceramics which has a thousands-year-old history impossible to ignore in contemporary practice, studio glass practitioners are perhaps less constrained by tradition in their work. The dual mainstreams in ceramics, the vessel-orientated 'truth-to-materials' tradition, and the 'anything goes', expressionistic stream, appear less defined in contemporary glass practice.

Nevertheless, similarly to clay artists, glass practitioners are drawn to the exploration of the vessel, its aesthetic, functional, cultural and metaphorical vocabulary. The dynamics of the glass vessel are linked, for example, to its long traditions in a number of cultures including those of Roman, Italian, German, Finnish, British and Czechoslovakian nations. In any assessment of contemporary work, the stylistic influence that these traditions exert cannot be ignored.

Today, glass practitioners have a more sophisticated understanding of the interaction between skills, process and idea. The emphasis now is on integrity — in both maker and object — as well as originality.

The following text sets out glass practice according to its predominant technical approaches which may be conveniently divided into three categories: glass blowing, kilnforming and alternative practices. There is, however, considerable overlap between these approaches — blowing and kilnforming are frequently combined in single works — hence the following sections merely provide a framework in which the practitioners and their works are presented.

Glass Blowing

Of all the forms of studio glass activity in Australia, glass blowing has had the longest development with over twenty-five years having passed since the techniques of glass blowing in the studio mode were demonstrated in 1970 by glass artist Stephen Skillitzi. Following reinforcement through waves of American blowers visiting Australia, the fascination for blowing abated somewhat over the mid-1980s as kilnforming processes became more popular. By the early 1990s, glass blowing has once more come into its own.

The dance-like orchestrations associated with glass blowing, its dependency on the human breath, and the need for practitioners to work together in combining their skills towards a common aim, are all distinguishing features. This latter facet of glass blowing, of people working together, continues to exert a powerful attraction to seasoned and young glass makers alike. Glass blowing is a volatile practice which places considerable physical demands on the practitioner who must be intuitive in a moment-by-moment process of appraisal of how form is emerging. It may seem that the embryonic bubble form, which always first results from glass blowing, places some restriction on the possible range of expressive shapes, but the imagination of the practitioner and the combination of this technique with others, surpasses this suggestion. Indeed, team approaches are considered a useful means of overcoming any of the limitations of individual blowing, broadening the potential range of expression in glass.

A revival of historical forms, especially Roman and Venetian glass, has accompanied this team model; its benefits include an investigation of classical forms with their timeless, intrinsic elegance, together with a heightened technical ability and showmanship. The stylistic influence of the design approach of the Italian glass masters, of old and the present, has seen a fusion of tradition with contemporary post-modernist attitudes. Makers may choose to combine contrasting strong colours or watery translucent effects with textured surfaces, which range from bold wheel-cutting to satin finishes achieved through sand blasting or acid etching. Dialogues between decoration and surface, form and colour, texture and meaning are as varied as the personality and intent of the makers.

The expressive potential of glass blowing may also be extended through its merging with other hot and cold-working techniques, and novel combinations are constantly being investigated. Even so, the allure of its links to history is sustaining and driving much of its vitality today.

Robert Wynne (b. 1959) is one such blower who is extending the decorative aesthetic of the blown form through the use of various surface techniques, especially through iridised patterning. To produce his sophisticated luminous works he begins by blowing the form, then iridising its entire outer surface in gold. After applying vinyl masks, of either abstract or leaf shapes, the surrounding iridescent surface is removed by sandblasting. The finished works combine the elegance of refined, simple forms with an almost luxuriant surface ornamentation. Sometimes he departs from the purely decorative to produce sculptural works; these often combine the blown,

PLATE 45
Nick Mount (b. 1952)
Murrini Vases, 1996
Freeblown glass with
red Murrini lower
portion and encalmo
join to shoulder
Ht: 27 cm
Photo: Grant Hancock

PLATE 46
Elizabeth Kelly (b. 1960)
Three Standing Columns, 1995
Drop cast, clear glass with spun
powder-coated steel base and neon core
200 cm

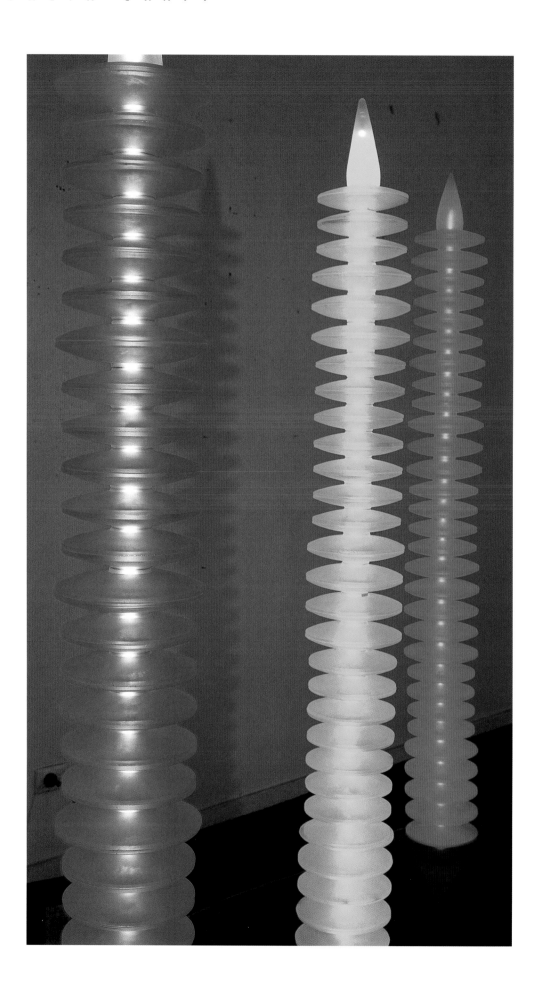

iridised vessel with steel and stone in startling juxtapositions as statements or comments on showmanship, or of the vessel's timeless qualities.

Glass blower Clare Belfrage (b. 1966) accepts wholeheartedly the seduction of the medium, especially its functional and colourful potentials. She aims to capture the 'rhythmical qualities' she perceives within this medium, and attempts to emphasise the intrinsic connection between object and the sensuality of the material: 'I see within the fluidity of glass a sense of order, one which beckons sensitive expression'. Her lively glass tablewares are designed around simple, functional forms and vibrant colour combinations which express this quality of movement or 'dance', as she puts it. Certainly, a title such as *The Party* appears perfectly apt for her group of dynamic drinking glasses which seemingly appear to be enjoying the latest dance.

Jane Cowie (b. 1962) is a prolific worker whose passion for glass is evident in the diversity of sculptural forms she creates. One of these approaches produces work consisting of contorted human figures presented in a myriad of poses. Through their striking clarity, high reflectivity and embodied fragility, these watery glass figures (sometimes placed within metal 'cages'), convey a sense of the balance of emotional precariousness and the dichotomy inherent in the human condition. On the other hand, her inflorescence blown forms are an energetic riot of colours, a showmanship-in-glass, and demonstrate an alternate, contrasting vision.

Cowie's starting point for these open vessels is a notion of organic life, based about the representation of rare, exotic plant forms. Small globular bowls suggest the embryonic beginnings of flowers, buds of modest colour and size. Progressively, from that point, other forms take on tubular, elongated, larger, and green and mauve-coloured tints, eventually bursting into fully-open flower-like vessels of glorious and intense oranges, reds and yellows. *Muscipula* are virtuoso works of blown glass which retain a spontaneous, free-flowing aesthetic reminiscent of the work of the American glass artist Dale Chihouly. Their strong colours, in combination with a resemblance to overblown flower forms, suggest a deliberate play on metaphors of growth, decay, decadence and excessiveness.

> I use glass for its vital colour, the threat of fragility and the surfaces that are tantalising to the touch. The pure colour and light captured by three-dimensional forms in glass make it a fantastic material to work with: it responds directly to heat, gravity, and the movements of my body — and my desires; it is an exciting medium with which to communicate.

Chris Pantano (b. 1948) is a master of a number of glass techniques including fusing, blowing and casting, applying these to express the rich diversity of Australia's natural and man-made environment through the qualities of glass. Elements for his decorative and sculptural work are drawn from the Great Barrier Reef and Queensland's rainforests, but he also explores Australia's Aboriginal and other tribal cultures, developing designs which are expressed through textural and other surface effects produced by sandcasting and other techniques. Through these applications he

PLATE 47 (opposite)
Bettina Visentin (b. 1965)
Cacti Bowls, 1996
Hand-blown and hot-worked glass
15 x 27 cm

is creating a distinctive, personal idiom which ranges from his iconographic 'Dreaming' totems to decorative vessels with richly layered image and colour effects.

Pantano's sources include detailed observations of natural markings which he considers as the same 'primal patterns' which were used by past cave artists to create their cultural images. From this universality of sources and beliefs he develops the forms, symbols, textures and colours which characterise his works, such as the potent *Tribal Mask*.

My Primal Image series expresses a continual process of development with its
roots stretching back from the Dreamtime of past cultures through to the present-
day of our own 'dreaming', and into the future.

As one of Australia's longest practising studio glass blowers, Nick Mount (b. 1952) has remained relatively diverse in his exhibition work and production output, yet nevertheless has developed a characteristic signature style. His travels in the United States have confirmed this as one of the strongest sources of influence on his work: included among the celebrated American glass blowers he has had contact or worked with are Dick Marquis, Steve Smyers, Lino Tagliapeitri and Dante Marioni. And while Mount's exhibition work tends to be idiosyncratic and sculptural in form, his prolific and distinctive production pieces especially, exhibit strong visual and historic links with the work of the Venetian tradition and aesthetic, fused with the contemporary exuberance of his North American experience.

Mount often works within the cooperative teamwork approach, with either glass trainees or seasoned glass blowers, both here and overseas. His blowing skills have focused on developing a line of vessels whose unifying characteristic is the consummate combination of refined profiles with luminous colours. These qualities pay homage to the traditional glass produced at Murano, Venice, as well as expressing his appreciation of the 'bonds found between glass blowers', and their links to the history of glass blowing. Mount's glass vessels exhibit a mastery of control of line and form, while his virtuoso encalmo work, as seen in *Murrini Vases*, is especially voluptuous in its aesthetic explorations of colour combinations and pattern.

Aside from this investigation of the play of light, colour and function, as seen in his ongoing vessel series, Mount also utilises his blowing skills for the sculptural exploration of the human figure. These are created by first making copper wire frames which embody prior line drawings into three dimensions. In one gestural action, glass is blown into these wire outlines expanding into the form. Mount's glass torsos invoke the earth goddess icons of early humankind with the various parts of the anatomy exaggerated as in the primitive antecedents. In these contemporary expressions, the copper matrix restrains the body yet emphasises the conjuncture of breasts, buttocks and stomach to produce an image of a curvaceous, powerful torso with strong sensual appeal; these handblown, wired and frosted torsos present the figurative form with a hint of the classical.

Mount has been working on these sculptural forms as an evolving series since 1991. The more

PLATE 48
Benjamin Edols (b. 1967)
and Kathy Elliott (b. 1964)
Vase Forms, 1995
Blown glass, wheel-cut
58 cm (tallest)
Photo: Ian Hobbs

recent pieces are 'self-portraits' which utilise additional features such as surface textures and overlaid photographic imagery which addresses issues of 'imposed expectations'.

Elizabeth Kelly (b. 1960) has an affinity with the clarity and colour of glass and takes two paths to creating glass works: one consists of more recent columnar sculptural works, including *Three Standing Columns*, which combine glass with other materials, such as powdered steel and include neon cores, the latter especially enhancing the colour and form dialogues she explores. She is she also a master at free-blowing glass bottles which combine bands of watery, contrasting and luminous colours: these vessels especially celebrate the spectral qualities of the medium.

> My practice is informed by material processes through a diverse range of applications. Contemporary craft cannot be positioned without a constant dialogue involving philosophies of design and fine art; my preferred strategy is a methodology which embraces all three strands.

Bettina Visentin (b. 1965) similarly revels in the clarity and variety of colours glass is capable of assuming. Her specialty is to make glassware which is functional, yet celebrates the qualities of its material and the processes used to bring it to life. As a first generation Australian born to Italian immigrants, she has been strongly influenced by her parents' Italian culture and traditions.

> I began a career in glass blowing after returning from a trip to Italy where I was taken to Murano, in Venice, to view the glass blowers. My work is therefore strongly influenced by Italian techniques, forms and attitudes, driven by the challenges of contemporary Australia.

In this way, she retains and celebrates her heritage as a major part of her life. Her recent vibrant glass work, such as *Cacti Bowls*, reflects this strong sense of identity and history, simultaneously pushing the limits of this genre.

Kathy Elliott (b. 1964) and Ben Edols (b. 1967) combine specialty skills with a strong aesthetic sensibility to produce a distinctive style of collaborative work which is inspired by a number of Italian designers such as Paolo Venini, Archimede Seguso, Carlo Scarpa and Fulvio Bianconi. Whereas Venetian glass has formed the basis of much of their work, they have lately begun to be influenced by a more diverse range of sources including sculptors, architects and other designers such as Isamu Noguchi, Gaeto Pesce and Tim Sarpeneva.

Elliott and Edols's glass vessels consist of vases and bowls in a range of refined shapes combined with subtle yet distinctive colours, and finished with richly textured surfaces. After Edols free blows the vessels, he and Elliott then work on the surfaces using a glass-engraving lathe, deeply cutting, rough grinding then recutting with a smooth wheel. These processes create a satin though textured surface with a very seductive, tactile feel, and with soft refractive effects which enhances the subtle colours and sophisticated forms of the glass. The extraordinary allure of this partnership's distinctive vessel-oriented work has led it to become well known and received in Australia and the USA.

PLATE 49
Maureen Williams (b. 1995)
Transition series, 1996
Free-blown, painted parison
57.5 x 25.5 cm
Photo: Robert Colvin

We have an overriding philosophy that we make what we like to see in the world trying, in this manner, to contribute to the domestic environment, as well as contributing to the long tradition of the decorative arts.

Maureen Williams's (b. 1952) approach to glass uses the medium and its forms as a painter would use a canvas. Her earlier *Coloured* series of works relied on intense and luminous primary colours arranged as large masses for striking decorative effect. Williams's present 'painted' vessels have developed a toned down colour range applied with daubist brushwork; as such, the *Transition* series are, in effect, abstract paintings in glass. These recent works have tended towards more personal expression, as this process has become developed into a more sophisticated level of expression. They retain their abstract patterning, yet express personal narratives through her visual interpretation of 'the interaction of shapes of life and dreaming states'. Painted in a cold state, reheated and free blown, these large-scale works are complex and alluring creations requiring a team approach, and were made with the assistance of glass artists Scott Chaseling and Nick Wirdnam.

Tom Moore (b. 1971) brings a fresh exuberance and wit into studio glass. His combined blown and cast forms, usually bottles of a variety of unusual shapes finished with whimsical zoo or anthropomorphic-shaped stoppers, express a sense of fun. They also reveal his delight in exploring the possibilities of the medium and its links to history. Although blowing is his predominant activity in so far as it produces the main forms, he applies other intensive hand processes and techniques including: hotworking, engraving, casting and sandblasting. Combining these techniques and stylistic approaches, he translates his imaginative visions into enticing assemblages which juxtapose function, figurative form and decorative imagery.

Gerry Reilly (b. 1958) has a strong commitment to teamwork, working with up to four trainee glass blowers to produce a large range of functional and decorative glasswares in his studio. He is especially skilled in Middle Eastern and Venetian techniques, taking his inspiration for his lyrical designs from patterns he observes in the natural environment. Although the works produced in the studio reflect the combined efforts of the team and are not so much complex exhibition works than functional glasswares made for commercial outlets, their Venetian swirls and lustrous gold to blue effects lend the workshop's wares identifiable characteristics and extend the availability of studio glass art to a wide audience. *Aladdin's Fruits* are an exhibition series which especially celebrate the opulence of glass and the craftsmanship of the glass blower.

Colin Heaney (b. 1948) similarly employs a team of some ten people working in the production of various forms to his designs, though much of the work is also handblown by himself. He has successfully developed an extensive range of decorative and functional glass types which have been especially sought after by tourists. His research has led him to the development of the iridising process, considerably expanding its colour range. The gold-brown glass base creates alluring iridised colours, although a recent departure into cobalt blue is giving an even greater

depth in the iridised effects. Heaney has lately extended his colour range and forms into making decorative works, specifically of flowers. This series, referred to as the *Wildflower Sculptures*, are generally presented as groups or bouquets, such as *Pastel Flowers*, which are colourful arrangements exhibiting a singular exuberance only glass can confer.

Richard Clements (b. 1950) has similarly had a long involvement in studio glass. He specialises in glass lampworking techniques to make two distinct types of glassware: strongly lustred, metal oxide coloured scent bottles and sea-shell forms; these can only be distinguished from those made through furnace glass-blowing methods with some difficulty. These pieces are made using dense colour applications developed through his considerable research over the past decade. They employ a complex matrix of colour and texture which produces a delicacy especially suitable for the making of perfume bottles — a specialty of his.

PLATE 51
Gerry Reilly (b. 1958)
Aladdin's Fruits, 1996
Handblown
Diam: 40 cm
Photo: John Austin

PLATE 52
Colin Heaney (b. 1948)
Pastel Flowers, 1995
Handblown vase with crackle
throughout;
flowers off-hand, hot glass
Ht: 58 cm
photo: Suzanna Clarke

Clements's other work consists of a line of sculptural and decorative forms in translucent colours: these range from goblets to teapots to non-functional objects which are imbued with a sense of whimsy and his philosophical outlook on life. The latter qualities are evident in *Sword Fish*, a work which reveals his glass-making virtuosity combined with the visual pun: a fish swallowing a sword! *Mystery Of Life* is a figurative work of a chicken contemplating (backwards between its

PLATE 53
Richard Clements (b. 1950)
Mystery Of Life, 1996
Lamp-worked glass
with translucent colours
18 x 10 cm
Photo: Terence Boag

legs), a square egg of clear glass. It is an amusing image which illustrates Clements's following statement:

> It seems to me that life is not complicated ... we simply go to bed, get up in the morning, go to bed etc., for some 25 500 times. The trick is what to do in between. This is where I have found glass making to be the perfect solution. It is an activity which has given me many years of fun and fulfilment, and will hopefully continue for the next 9 125 days.

Kilnforming

By the end of the 1980s, the shift from glass blowing and cold techniques to kilnforming, especially casting, altered the character of studio glass practice to the extent that it is recognised as one of the strongest themes in Australian studio glass today. The reasons for this shift of emphasis from one technique to another are varied, but they partly reflect overseas changes, as well as the arrival

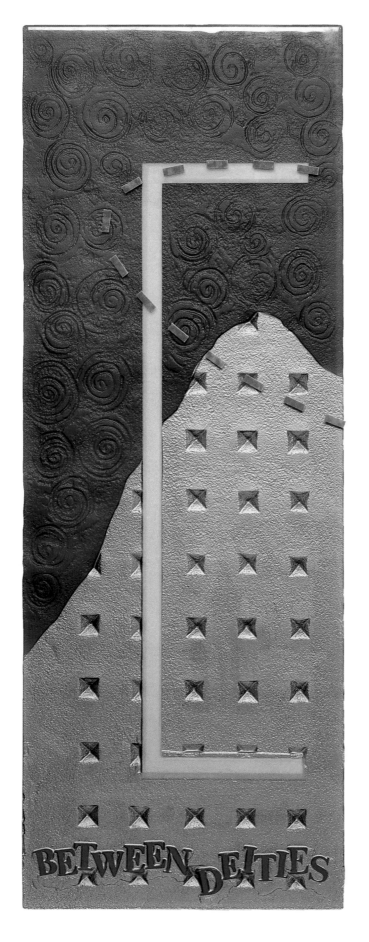

in Australia of glass masters such as Klaus Moje, who promoted the creative potential of kilnforming approaches. Towards the later 1980s, many practitioners who began their careers in glass blowing in the first decade, embraced kilnforming and other areas of activity; some have simply dabbled in the latter while others have taken to working in both areas, combining aspects of the two fundamentally differing approaches to studio glass.

Kilnforming techniques and processes especially broaden and intensify the expressive possibilities of glass. Certainly, the crystalline, spectral and sculptural qualities of kilnformed work set it apart from the mercurial and organic nature of blown glass forms. Kilnforming is particularly suitable for individual approaches in the exploration of sculptural or figurative concerns, of decorative effects such as colour and textural treatments, of the metaphoric investigations of the vessel, and of symbolic and cultural representations. It also facilitates the investigation of the connections between historical and contemporary glass processes and traditional forms and functions.

The relative ease with which kilnforming permits ideas or figurative imagery, to be translated into glass, is yet another reason for its popularity. Step-by-step handskills permit the maker's thinking to be translated at a controlled pace, and hence be more precisely interpreted and expressed through the medium: the process of 'making' itself is thus magnified. As such, kilnforming techniques and processes allow a broad vocabulary to be developed, one closely allied to the maker's intent and identity.

There are a variety of fusing and kilnforming processes including the sensuous qualities of *pâte de verre* (literally glass paste), casting with its crystalline chunky and prismatic qualities, and fusing with its colourful collage and mosaic possibilities. Any or a combination of some or all of these techniques may be used to make a broad range of forms from glass jewellery to vessels, as well as figurative or abstract, sculptural work.

Typical of the other media, practitioners these days tend to settle on a particular set of skills which they hone and apply to exploit the expressive potential of kilnforming. Out of this endeavour emerges a multiplicity of representational imagery embodying personal or domestic concerns; or dealing with broader social or political issues; or simply exploiting the subtleties of the medium's relationship with light, the shifting translucency, opalescence or transparency; and the interaction of these qualities with surface, texture and colour.

Warren Langley (b. 1950) is a master in kilnformed glass, producing work which embraces three separate but interrelated areas: personal, exhibition work; site-specific artworks for public spaces; and design-based work for application in architectural settings. Of the latter, Langley is an acknowledged pioneer, developing, between 1979 and 1982, large-scale technological processes in kilnforming, and initiating contemporary commercial applications of this in Australia and overseas.

The successful transition from studio craft practice to mainstream design-based

PLATE 54 (opposite)
Warren Langley (b. 1950)
Mountain (Between Deities and Mortals),
1996
Kilnformed glass, enamels and paint
160 x 130 x 3.5 cm

PLATE 55
Stephen Skillitzi (b. 1947)
Snappy Thoughts - A Self-Portrait, 1996
Lost wax cast glass, gold and copper
electroform
40 x 20 cm

manufacturing of kilnformed glass, has given Langley the ability to produce architectural and exhibition works on a very large scale.

> Stylistically and often thematically, there is a distinctive cross-over between these three areas; they are, in fact, designed to catalyse one another, even though their intended use and intellectual content differs in all three instances.

Langley's exhibition work especially elevates the imbuing of the material with complex narrative and symbolic content. Beyond these intentional elements, the quality of Langley's kilnformed, cast glass, its colour and tonal ranges and the texture of the glass itself, enhance its sculptural and iconographic imagery. Invariably, the works reflect their creative origins through their dense translucency, or high-gloss finishes, and through the abstract juxtapositions of colour and formal insertions, as well as through impressed or moulded graphics and signals.

Langley's creations from the early 1980s determined his ongoing conceptual approach which takes various cues from a number of sources such as anthropological, archaeological and geological science, as well as from various past cultures; out of this fusion came a number of exploratory themes including the *Druid, Games, Puzzling Evidence* and *Map*, series. These embody ritual intent, irony and metaphor, as well as expressing various intellectual and social concerns, qualities to be discovered in the work *Mountain [Between Deities and Mortals]*; but perhaps the strongest point of communication Langley wishes to convey is one of a sense of inquiry, a challenge to comprehend, on both a personal and broader scale, the paradoxes of making and ways of communicating meaning.

Stephen Skillitzi's (b. 1947) long involvement in studio glass in Australia since 1970 has seen him become a master of one area in particular, that of kilnforming, and specifically in casting methods such as the lost-wax and *pâte de verre*. Lately, his more modestly-scaled pieces, invariably figurative, have taken on heroic, life-sized dimensions, as he exercises his command of the medium to produce complex allegorical and symbol-laden works.

Although he regularly turns his attention to explore various perennial themes as well as political, social and environmental issues, Skillitzi's work is often also autobiographical, or at least carries the viewer to deeper analytical levels of the psyche or the archetypal. Whatever the subject, the quality of his glass work always reflects its handmade origins as well as the historical and physical processes of its creation. A recurring image is the mask, which Skillitzi constructs as a metaphor for projecting various meanings or moods: ambiguity, illusion and symbolism pertaining to duality.

Sometimes his masks appear to be in a stage of metamorphosis into, or out of, a fuller figurative representation of the face (usually the artist's), which, in combination with architectonic or other figurative motifs or fragments, combine to create sculptures of considerable complexity. *Snappy Thoughts — A Self-Portrait*, for example, is a work which, like the proverbial 'fish out of water' visualises a Piscean tug in opposing directions, and representing those overwrought

cognitions of 'a self-conscious glass artist', as Skillitzi puts it.

Skillitzi's work exemplifies the expressive potential of glass, especially in the manner that he utilises the medium's properties to communicate mood or suggest ideas through textural manipulations. In this respect he has also extended his *oeuvre* through his application of electroforming, a process which deposits copper or silvered nickel metallic deposits on glass surfaces; this confers a further metaphorical layer, or an 'aura' as he puts it, to his sculptural works.

> Media, techniques and concepts form an unstable trial whose elasticity accommodates my three decades-long glass and metal odyssey. Visual content assaults the more stoic economic and technical restraints: nevertheless, surrealistic glass sculpture sits comfortably within the contemporary Studio Glass Movement.

Richard Morrell (b. 1953) has a strong affinity for the vessel

PLATE 56
Richard Morrell (b. 1953)
Bowl of Passion, 1994
Kiln cast glass, metal oxides
and coloured glass-shard inclusions,
acid-etched and cold-worked
Ht: 36 cm

form which he explores and celebrates through a central image he has developed and honed over the years. A blower and caster, Morrell has combined these two approaches into a unified form of considerable power and allure. His monumental vessel forms have thick, heavily textured glass walls which hold a seemingly hollowed-out central bowl, the latter often glowing red or some other colour which acts to set up a contrast with the massive, structural walls. Such a distinctive form very strongly suggests a crucible, the bowl used by a metallurgist or chemist, or even the alchemist, hence evoking allusions of transformation; or else, its votive imagery solemnises the craft practitioner's skills in this or some other respect.

> Using the bowl as a vehicle for exploration, I utilise the elements of structure, surface and space to create compositions which are aimed at the senses rather than the intellect.

Bowl of Passion is one such work which exemplifies Morrell's mastery at casting and working glass to embody it with a strong physicality and sensuousness, as suggested by its title.

PLATE 57 (opposite)
Rob Knottenbelt (b. 1947)
The Healer (Totemic series #5), 1995
CAD CAM generated, sand-blasted,
acid-polished
58 x 42 x 5 cm
Photo: Robert Colvin

Alternative Approaches

While glass blowing and kilnforming constitute the two pillars on which studio glass rests, there are a variety of alternative approaches and techniques which extend its diversity of expressions. Glass can also be melted and poured into impressions in sand, or else, blowing and casting may be combined to produce works. But glass does not necessarily need to be hot-treated to be

PLATE 58
Brian Hirst (b. 1956)
Offering Bowl Form
(Object and Image series), 1996
Assembled sheet glass, engraved and
carved, polier gold, aluminium, enamel
53 x 82 x 13 cm

manipulated into an expressive art form. This does not mean that leading and staining or other flat-glass working approaches are the only other alternatives to kiln or furnace-working. There are an increasing number of other, cold-working techniques, sometimes in combination with hot-working approaches, which provide alternative ways of handling and manipulating this medium. These include innovative developments in traditional leaded and stained glass, lamp-working, glass-engraving, optical glass, laminated glass, and sand-casting to name a few.

New ways of dealing with glass include the application of cutting-edge technologies such as the use of computer aided design or other software, sometimes in combination with industrial processes. In this respect Robert Knottenbelt (b. 1947) is a master in a very specialised area: he has developed considerable skills and techniques which combine computer programming with high pressure water jets to carve architectonic shapes out of plate glass which he then assembles into intricate sculptural works; a final stage of sand-blasting and acid-etching gives the work a seductive translucent, satin-like finish. Given this unusual approach, Knottenbelt's works stand out as unique in the area of studio glass practice — for their technical achievement, as well as for their sculptural forms and artistic content.

His crisp, interlocking forms can suggest a considerable degree of delicacy and complexity, or else they may appear deceptively simple through their powerful graphic imagery. Beyond their aesthetic allure, they encode a cryptic vocabulary which is at once organic and mechanic, articulating a mythic iconography charged with meaning for individual and society. Knottenbelt's totemic series are especially forceful in their iconography. *The Healer* is one such work in this series which projects a dual symbolism: on the one hand there is the notion of the technology available to the healer in the late twentieth century and in the future; and on the other hand, of a backward looking into the past at the traditional healer of herbal remedies. Entailed in this are the concepts of knowledge transmitted through written and oral means, and the latter's implications of female collective knowledge. In this work, the chest cavity represents the heart with its life pulse represented as a screen monitor; while tool-like arms act as ciphers for contemporary surgical implements.

> To be 'a healer' is to be pro-active, a doer, to take risks, to think, and if possible,
> to find some kind of working solution.

Brian Hirst (b. 1956) similarly works in novel ways when dealing with glass, and has mastered a set of skills which permit his artistic intent, generally a complex concept which explores the relationship of a three-dimensional glass object with its two-dimensional representation as an image. Cycladic art was the initial inspirational source of Hirst's ongoing imagery, the iconography gradually developing into its refined characteristic form.

Hirst's central work, his *Object and Image* series, have been evolving over a period of some ten or more years, their main focus being the investigation of illusion and relationship, and the dialogue generated through the juxtapositions of the two. His free and mould-blown glass vessels, often conceived as votive three-legged bowls, are celebrated for their powerful form and symbolic imagery. These, and his two-dimensional panel images, involve the application of a number of

PLATE 59
Deb Cocks (b. 1958)
Grace's Ark (Series: no 4 of 5), 1996
slumped and enamelled glass
Diam: 32 cm
Photo: Peter Schardin

PLATE 60 (top right)
Roger Buddle (b. 1940)
In Vitro II, 1996
Kilncast glass
27 x 25 x 8 cm
photo: Michael Haines

PLATE 61 (above)
Mies Grybaitis (b. 1968)
Considerations of Matter, 1995
Lost wax crystal, blown glass, engraved
and polished
41 x 10 cm

techniques and processes including engraving, acid-etching, sand-blasting, gold application, carving, and enamelling. The result is work which is extraordinarily rich, yet elegant in its presentation of decorative and symbolic patterning. In particular, his mastery of these multiple glass practices, confers to his work an aura of age and meditative intensity.

Lately, Hirst's *Object and Image* series have included the presentation of one or the other of the works without their counterparts: *Offering Bowl Form*, for example, is one such work which consists of a thick piece of sheet glass formed and treated with his standard set of techniques to create what, at first, seemingly appears to be a bowl; it is an illusion which is accentuated by the absence of his usual pairing of this series. The dimpled bowl surface, the gold and engraved treated rim, the shadowing and curves and other features as seen in his three-dimensional works are all there, although this two-dimensional image represents the three-dimensional object. Aside from this complex intellectual and visual play on imagery and the physical and functional aspects of the object, or the historic and metaphoric allusions evoked, it is the crystalline and textural qualities of the glass and its contrast with the gold-treated surfaces that act to seduce our aesthetic sensibilities.

Deborah Cocks (b. 1958) is best known for her enamelled and engraved glass bowls, although she is also skilled in casting techniques. In particular, she has developed a characteristic graphic technique which includes a specific palette of colours and textures which she applies to illustrate narratives on large platters. Her subject matter is eclectic, but her favourites are female nude figures, barnyard animals, birds, or compositions of animals and richly decorative, botanical backgrounds.

Movement is often effectively captured in her compositions, either in the motion of animals or birds tumbling about, or else in the rhythmic patterns created from repeat motifs. The idea of the safe, fantasy world is another favourite theme, which she represents with an ark which carries an overflowing menagerie of animals, humans and birds, sailing through fish-filled seas amidst a chaotic background sky of drying clothes, safety pins, clothes pegs and other domestic items — the imagery of *Grace's Ark*. Cocks's vignettes often capture a familial warmth, psychological intensity, or other moods which successfully engage or draw the viewer into her whimsical, and often endearing, snapshots of life.

> My work reflects my life. Bits and pieces put together, sometimes real, sometimes fictitious, sometimes the fiction becoming reality. Domestic things: animals, flowers, foliage, fruit and veg and Gracie. A child to make you see and laugh. My attitude to craft? Wonderful stuff to make, to have, to use, to integrate in the normal patterns of life. No home should be without it.

Sculptural or painterly, Roger Buddle's (b. 1940) ambidextrous versatility in the medium of glass is immediately apparent as he shuttles from figurative kilnwork to brilliant colour compositions on slumped glass, exploring aesthetic, abstract and metaphorical ideas.

Buddle achieves the necessary balance between craftsmanship and artistry, permitting the medium to display its inherent qualities, yet clearly expressing idea or aesthetic aim with verve and confidence. His painterly design work includes functional sushi dishes or platters produced by fusing and slumping techniques. These emanate from his technical background in electronic design, where 'most issues are clear-cut and unambiguous'. They also draw their inspiration from the works of painters such as Klimt and Mondrian. These works exploit the clarity of colour, as well as the precision of colour hue which is possible with glass. The canvas in this case is the shallow glass bowl, often triangular or square, with angular and contrasting colour compositions further

PLATE 62
Anne Dybka (b. 1921)
Parrot Cameo Vase, 1995
Red glass with white casing, cameo carved decoration
30 x Diam: 13 cm
Photo: Bruce Alexander

accentuating the geometry of the overall form. The visual strength of such work demonstrates that glass may transcend the decorative art barrier to become contemporary art, yet retain its practical utility within the domestic setting.

From the flat glass sheet to the three-dimensional form, Buddle's dramatic and conceptually forceful sculptural pieces are similarly impressive. Created in clear cast glass, these *In Vitro* works develop an earlier concept that explores aspects of the creation of human life, whereby the form of the human embryo is used to elicit a range of emotional responses. 'It attempts to deal with the paradox that is the struggle by some to create new life while others battle with the dilemma of terminating it.' Indeed kiln-casting, with its crystalline and prismatic qualities, is at once brittle and alluring, hence suggesting the vulnerability and wonder of human life, qualities Buddle effectively exploits. And although the seductive qualities of glass can easily tempt the maker to sacrifice content over showmanship, Buddle's strong and critical design sense resists such indulgence in his harmonious compositions.

More conventional in approach but no less expressive, Mies Grybaitis (b. 1968) combines glass blowing and kilnforming to produce figurative works which demonstrate an incisive ability to embody complex ideas in glass. Grybaitis has an interest in exploring and visualising psychological states and their relationship to the professions which have developed a mystique of treatment through therapeutic processes and other means. The conflict between the intellect and the heart is a particular focus.

She begins with the vessel forms, produced by blowing, creating a 'communication' bubble — actually funnel shaped — and attaching these to the heads of her figures from which they seemingly emerge as thoughts. These vessels provide surfaces for engraving graphic imagery and text, including medieval schemas of the construct of the intellect and emotions, as well as cross-sectional drawings of the human brain, site of the intellect. In *Considerations of Matter*, the figurative portion is produced from the lost wax casting method: swirling bubbles captured within its cranium seem to suggest the seeds of thought. By leaving two specific areas clear — the cranium and a heart shaped area on the chest — while acid-etching the rest of the figure, Grybaitis gives it a greater sense of solidity, as well as contrasting it against the clarity of the emerging thought bubble. But more significantly, she emphasises these two sites, the heart and intellect, as the loci of her interrogative imagery. A touch of grey staining around the temple further defines this region: it's a complex, intriguing work which demonstrates the degree with which ideas may be translated and expressed into sculptural form within the medium of glass.

Anne Dybka's (b. 1921) work pursues another pathway of expression in both her technique and her visionary intent. As a glass engraver, her decorative work exemplifies the development of the European engraved crystal-glass tradition in Australia, especially in free-standing glass carving and cameo glass. Her wheel-engraved lead crystal upholds traditional techniques whereby mastery in this craft strives to achieve a refinement of the design and its execution in the medium,

PLATE 64
Pamela Stadus (b. 1953)
Interlude in Blue, 1996
Sand and kiln-cast glass
42 x 28 x 7 cm
Photo: Robert Calvin

PLATE 63 (opposite)
Tony Hanning (b. 1950)
The Sun, 1991
Cased glass, sand-blasted and engraved
Diam: 21 cm
Photo: David McArthur

PLATE 65
Shaelene Murray (b. 1960)
Glamour, 1995
Cast-glass,
recycled and electrified iron
28 cm

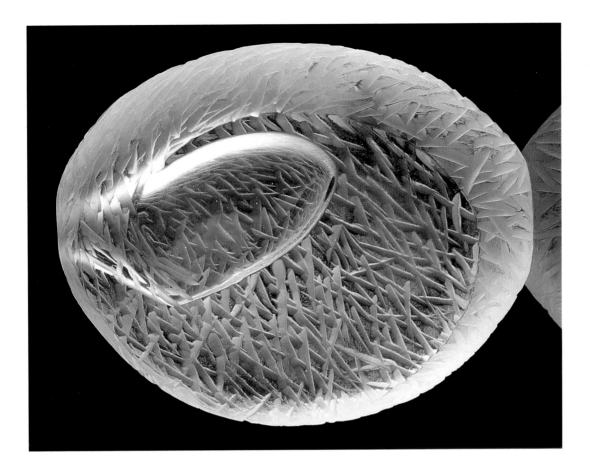

PLATE 66
Lienors Allen (b. 1972)
Featherliness, 1995
Blown, cut, polished, engraved glass
9 x 6.5 x 3 cm
Photo: Stephen Procter

to control light and enhance texture and tone; her work demonstrates considerable precision, discipline and restraint.

Dybka's subject matter varies considerably, and includes figurative work such as the representation of Shakespearian characters in crystal glass, through to native flora and fauna in a realistic style. She also works with novel combinations of various techniques to create illusionary effects. Ultimately Dybka hopes that, through her work, she can 'restore, to a degree, our separation from the natural world, to give people a chance to stop and be aware of the beauty and harmony still to be found, and take a rest in that...' Her virtuoso engraving embodies a meditative calmness which can provide such a respite.

Tony Hanning (b. 1950) similarly focuses on creating various representations through the skilled carving of encased or layered coloured glass vessels, with a strong personal inclination favouring illusionary imagery. As he is actually manipulating the glass to produce the varying shades which parallel the graphic or painterly intent of drawing or oil paining, he refers to this process as a kind of 'painting with light'.

The actual imagery appears as a three-dimensional form yet, because it is clearly embodied over the surface, the illusionary aspect is magnified. The process becomes a formalist game where illusion, metaphor and reality coalesce into the form of the three-dimensional vessel. The

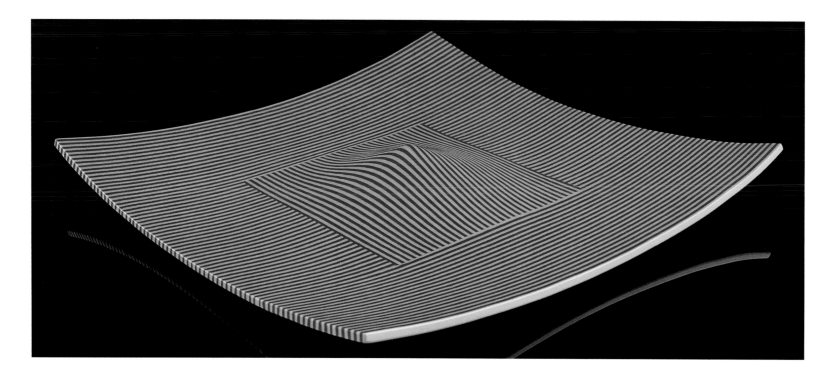

PLATE 67
Claudia Borella (b. 1971)
Striped series 2, 1995
Bullseye Glass, kilnformed, latheworked
50 x 50 x 5.5 cm
Photo: Stephen Procter

prevailing image is often a haunting one, usually focusing on the urban landscape and its architecture which appears perfect in its classical geometry, yet its citizens are often mysteriously absent. In the work *The Sun*, human representation seems to be suggested by the newspaper sheets he has engraved, blown away from the newspaper stand and now drifting amongst the seemingly deserted buildings.

Departing from these preceding techniques, but still focused on metaphoric allusion, Pamela Stadus (b. 1953) produces monumental sculptural works using sand-casting and kilnforming processes. These are generally representing 'mind-scapes' as she puts it: *Interlude in Blue*, for example, is an expression of an idea, emotion or passing passage of time, contained within an architectonic framework.

Sand-casting is an ancient technique which produces crystalline, highly textured qualities in the cast glass which, together with bubbles and colour inclusions as well as engraved surfaces, can heighten the processes and physicality of the medium which, in turn, can enhance intended symbolic references. Stadus's work suggests emotional mood shifts through its bold articulation and contrasts of colour and shape which 'convey the difference between ethereal space and dense matter; lightness and intensity; and movement and stillness'.

Still sculptural but multi-media in approach, Shaelene Murray (b. 1960) takes various domestic appliances — functional objects of industrial mass production — and elevates these into domestic icons. Reinterpreting everyday objects through a kind of sculptural sleight of hand, Murray transforms the mundane imagery of second-hand, 1950s irons, toasters, egg-beaters or hot-water jugs, into other items with new — often glamourous — functions: the toaster, hot-water jug, and iron become electric table lamps; others become handbags or simply sculptural objects.

PLATE 68
Giles Bettison (b. 1966)
Murrini Vessels, 1995
Mosaic techniques
21 x 11.5 cm (large)

Kitsch and glass are seemingly incongruous, but it is this very dissonance that Murray exploits in her challenge of the domestic icon.

Murray has only relatively recently entered the field of studio glass, having originally worked as a clay practitioner. Now she casts glass and combines it with recycled industrially made domestic appliances to make sculptural forms which address feminist issues. *Glamour*, for example, is a 1950s appliance which has had its working metal plate removed and replaced with

a cast-glass replica; an electric light within the iron causes the glass 'plate' to glow with a greenish tinge. We all know that the iron can no longer perform its original function, but now it provides intellectual and aesthetic satisfaction in its new role as a surreal table lamp: a fusion and parody of gender and icon. It is also an approach which utilises handcraft skills to convert — and subvert — the industrial, mass produced and obsolescent object into one-off, unique works. In this manner, the superficial allure of the technological gives way to the sign of the hand.

Annual waves of graduates from the numerous art institutions around the country are constantly entering and invigorating the field of studio glass practice. It is not possible to select a comprehensive representation of them in this text, but a number of recent graduates from the Glass Workshop of the Canberra School of Art serve to illustrate the verve many of these young, would-be masters exhibit. Lienors Allen, Giles Bettison and Claudia Borella are already demonstrating the capability of translating strongly defined artistic visions into the medium of glass with considerable skill, sensitivity and enthusiasm. All have chosen specific sets of techniques and areas for aesthetic or sculptural explorations of the medium.

Lienors Allen's (b. 1972) work seeks to explore the sculptural qualities of glass using blowing, cutting and engraving techniques. The forms are conceived around the theme of what he refers to as 'birdliness', and are directly expressed in some pieces, while they become the starting point for others.

> Clear glass is responsive to the mood of its surroundings: it reflects the luminous warmth of sunlight, it glimmers coldly at night, or can assume an overcast melancholy. Surface textures collect and disperse light. Facets reflect direct light making the forms glow and sparkle. Tactile surfaces draw people to contemplate, hold and feel the pieces.

Allen's works demonstrate how the medium may achieve this variety of moods, and succeeds in expressing the sought-after qualities of the avian species: the detailed textural complexity of feather (as in *Featherliness*); the rounded, embracing warmth of plumage; and the beaked and streamlined form of birds.

Claudia Borella's (b. 1971) vibrant work is a technical *tour de force* which challenges the boundaries between art, craft and industrially produced objects — her proclaimed wish. Her recent development of kilnformed work entitled *Striped* series, explores the interrelationships between pattern, colour and form. She achieves this through clean, finely striped patterns of contrasting colours which suggest, to a degree, the structural lines visible at close range on television screens. The curvatures of her immaculately made work accentuate the close precision with which these effects are obtained, as well as conferring an optical, colourfield illusion. Both design and its conception are executed with an impressive skill.

> When reduced to their essential components, pattern, colour and form, these elements become integral in linking structural qualities to the aesthetics of the

PLATE 69 (opposite)
Klaus Zimmer (b. 1928)
Dresden 13. 2. 45 (The Inferno), 1995
Antique glass, lead, paint and stain
painted and stained centre, partly
double-glazed; metal surface raised
with articulated texture
67 x 67 cm
Photo: Andrew Barcham
(Monash University)

work. The series is based around the concept of production, unlike the machine-made object which produces multiples of the same object, the freedom afforded by the designer/maker permits multiple pieces to be individually unique.

Giles Bettison (b. 1966) creates lyrical works with rich patterning and colouration following the complex Murrini mosaic process. Highly demanding and time-consuming, this technique involves a number of stages, beginning with the stacking and stretching of coloured glass sheets which are then bundled up and restretched. The resultant glass canes are then sliced in cross-section to create tiles or Murrini. The Murrini are now fused into a sheet which is either blown or slumped into the desired vessel form. Finally, the surface is ground to enhance the colours and pattern, and to further shape and finish the work.

Bettison's efforts are directed at exploiting the richness of the visual effects obtained through this process: the rhythmic patterns and intense colours change as one approaches closer to these vessels, their vibrancy and sensuality engaging the viewer.

The colours I use and the way I use them are inspired by my experience of the Australian landscape. Many of these colours are subtle yet contain a richness through their contrasting effects and through their setting. It is this harmony I wish to interpret in my work.

Flat Glass

From its apotheosis in the Middle Ages, the contemporary art of stained glass descends from a long tradition extending from an unbroken lineage to the present day. It is not difficult to see why stained glass has retained its popularity for so long: we have all experienced that moment of inspiration when light, filtering through the pattern and colours of a stained glass window — be it church, home or public space — enlivens and charges the space with warmth and vitality. As light changes throughout the day, and over the seasons, so too does the beauty and drama of a well-designed and positioned stained glass window. Light, therefore, is paramount to the expressive power of stained glass as it enlivens, colours, creates jewel-like effects, and brings images to life — and hence, communicates meaning, be it historical, social, religious, or even political.

While the term 'stained glass' conjures up the typical Victorian style of traditional leaded and painted glass, contemporary personalised strategies have adapted the medium to the demands of late twentieth-century architectural practice. Today's designer-makers see themselves as manipulating glass, light and space, balancing these qualities, juxtaposing texture and colour, and orchestrating suitable tension and release in the design and its expression in the given space. By exploiting these qualities they create architectural works which decorate, make statements, evoke moods, or construct narratives.

Stained glass has a number of elements that determine its unique character: after cutting glass into the desired shapes according to design, extra details are painted with vitreous enamels and

PLATE 70
David Wright, (b. 1948)
*Crucifixion, Resurrection and Life
Everlasting*, 1994
Central panel of Cabrini Hospital Chapel
Windows
Kilnworked, leaded glass
360 x 360 cm
Photo: Sandy Nicholson

then fired onto the surface; the pieces are finally fitted together and joined with strips of lead —
this gives the image its dramatic, bold outlines. However, only a book devoted to stained glass
could represent its numerous practitioners: this text presents only a handful of practitioners with
a focus on those who have extended the basic process of stained glass through innovative
techniques and approaches.

A key figure in Australian architectural glass, Klaus Zimmer's (b. 1928) lifelong involvement
and achievements in the field have included the establishment of the first tertiary course in the
country; the pioneering of innovative approaches to design; and the spear-heading of the use of
hot-glass and other processes in contemporary work.

In particular, Zimmer has developed the use of laminating and fusing techniques to the point
that they are an integral and distinguishing facet of his work. His philosophical approach is
clearly defined.

PLATE 71
Cedar Prest (b. 1940)
Araluen Aranda (Foyer Window), 1989
Leaded, stained, painted, enamelled and
kilnworked glass,
and small areas of fused glass
17.3 Sq m (total of 12 panels)

Exquisite handcrafting is common to most, if not all, civilisations. While ours is no exception, the artist/craftsperson's responsibility is now greater. To continue to delight society with the pleasures of the handcrafted we must produce what computers and technology cannot make. I have made extravagant decoration a form of artistic expression for the post-modern era. Over five decades I have developed a language of abstract curvilinear images and calligraphic marks and invented the studio techniques needed to express them in lead and glass. The resultant textures, colours and transparent/translucent effects, finely crafted, are intended to provide pleasure, promote contemplation and excite the senses.

Zimmer's techniques centre about this development of decorative surface structuring of both the glass and the lead elements in his work; he refers to the latter as lead embroidery. Beyond his celebrated architectural works, his autonomous panels provide another means to expose the results of his artistic explorations. Through their characteristic, richly textured and lustre surface qualities, these alluring panels construct an engaging, meditative iconography. *Dresden 13. 2. 45 (The Inferno)*, is an arresting work which, as its title informs us, recalls, through its searing colours and fused surfaces of its glass and lead, the horrors of that infamous day of unwarranted destruction.

David Wright (b. 1948) has also invigorated the area of architectural stained glass through his innovative fusions of a technological approach with a distinctive stylistic and symbolic imagery. Coming into the area from an architectural background, Wright has freely adopted kilnforming techniques and processes to develop a personal vocabulary glass centred about texturing and colour.

Wright's interest in creativity, birth and science forms the basis of his designs, with imagery often derived from microscopic studies of nature and human biology. His background training as an architect has also directed the successful integration of his work with the built setting. Commissions for church windows in the early 1970s allowed him to initiate his lifelong interpretation of this creation theme 'into a more human philosophical sense'. At this point, embryonic forms began to emerge as part of a characteristic imagery. For Wright, humankind's growing scientific understanding was not diminishing any sense of the wonderment of creation. The latter theme has been interpreted by Wright into a symbolic language which contextualises science and its ongoing technological development. This is a specific visual language constituted through the careful layering of intricately textured glass, which seemingly fuses medium with form: idea is bound to technique.

However, his cellular imagery is not restricted to the larger architectural panel, and he also makes small-scale works which fit the exhibition format.

> My exhibition work allows free experimentation of idea and technique which then feeds into my commissioned pieces. The latter offers me the privilege of being allowed into people's inner lives, their systems of faith, belief, as well as symbol and work practice. The integration of these elements is complex but is an exhilarating activity.

Crucifixion, Resurrection and Life Everlasting, is a more recent virtuoso work of cogent imagery which embodies Wright's philosophical, artistic and craftsmanly urges.

Considered to be one of the doyens of the medium, Cedar Prest (b. 1940) has worked for over thirty years as a stained glass artist. Challenging the boundaries of 'flat glass', she has constantly aimed for an 'Australian school' of stained glass, her large-scale work expressing community identity, Australian iconography, and a sense of place. To this end, she has applied her imagination in design and handwork, experimenting to combine traditional and modern techniques, developing her own distinctive approach and style.

Her work in communities especially underlies her philosophy that art should be accessible to all members of any regional or urban group. Prest contends that 'community art projects can demystify stained glass'. The key to translating stained glass into an accessible and symbolic cultural feature of any community is based on this perspective. She believes that Australia is 'very much the land', itself a mosaic of regions, and therefore, that it is necessary to live and work within the local landscape and its community if the work is to be imbued with 'the sense of place'.

> In my commissioned work I am continually striving to produce a suitable light atmosphere (both colour and its projection) for the space and use of the building.
>
> My work celebrates a sense of being Australian — our place and its plants, landscape and history.

Prest has therefore constantly worked to develop an Australian palette, softer grey, with green colours in particular, that would project a suitable light atmosphere, especially, the sense of the 'bush'.

Among her main collaborative projects executed within various communities is the Araluen Arts Centre in Alice Springs. This project involved working with the Aranda people to guide and assist them in the designing and making of a distinctive 'spirit of place' series of works. The project saw dreaming stories which crossed the Araluen site, translated from Aboriginal sand painting styles, into glass as the vast panel *Araluen Aranda* for the main foyer window.

Other major commissions include works for numerous ecclesiastical and secular public spaces: the clerestory of St Peters Cathedral in Adelaide in 1991–92, was a lyrical 'hymn' in praise of creation and settlement, based on themes from South Australian history; while the Sydney International Airport involved her in the making and designing of the glass and its special colours (in association with Frank Moore at Freedom Western Australia), to produce a major work of dramatic power and luminosity. More recent work includes the Mary McKillop windows in St Kevins, Sydney, the design representing the first school in Penola, its vineyards and Aboriginal influenced stencilled handprints.

Lance Feeney (b. 1948) may be considered as a representative of the numerous stained glass artists in Australia whose design and work accesses the traditional within the contemporary setting. He is especially a master of the stained glass painting technique and has restored numerous ecclesiastical stained glass windows in Australia, using the traditional approach and style according to the nineteenth-century period context of the buildings. These works glow as jewels, while the figurative imagery is imaginative within the constraints of convention.

Manipulating light and texture, he also utilises a more contemporary approach to make stained glass windows for domestic, as well as public, settings. Feeney particularly enjoys combining leaded glass panels which are moulded with ripple lines, with plain and tinted glass to

PLATE 72
Lance Feeney (b. 1948)
Hands of Compassion, 1990
Salvation Army Citadel, Sydney
Painted, leaded glass
3 x 2 m
Photo: Stephen Wilson

create dramatic conjunctions of texture and graphic form. But it is his religious imagery which particularly commands our attention: *Hands of Compassion*, a large work commissioned by the Salvation Army Citadel in Sydney, uses painted and leaded glass to convey its repeat imagery of human hands reaching towards one another, while the textured and coloured glass background panels complete this understated though powerful work.

This and the preceding examples show that, whatever its subject or thematic focus, contemporary stained glass has the power to reinstate human values into the built environment.

CHAPTER FOUR
METAL – FORGING IDENTITIES

Hammered, pulled, beaten, oxidised, alloyed, anodised, embossed, braided, patinated, pierced, bent, moulded, enamelled, and melted — the numerous techniques and processes utilised to fashion metal, and other materials, into the infinite shapes and signs of contemporary jewellery and metalworking, be it body pieces, exhibition objects, flat or hollow-ware, or furniture — distinguishes this practice from those concerned with wood, ceramics, fibre and glass.

This chapter surveys the centrality of metal within the broad discipline of contemporary metalworking which embraces skilled handcraft activities as diverse as jewellery, hollow-ware, silver and goldsmithing, as well as blacksmithing. Yet, beyond the precious and non-precious metals of gold, silver, titanium, iron, steel, and aluminium, jewellers and metalsmiths have always had the freedom and imagination to extend their creativity beyond the manipulation of one medium into other substances as diverse as glass, plastic, gemstone, bone, shell and wood. Today, for jeweller and metalsmith, it is attitude and artistic intent, more so than convention, that determines the choice and combination of materials, as well as the form and function of the objects fabricated.

In addition to widely casting their net with respect to the materials they use, these practitioners may further extend the possibilities of their work through the manipulation of the social and symbolic values ascribed through tradition to materials such as gold, silver and precious stones. These may be accepted and celebrated, or else constantly questioned or subverted — as is usually the case with much contemporary, cutting-edge metalwork. Thus while the foregoing embody wealth, power, status and ritual, their recontextualisation with common materials into novel designs constantly challenges our perceptions of the value, symbolic meaning and function of particular materials. Similarly, they may take advantage of the rich cultural or historical associations linked to particular forms or objects such as the talisman or ritualistic vessel, to charge their work with meaning and vitality. Beyond this role, contemporary metalworking seeks to surf on the waves of contemporary culture, examining, provoking, critiquing, proclaiming, or simply beautifying the body or our environs, through its myriad expressions and contradictions.

Jewellery

Seemingly more so than any of the other crafts, contemporary jewellery has extended its defining boundaries to the far edges of innovation and imagination. In the 1960s, jewellers began to break

PLATE 73 (opposite)
Robert Baines (b. 1949)
The Entropy of Red — Table, 1995
Sterling silver, gilt, lacquer,
soldered and diffusion bonded
53 x 28 cm
Photo: Gary Sommerfield

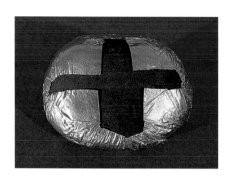

PLATE 74 (above)
Margaret West (b. 1936)
Memorandum II, 1995
Stone, 24-ct gold
Photo: Margaret West

PLATE 75
Rowena Gough (b. 1958)
Mobius, Circles and Discs: Bandoliers, 1992
Two-hole antique mother-of-pearl
shell buttons, blued mild steel,
mesh construction
66 x 8 x 1.5 cm
Photo: Ian Hobbs

from the traditional perception of jewellery as a craft activity centred about the combination of precious metals and gems for ornamental and status-conferring uses. As well as extending their *oeuvre* and the range of materials which they incorporated into their creativity, jewellers began to question the role of jewellery as simply body accessory or emblem of power and privilege, to produce ever-challenging and inspiring multi-functional objects. Now, in the 1990s, much of their work may be destined never to be placed on the body and, instead, is intended to be viewed as a gallery installation or art object. Such work may simply make references to its past traditional functions, or else act as semiotic markers for group, gender, political or otherwise sub-cultural, urban-tribe identifications. Other work may focus on the exploration of aesthetic, conceptual or sculptural realms. Whatever the intent, jewellery has been well and truly emancipated from any past cultural or traditional roles.

This does not imply a jettisoning of the wealth of imagery and meaning that the past and tradition may offer for contemporary creativity in this area. Compared to the other crafts, jewellery may appear superfluous in terms of its practical functioning — we can live without brooches, bangles, necklaces and earrings — but is life as satisfying or comfortable without clothes, furniture, glass and ceramic vessels? Certainly, the issue of wearability, addressing the interaction of the body with jewellery as ornament or complex signifier, remains a central focus for this practice. Situated on, encircling or piercing the flesh, or pinned or otherwise attached to clothing — jewellery evokes intimate moods and many readings.

Jewellery originated as a body-specific article, a locus which sets it apart from the usual kinds of roles of the crafts in so far as its practical functioning had little, if anything, to do with the basics of human existence. Yet the earliest jewellery may have been the talisman, perhaps a special crystal or pebble imbued with magical, protective powers, and worn around the neck or arm: surely this use was as critical to the wearer as were the practical functions of clay vessels or iron knifes? Later still, the amulet evolved as a purpose-made piece of jewellery specifically functioning as a charm. These ancient conjunctions of the body with mystery, ritual and magic continue to inform modern perceptions of jewellery as an aspect of contemporary material culture which is still associated with such esoteric qualities. Then again, jewellery's intimate scale and power as a repository of memory and meaning, acts to focus its primary functions within the ornamental, psychological, social and semiotic spheres. Jewellery decorates and complements the body; it enhances the erotic; it psychologically assures; and it socially identifies or distinguishes the wearer: these dynamics project a diorama of human culture revolving about sexuality, spirituality, and power and fame, signalling these qualities and other meanings to its intended audience. Invariably, jewellery has the power to draw people together, pronouncing identity, establishing links, delimiting territory, and generating intimacy.

No longer simply functioning as body accessory, cutting-edge contemporary jewellery can act as a metaphor for experience, memory, mood, identity, status, class, private mythology, political

PLATE 76
Carlier Makigawa (b. 1952)
Red Field Pendant, 1995
18-ct gold
16 cm (approx.)
Photo: Kate Gollings

PLATE 77 (above)
Anne Neil (b. 1951)
Power Dress, 1994
Woven electrical power cord and steel
70 x 50 x 25 cm
Photo: Andrew Lelong

PLATE 78 (right)
Helge Larsen (b. 1929)
and Darani Lewers (b. 1936)
Candlesticks, Paten and Chalice, 1990
Chapel of the Holy Spirit, St James
Church, Sydney
Silver

affiliation, gender inclination, narrative, or any of a gamut of cultural meanings.

Jewellers may seek to explore any one or combination of this rich cultural matrix, or else select a variety of other issues or areas which warrant investigation. These include an exploration of the process of design and fabrication of jewellery; scale in relation to human form; the sentimental attachment we have to precious or heirloom pieces; the symbolic and emotional associations and meanings of particular items such as the ring — marital, friendship or otherwise; the power or role of jewellery to draw attention to the wearer; personal narratives as extolled by jewellery; and jewellery as social facilitator.

One result of this breadth of possibilities is the name contemporary jewellers may assume and which often include silver or goldsmith, designer-maker, or art metalsmith. Today, fine art, clothing and fashion, new technologies, traditional forms and skills as well as traditional links with precious materials continue to act as sources for jewellery's ongoing efflorescence. But

PLATE 79
Phill Mason (b. 1950)
Little Dipper For Catching Falling Stardust,
1995
Hollow-fabricated sterling silver,
18-ct gold, 24-ct gilt
rivetted titanium wheel
15 x 5 cm
Photo: Uffe Schultze

perhaps the constant, central feature which continues to pull jewellery to its core, is its body-connectedness and hence, its intimate scale and roles within the human 'bodyscape'. There is a singular tension which is generated between the body and the placement of the object which is peculiar to this discipline, and which charges the works with additional meaning. Surely it is through a reaffirmation of these links with the body that the practise of jewellery is constantly reinvigorated.

The appropriation of imagery and motif from a grab-bag of material cultures, has also extended the vocabulary of jewellery well beyond the powerful and enduring traditions of European jewellery — centred as they are in the precious metals. Contemporary urban life itself provides a rich source of ideas for jewellers and some of the more unusual sources which have or continue to inspire the practice are: medals, cuff-links, body-piercing, spectacles, the walkman, dental braces, security badges, and even, hearing pieces.

Practices are diverse: some take an intellectual, conceptual or design approach, while others enjoy a playful path, and yet others explore sculptural directions. All result in meticulous works which extend from the metaphorical and the decorative, to the harmonious and the functional; these can be exquisite, alluring, puzzling, amusing, impressive, poetic, and wearable or non-wearable.

Today, the jeweller's point of departure can be, and usually is, entirely personal, with ideas sourced from practically any subject or any period, the material choice similarly being decisive and based on idiosyncrasy rather than tradition. Yet, despite the increasing use of hi-tech processes and eclectic sourcing, the allure and satisfaction of taking a traditional approach to jewellery and metalsmithing continues to influence a large proportion of the work in Australia. In this respect, many influences continue to be transferred and reinforced by the constant flow and exchange of

PLATE 80
Marion Marshall (b. 1948)
Steel Brooches, 1989
24-ct gold chisel inlay in steel
5 x 5 cm
Photo: Daniel Jenkins

jewellers and information between Australia, North America and Europe, as well as by travelling exhibitions of contemporary international work.

While the latter have been regular, the 1995 Italian Gold exhibition, for example, is but one of a number which serve to illustrate how historic and contemporary design sources may be fused into works of timeless beauty and technical excellence, and how the fruits of an ancient tradition of goldsmithing become exposed to practitioners in Australia. In this instance we may note the influences of the Renaissance combined with contemporary Italian goldsmithing design, itself linked to sculpture, as well as the trends initiated by the new-wave jewellery of the 1960s and 1970s crafts revival movement. Undoubtedly, the Italian goldsmithing heritage which continues to inspire contemporary works in that country, has also prevented the often unbridled eclecticism and lack of cultural focus sometimes seen in cutting-edge contemporary Australian or North American jewellery. Yet where the contemporary practitioner has delved into the past in a more sustained manner, work has emerged which challenges the traditional superiority of the European masters.

Robert Baines (b. 1949) is a goldsmith whose integrity and virtuosity of practice exemplifies the extent to which early jewellery traditions may inspire and inform contemporary work. His world-wide studies of ancient Greek and Etruscan gold work, as well as the nineteenth-century revival of these traditions, have led to a body of work which is not only extraordinary in its aesthetic allure, but also powerful in its conceptual embodiment.

Baines's work has been especially informed by the techniques and processes of construction that he has discerned and teased out as fundamental to the ancient goldsmiths of the Mediterranean region. By analysing and mastering these traditional skills, he determined how the ancient goldsmiths arrived at and constructed the stylistic features of their work; beyond these

PLATE 81
Mascha Moje (b. 1964)
Elipse and Cable, 1995
Mild steel, steel cable, silver
3.8 x 4.8 cm
Photo: Johannes Kuhnen

PLATE 82
Pierre Cavalan (b. 1954)
The Aesthetic of Distinction, 1994
Brooch/Pendant Shell, enamel badges,
anodised aluminium, glass, gold,
military paraphernalia, silver
22 x 11.5 cm

processes Baines has extended ancient traditions into a contemporary idiom through his own creative imagination.

Baines's works are typical in their highly sculptural forms and large scale: the intricate complexity of *The Entropy Of Red — Table*, for example, is based on a refined woven complexity in silver and gold, its enlarged decorative and rhythmic patterning communicating its historical and cultural links, while the intriguing form — and petal of red lacquer — is a highlight which instantly signals a post-modernist sensibility. Lyrical in its unity and semiotic in its projections, this engaging work is an inspiring visual and intellectual feast.

> Working as a goldsmith/artificer I am constructing artefacts as a vehicle to convey
> meaning, or through the process of making to express values. The conceptual
> basis is usually Christological in its intention.

By way of contrast to the former's approach, Margaret West (b. 1936) is especially known for her intellectual and poetic approach to jewellery which is usually considerably esoteric, and often, about as far removed as possible from the idea most people hold of jewellery. West's work, however, is not simply an academic's exploration of the concepts associated with traditional jewellery, but rather, she uses it as a focus for inquiries into emotions, desires, materiality, or other abstractions.

> I listen attentively to the presence of the present and the equally weighty absence
> of the past, as well as to form, to material, and to the poetic imperative that drives
> (me and) my work.

She investigates these various concepts through a strategy of juxtaposing the unusual where the usual is expected and dramatic changes of scale and form. For example, in a recent exhibition of her work (called 'Interstices'), instead of finger rings, precious stones, brooches or similar articles, she showed objects such as *Poem*, a work consisting of seven book-sized sheets of lead with difficult-to-read engraved text alongside an open, book-sized box; *Five Caskets for Galah* comprised five thick-walled boxes of iron and lead with small cavities filled with galah feathers, while another series was filled with sand; *Twelve Bibs* consisted of sheets of lead hung on the wall with one piece covered in gold leaf; and finally, perhaps the most surprising piece one would expect to encounter in a jewellery exhibition was a work called *Slough*, a full-scale human figure cut out of a lead sheet and laid out on a circular bed of white sand. All of these intriguing items were meticulously crafted.

With the exception of *Eight Stones with Steel*, a necklace of beach stones hanging on wire which would cut your neck if actually worn, none of these preceding works even suggested the wearable qualities of jewellery: they were either too big, too heavy, ungainly, and lacking means of attachment. Instead of modernist aesthetics and functionalism there was post-modernist angst, anthropology and semiotics. The meanings of these enigmatic works were difficult to read, forcing the viewer to ponder his or her own projections — perhaps the artist's intention.

'Interstices' was an exhibition which drew the viewer's attention to the gap between opposites, to the searching of ambiguities, the probing of content between the precious and non-precious and between the recalled and the forgotten. As such, the works are related more closely to the notions of poetry than jewellery, with West presenting sculptural forms and installations as the particular grammar of her visual language.

Memorandum II is yet another such example which, in presenting a stone wrapped in gilded silver foil with a cross cut-out revealing the stone's surface, further typifies West's intellectual and symbolic approach. This and her preceding works indicate the extent that jewellery can depart from its conventional format to be used as a means of exploring the boundaries of its own practice to the point that, such 'jewellery' is not so much intended to interact with the body, as with the mind.

Rowena Gough (b. 1958) similarly pursues an intellectual approach to jewellery, with feminist issues strongly expressed in her sculptural works. These invariably directly address the body enveloping, protecting, draping, hanging or gesturing, and ultimately drawing attention to particular ideas or narratives.

PLATE 83
Sue Lorraine (b. 1955)
Coiled Heart, 1994
Brooch: rusted steel, stainless steel pin
28 x 41 x 0.3 cm

> My interest stems from the conceptual, physical, emotional inter-relationships between jewellery and the human body. Jewellery and body ornament is the most ancient and poetic form of art-making: it is simple and complex, it is craft, it is a symbol, it is a metaphor, it is experience and memory. It acts as a cipher of the language of culture: it speaks on an intimate scale.

Gough abhors jewellery without meaning: instead, her practice strives to access these rich corporeal and cultural evocations. She is drawn to make work which is rich in its narrative content, using simple, refined suggestive and sensual processes and materials. The latter range from papier mâché, paper, mother-of-pearl, silver and other metals. She often combines specific units in multiples — discs being one favourite motif — to produce works which are elegant and often strongly rhythmical in appearance. *Bandoliers* is a work which exemplifies Gough's approaches and concerns. Its appearance, as the name suggests, is of a soldier's broad shoulder belt, although this bandolier is not made of leather but of mother-of-pearl discs seductively linked with fine metal wiring. She presents this work draped seductively over the body, suggesting the decorative or show sash; and while the bandolier normally functions as a holder of deadly bullets, Gough's version leads it with buttons, hence evoking a theme of domesticity.

Carlier Makigawa (b. 1952) is concerned with making jewellery which explores the relationship between architecture and body, volume and void, and 'the metaphors of

psychological containment: inside/outside'. To this end she creates brooches, neckpieces and other works including hollow-ware, using metal to outline and define spaces in conjunction with solid forms. The resultant effect can be like a stylised X-ray in three-dimensions, or cage-like, the forms always appearing elegant and expressive.

> Relation does not simply refer to how the body is situated in an architectural context, but also the contrast of man-made structures and nature. My works explore a symbolic, ritualistic and sensual expression within the object, as well as its placement on the body.

Makigawa's forms may include the human heart, but more often they are derived from nature: seed pods, buds, flames or leaves. She sees her jewellery as a kind of talisman, encapsulating and protecting the memories of its wearer and, in turn, becoming a reflection of his or her personality.

Typical of a growing number of craft practitioners, Anne Neil (b. 1951) is creative across a wide diversity of practices, from wearable jewellery to sculptural art works, as well as public art commissions. This diversity of application is also reflected in her techniques and processes which may range from fabrication, assembly, multi-media and even weaving.

Recurring themes in her work deal with self image, identity and classification, as well as aspects of dislocation. Feminist concerns are strong and is the focus for *Power Dress*, a work made for an exhibition titled 'Reveal and Conceal' at the Adelaide Female Writers Festival (in Adelaide, 1994). The use of recycled power cords woven into a woman's frock creates a strident metaphor which addresses domesticity, power and gender relations. Perhaps more appropriately located in sculpture rather than jewellery, or for that matter within the realm of weaving, Neil's work serves to illustrate the diffusion of boundaries and expansion of craft practices beyond conventionally accepted areas.

On the other hand, the work of the celebrated partnership between Darani Lewers (b. 1936) and Helge Larsen (b. 1929) sits well within the functional, symbolic and decorative boundaries of contemporary jewellery and metalwork. As a body of work which has developed over a thirty-five year period, their characteristic jewellery and hollow-ware is indelibly stamped with the many influences encountered over that period, and represents the fusion of a number of elements: Larsen's Danish and Lewers's Sydney background; a commonly inherited, traditional metalwork European heritage; respective modernist and post-modernist design sensibilities; and their personal insights, skills and experience of life.

Above all, their willingness to explore and take risks, yet retain a strongly defined philosophical basis which stems from their sensitivity to materials and processes, as well as a recognition that the cultural role and values of craft has sustained their creativity throughout this

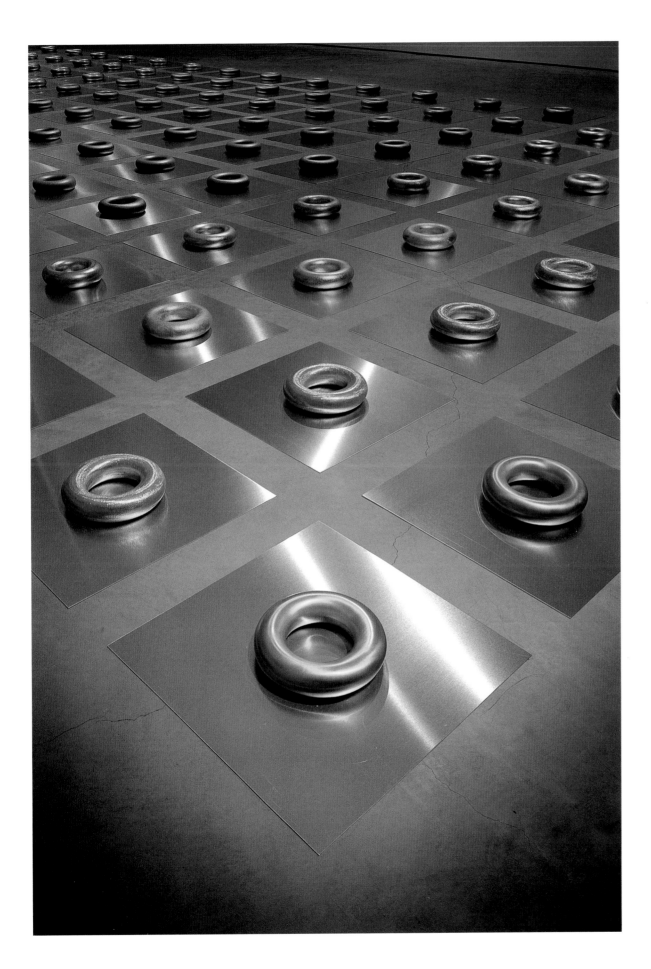

PLATE 85
Susan Cohn (b. 1952)
Way Past Real, 1994
Fine gold, natural
aluminium, 24-ct gold-plated
brass, gold anodised
aluminium, 22-ct gold
leaf, Dutch gold leaf,
24-ct gold-plated brass,
gold dust, gold paint and
theatrical lights;
Stamped aluminium,
brass or fine gold forms
constructed together and
finished with a variety of
gold surfaces
Bracelet size: 3 cm diameter
section x 13 cm diam
Installation size: 6 x 1.5 m
Photo: Kate Gollings

PLATE 86
David Walker (b. 1941)
Morph series, 1993
Set of five brooches
18-ct gold, 925 silver, Argyle diamonds,
stainless steel, paper, graphite
average size: 16.5 x 7.4 x 2.0 cm
Photo: John Leeming

period. Their work, therefore, retains freshness and exuberance as well as a relevance to everyday life not always encountered in the contemporary crafts.

> The social value of the crafts underpins all our work as does the process of working in collaboration. We believe the jewellery is only complete when worn on the body, reinforcing the personality of the wearer. It acts as a messenger between the maker, wearer and viewer marking an occasion, a ceremony or a rite of passage.
>
> Our silversmithing practice which includes large-scale religious and ceremonial work involves the reworking of symbols in a contemporary context to give fresh meanings to spiritual and social values.

The visual imagery of the work of Larsen and Lewers has certain recurring motifs and qualities: a preference for sterling silver and a Danish or northern European modernist simplicity is especially noted in their larger commissioned works; wearable, ornamental jewellery of complex assemblages of silver and other materials including glass beading, but especially natural materials such as amber, bone, shell, horn, wood and opal are also utilised. The latter materials have become prevalent in their more recent work, in part due to travels in the south-east Asian region where observations of the role of craft in Oriental culture underscored their desire to make work which celebrates diversity and recalls the spiritual, ritualistic and ceremonial richness of life.

The latter qualities are also expressive in recently commissioned liturgical works for the parish

PLATE 87
Robert Foster (b. 1962)
Teapot, 1995
Raised and anodised aluminium
Ht: 30 cm (approx)

Church of St James in Sydney, and for the Chapel at Cabrini Hospital, Melbourne. Sterling silver candlesticks, paten, chalice, ambry door, and sanctuary lamps assume a strong modernist influence, their sleek designs based on wrapped metal sheets, their decorative appeal emerging from the functional constructions of overlapping planes, reflective surfaces and apparent function.

The ceremonial and the ritualistic also figures strongly in Phill Mason's (b. 1950) jewellery and metalwork. Highly experimental while retaining its links to mainstream, traditional practices, the challenge in Mason's work emerges from the creation of new, often fantastic forms. He employs time-honoured precious metals and gems, rather than the novelty imposed by the trend for new materials and processes. In the past this approach led him to setting faceted stones upside down, so that the form predominated over the sparkle. Currently, the use of chenier has become a signature of his work, the pointed stones being especially cut to his specifications, ranging from the acutely pointed angular through to his development of the geometric annulus.

Underpinning the majority of my work is the attempt to symbolically address the resolution of duality. It might be by motifs such as squaring the circle (more abstractly by curving the angle), or by the simultaneous influence of, say,

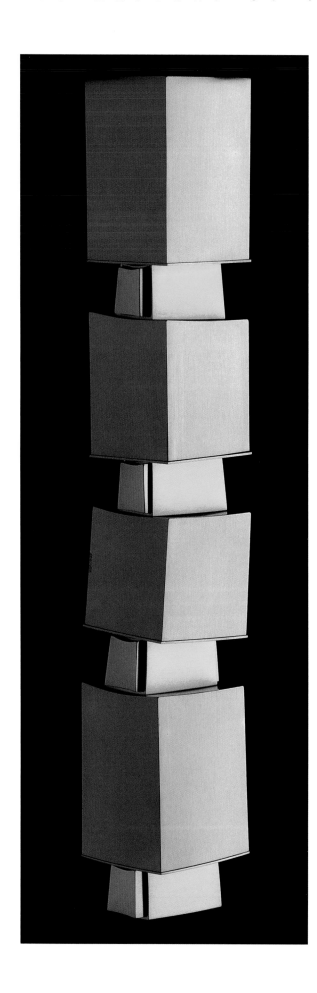

space-age geometry and historical architecture, yielding pieces on occasion which feel both futuristic and archaeological. Either way, the work frequently also addresses issues of emotion and power.

Mason imbues his work with passion, the richly worked, textured surfaces of silver, gold or titanium, often resplendent with amethysts, pearls, rubies, lapis lazuli, quartz or garnets. These works, typified by *Little Dipper For Catching Falling Stardust*, often suggest a baroque opulence, and although their strong design sense alludes to, but avoids, mere ostentation, their glittering complexity project a personal and singular, imagery.

Marion Marshall (b. 1948) is a jeweller who is not so interested in complex symbolisms or metaphorical expressions but in exploring the decorative potential of the more conventional processes and materials of the discipline. Her work consists of wearable jewellery — usually abstracted geometric shapes with cool surfaces and colours — which combines precious and non-precious materials, especially gold, jade, silver and iron. Another distinguishing feature is her frequent use of chisel inlay work, especially gold line in steel, the rich colour of the precious metal creating visual highlights and interest within the dark, base metal.

> Contrast and visual dichotomy are at play in my chisel-inlaid steel and precious metal jewellery. I have a fascination with the graphic play of line and the contrast of colour which merge as drawn lines on the surface of the steel to be accentuated by the occasional dot of colour achieved through the use of precious coloured stones or slabs of black jade in pure gold.

Mascha Moje's (b. 1964) work is instantly recognisable as the end-result of a relentless, intellectual and technical approach, one which has sought for a formal resolution which retains its functional intentions yet signals an invitation to further engagements. Furthermore, it has a curiously anonymous, rather than personal or intimate character, the emphatic forms inviting the wearer or viewer's personal projections: indeed, the work appears classical yet is innovative; primitive yet highly sophisticated.

Her material language is almost exclusively based on a distinctive and well-defined design intention of using stark combinations of steel and silver; pure geometric forms such as rectangles, squares, ovoid or circular segments; and (mild steel) cables — as seen in *Elipse and Cable*. Aesthetic properties emerge from these minimalist forms, from the gentle glow of burnished, dark steel or from the cool radiance of finely textured, matt silver surfaces.

Moje's visual imagery is gentle yet determined in its allure, a result of the strict yet subtle control that is evident in the assured articulation of a carefully selected vocabulary of material and process.

Sculptor Glen Dunn points to Moje's systematic approach in producing work 'in series, exploring all possible variations, views and compositions to any given concept'. Invariably, her earrings and pendants make strong statements, sometimes sculptural, sometimes graphic, but always attesting to their links with traditional values and contemporary developments in European jewellery and metalsmithing.

Eschewing the purity of the former's design approach, Pierre Cavalan (b. 1954) is surely a bricoleur master of jewellery. He combines assemblage and montage techniques with traditional jewellery skills to make elaborate and splendid medals, brooches, neckpieces and trophies from recycled institutional badges, tourist insignia and mass produced dress jewellery of the pre-war period.

The anthropological process of bricolage, as discussed in Chapter One, is a strategy whereby jettisoned materials and objects whose cultural meaning and original use have been surpassed, are reassembled into new objects which embody alternative, new cultural associations or meanings. In this manner too, the ordinary and often quite mundane can become extraordinary and impressive — precisely Cavalan's intention.

The Returned Servicemen's League, for example, once issued tens of thousands of badges as insignia for those members who 'served in the war', to be worn during official gatherings or during processions. Other badges identified members of other clubs and groups, institutions such as the military, bowling clubs,

PLATE 88 (opposite)
Mark Edgoose (b. 1960)
Stack III, 1995
Aluminium, 22-ct gold,
titanium nitride
31 x 6 x 6 cm
Photo: Sandy Nicholson

PLATE 89
Mari Funaki (b. 1950)
Container, 1993
Mild steel,
heat coloured,
fabricated
32 x 20 x 6 cm
Photo: Sandy Nicholson

PLATE 90
Beatrice Schlabowsky (b. 1958)
Oil and Vinegar, 1993
Pâte de verre, raised stainless steel,
gold-plated gilding metal
11 x 8 x 1.8 cm
Photo: Gary Summerfield

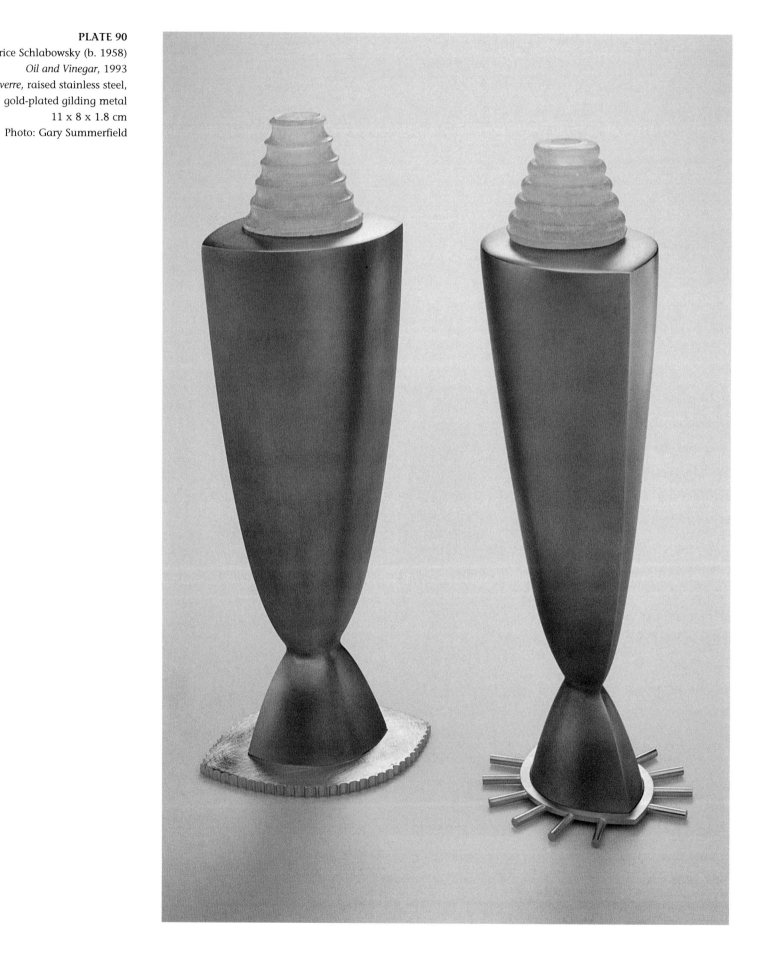

masonic lodges or football clubs, now irrelevant or defunct, and whose philosophical or authoritarian underpinning — once proclaimed through the imagery and text of the badge, in presses or cast metal, painted or enamelled — now belongs to a past industrial, imperialist age; these are the basic units, the motifs or vocabulary of Cavalan's visual language.

> From earliest times, people have gathered and treasured small organic objects such as shells, seeds, pods or animal claws, displaying these on the body as simple adornment. These objects connected the wearer with another place, or expressed an exchange or a winning trophy. The latter could be a feeling of victory in the case of the tribal warrior wearing the claw of a tiger. Modern day military decorations are the glittering remnants of such emotions. Persons in the army carry their 'body decoration' with pride. My jewellery celebrates a definite *joie de vivre*; my medals reward life itself.

The ceremonial or social values once signified by these pre-war and tourist badges and paraphernalia, now mostly exhausted, are subverted through Cavalan's action of recycling them into decorative assemblages, such as the brooch entitled *The Aesthetic of Distinction*. Although no longer capable of reissuing their original proclamations, these rather larger, opulent and even baroque works — whose component parts once lay on the dusty shelves of second-hand shops or languished among the detritus of garage sales — are held up to our renewed scrutiny. Symmetrical, colourful and splendidly baroque, these recontextualised medals and other works of bricolage jewellery, are destined to be mostly displayed in exhibitions or art museums where they elicit admiration, trigger memories, or rouse our curiosity.

The creation of jewellery which describes rather than decorates the human body is Sue Lorraine's (b. 1955) preoccupation. Her intent is clearly revealed in a recent series of works, which she refers to as 'em/body', she explored the metaphoric use of the body 'using the whole body as a site for jewellery and its parts as jewellery, to describe that space between the physical and the emotional'. Lorraine's highly disciplined approach investigated a number of possibilities and themes: the use of very rusted sheet steel; large (non-jewellery) scales; and the image of the cut-out heart, the human figure, or its intestinal shapes, as a site of transformation, for ritual, and for its metaphoric roles. There is a considerable boldness in the manner these forms have been created through minimal processes — mostly cutting and stencilling — and their controlled, forceful expression through the use of this base medium with its rusted surfaces.

Lorraine's point of departure for the work, her reading of thirteenth-century medical manuscripts, Eastern anatomical drawings, and the development of post-mortem science, illustrates the eclecticism of sources contemporary jewellers often draw on. Lorraine isolates a number of qualities and ideas, often as contradictory opposites: scientific learning and accuracy versus emotional symbolism; as well as historical allusion versus personal projection.

In a display which evokes a sense of the ancient, cadaverous anatomical theatre, this series of

PLATE 91
Peter Coombs (b. 1965)
Sangraal, 1993
Fabricated anodised aluminium,
sterling silver, UV plastic lens
15 x 35 cm

works included hearts with tendricular vessels curling into whiplash ends; hearts with their stumpy aorta intact; and hearts as negative cut-outs on articulated, almost life-size human figures. The symbolic meanings for this organ are evident: for love, a seat of the intellect, or as the source of the spirit. The negative cut-outs of intestines, as well as lengths of splayed out, sausage-shaped intestines, are metaphors for greed and vice. Yet another organ, the liver, has seemingly metamorphosed from a lobed, amorphous object, to a flower that may be mechanically fanned open or closed at will. Thus shifts from one form to another are mechanically simulated, while symbolic connotations are determined in the historical past as well as in the present.

These crisp organ and body images — executed in the rusted and rich textural qualities of steel which accentuate the skin-like effect — accumulate as metaphors for the personality or the emotions. Perhaps this is the most cogent aspect of this mostly, non-wearable jewellery: although sculptural and symbolic, it retains its links to the body, hence evoking the convention of wearing ornaments, placing them over parts of the body. In Lorraine's work, rather than expressing the usual notions of status or wealth, they conjure up historical belief, symbolic or psychological states, and personal allegory.

Glass could not be a more dissimilar material than metal, but its use in jewellery is well established, from the time glass-making was established and beads were made, to the present renaissance of the use of glass in this discipline. Blanche Tilden (b. 1968) considers her work to be jewellery, rather than specifically glass jewellery. In her work she combines glass with metals such as gold, silver, titanium and steel, challenging our perceptions of the use of glass as a material for this discipline.

Tilden is a master in solving the technical and design problems of bringing metal and glass together to make practical, wearable objects: indeed, 'Wearable Glass' has been the title of a number of shows in which she has presented such work. She rarely uses colour in her work, but mostly derives her design vocabulary from repeat linkages of glass components which vary from hollow or solid spindle forms, solid rings, interlocking u-shapes, and crosses. Neck-rings and 'chains' as she refers to her necklaces, are made up of these lamp-worked borosilicate components which are linked to each other with discs or wiring of stainless steel, titanium or silver.

The chains are especially alluring rhythmic forms: the interlocked components of clear or frosted glass capture the light, reflecting or refracting it in harmony with the movement of the wearer.

Susan Cohn (b. 1952) is interested in the cultural and social meanings and connections between the crafted object and day-to-day living. She has clearly articulated the philosophical basis for her work.

Well-crafted objects that serve as function are beautiful. Their special status derives from their very ordinariness, the way they quietly celebrate the daily routines and rituals of our lives. This is not only a simple matter of aesthetics, but it has to do with cultural connectedness, the reinforcement of values and the power of objects to reinvigorate social ritual. As a craft practitioner, I enjoy exploring the capacity of goldsmithing and jewellery to help redefine Australian popular culture, and to have some small, subtle effect on people's lives.

PLATE 92
Wayne Guest (b. 1956)
Vase, 1996
Sterling silver, coloured copper, fabricated
40 x 60 cm

In pursuing this philosophy, Cohn has become multi-skilled in so far as she not only makes jewellery (wearable one-offs, exhibition, or small batch production), but she also designs for industry, notably the Italian design firm Alessi; as a consequence her output includes, paradoxically, mass produced tablewares.

Her work is usually instantly recognisable by her trademark use of aluminium mesh which she crafts into precise, hi-tech functional forms which often appear to be made by machine. Certainly, the imagery in Cohn's work is often one alluding to the urban environment, its physical and psychological stresses and reality. This is so especially in respect to man-made control, its relentless pressured pace, and its anonymity. As a potent symbol of contemporary technology, Cohn's predominant use of aluminium emphasises these characteristics and acts as a sign for the city: in the past, she has crafted briefcases, walkmans, microphones and containers from aluminium mesh — all sleek and modernist in their machine-like finishes.

Yet her prime impetus, to imbue her objects with the characteristics which would in some way make cultural or social links with their owners, is assured — albeit sometimes in rather extreme or else subtle means. For the former consider her 'cosmetic manipulations', 'nose correction' brooches, or dental braces which she has crafted ostensibly, as 'ornamental' jewellery but which, in attracting attention to personal visual defects preferably left undisclosed, act to emphasise and interrogate social customs.

Her most recent foray into this thematic area are her *Insect Pendants*, a series of works which resemble large mechanical insects with a body made from telescopic segments of aluminium mesh, with industrially made components substituting for other parts, such as earplugs for the eyes and sunglass lenses for the wings. Cohn's social or cultural statement in this instance emerges from the fact that the hollow belly of each ornamental pendant contains a 'condom box'. Their functional intention is to provide the wearer with condoms at a critical point when the current social mores of sexual necessity arise. But Cohn's interrogations usually come in multiples, and the display of her *Insect Pendant* series in large numbers as an installation, also questioned the relationship, interface and role of craft and mass production. She instigates this dialogue by altering each of her insect pendants slightly: the colour or shape of the wings, the shape of the antennae or body, hence evoking the issue of handcrafted uniqueness versus uniform mass production.

PLATE 93
Mark Douglass (b. 1964)
Bullet Table and Chairs, 1996
Cast and polished aluminium,
Huon pine seats
Table diam: 140 cm; Chair ht: 87 cm

This line of exploration was also pursued in her jewellery installation exhibition 'Way Past Real', where Cohn displayed one hundred and fifty-three doughnut-shaped bracelets (a favourite form) about the gallery floor. These golden bracelets were either made of pure twenty-four caret gold, or else they were made to simulate the precious metal through various techniques such as gold anodised aluminium, twenty-two caret gold leaf, Dutch gold leaf, twenty-four caret gold-plated brass, gold dust, gold paint, and even gold light projected on aluminium. These bracelets were displayed individually on squares of natural aluminium arranged in a regular pattern over the floor. Which was the real gold bracelet handcrafted by Cohn, and which were the fakes which had been made in her production workshop? Because aluminium is a very cheap metal, whereas gold is valuable, Cohn forces a reassessment of our traditional ideas of jewellery, its value, its use and the feelings of desire or otherwise it may arouse.

Diversity is a hallmark of the contemporary metalworker: the considerable range of David Walker's (b. 1941) jewellery reflects the diversity of his background in silversmithing, design, architecture and craft. His intent is similarly broad: he seeks to integrate scale, material and process with references to the body, the natural landscape, elements of Australian culture and of the nature of jewellery itself.

Scale, for Walker, does not necessarily mean that his work must conform to traditional notions; instead, his work ranges from the wearable to the sculptural and the gallery installation. Processes and materials are similarly multifarious and include the use of hi-tech through to natural substances, their use not only extending the range of possibilities for construction, but they also become a means of imbuing further symbolic gestures into the work. Indeed, Walker structures his work to embody layers of meanings, the various metaphors peeling back, one after the other in a reading of his conceptual yet lyrical explorations.

The strongest formal basis for Walker's more recent work has been based on the idea of a stretched surface over a frame: these provide a variety of forms and surfaces which may be coloured or burnished at will, the textures, reflections and visible tensions providing a means to express philosophical, environmental or psychological concerns. In one series of works, Walker used this approach to stretch gold-leaf burnished paper skins over steel frames, the resultant forms being circular or canoe shaped. In this case his interest was in exploring the tensions between nature and technology; on another level, these explored the 'sense of collision between this ancient continent and its symbolic Aboriginal culture, and the threats posed by Western technologies … alternately, they demonstrate the immense potential for the synthesis of two opposites'. These works also allude to architectonic structures.

Walker's *Morph* series also explore this structure/tension approach, although in these works, the scale has been reduced to a wearable one. These *Morph* brooches have paper stretched over steel frames, the surfaces burnished in a dark graphite, while each piece includes the attachment of either a gold or silver bead and a diamond. The immediate impression gained from viewing these works, as intended, from above, is a sense of landscape, the brooches then evoking an impression of a cluster of ancient Australian landforms. These works are also specifically identifiable with Western Australia, given the specific use of an Argyle diamond. This structure and tension theme also highlights the fragility of this ancient landscape, just as the use of graphite, a pure carbon substance and the same element from which diamonds emerge, suggests genesis and a sense of timelessness — characteristics of the Australian landscape.

Hollow-ware

With its dazzling displays of design ingenuity, intellectual content, aesthetic sophistication, and consummate crafting, contemporary Australian hollow-ware is taking the limelight from metalworking. Rectilinear, curvilinear, architectonic, organic, ethereal, striking, sumptuous, pristine, complex and lyrical, beyond these parameters and qualities, enigmatic and virtuoso are two words which especially sum up the character of contemporary hollow-ware.

Although considerably diverse in its expressions, Australian hollow-ware often reflects its roots in nineteenth-century colonial silver and goldsmithing traditions. The 1960s and 1970s craft revival included a reinvigoration of the craft, especially following the arrival of a number of

PLATE 94
Marc Pascal (b. 1959)
Mimi Chairs, 1994
Powdercoated steel,
spun anodised aluminium,
back: ABS thermo-formed plastic
Photo: Oriander

European masters including Ragnar Hansen, Helge Larsen and Frank Bauer.

Reduced to its essentials, hollow-ware takes the box, bowl and cylinder, transforming their simple geometries into masterful articulations of surface, volume, weight and balance. While a proportion of contemporary jewellers specialise in the making of hollow-ware, others simply make occasional forays into this area, investigating and refining the conjunction of function, form and ornament in vessels and related objects for presentation, ornament, tableware, or for other traditional ceremonial, functional or ritualistic uses.

Hollow-ware entails particular demands and raises certain questions: is traditional function to be minimalised in order to be replaced with abstracted notions, or reduced to allusion? What metal is to be used, and are other materials such as wood or acrylics to be incorporated? To decorate or not? And ultimately, which approach is to be taken, minimalist, organic or eclectic? Influences on Australian hollow-ware include those emanating from traditional and contemporary European, and to a lesser extent, North American sources, as well as colonial metalsmithing traditions. Industrial design is also strongly influential in this area, with advanced techniques and processes constantly providing new choices for the making of forms and the treatment of surfaces.

Hollow-ware is also used as a vehicle for the exploration of more abstract artistic or design ideas; frequently, hollow-ware assumes forms which are a considerable departure from recognisable, traditional models. This split suggests two mainstream approaches to hollow-ware: a 'cool' modernist path which reduces form to functional, clean lines and geometric shapes or planes; or else an 'emotional' post-modernist strategy is taken, one which favours lateral solutions to design including the reduction of function to mere reference, eclectic sourcing for ornament and surface treatment, rich narrative content, and the reconfiguration of historical motifs and models.

But this is a simplistic view, and hollow-ware in the late 1990s is a complex, often paradoxical activity, sometimes combining minimalist principles with pastiche, humour with irony, feelings with memory. And as with the other crafts, the boundaries between the functional, aesthetic and sculptural have become blurred. As a result, the visual language of hollow-ware has become especially cutting-edge and highly-sophisticated: from Gothic to Renaissance, from sleek modernist to organic post-modernist, contemporary hollow-ware takes its cue from an eclectic range of historical or contemporary sources; it may refer to the crafting process, to past rituals, to its material origins, to architectonic forms, explore the idea of function, or virtually become sculpture. Often it's a case where one needs to jettison the usual notions of what teapots, coffee-pot, jugs and vases look like, and expect the unexpected.

Robert Foster (b. 1962) is a designer-maker who specialises in hollow-ware, combining function with fantasy to produce work which especially bends conventional notions of the genre. He applies design for the purpose of visual and emotive stimulation, as well as symbolic projection. Tendricular, jocular and funky, his vessels are exemplary of the cutting-edge of craft design in the 1990s. Foster creates his teapots, kettles and coffee-pots as organically based forms which evoke the archaic shapes of prehistoric life; or else, they suggest insects, the profiles of leaping dolphins, or even, Persian slippers; while some resemble exotic plant forms seemingly plucked from far-off worlds.

An element of Alice in Wonderland also appears to be a part of Foster's design approach: blink, or turn away for a moment, and there is an expectation that these extraordinary objects might spring into life, the tendricular plant-like handles and spouts waving to and fro, the low-humped and spiky trilobite vessels scuttling off their plinths, coffee-pots swaying and twisting their bodies, sake pots in mesh frocks bobbing and spinning, all to a silent fandango.

Foster's imaginative design vocabulary appears to be inspired from sources as far ranging as

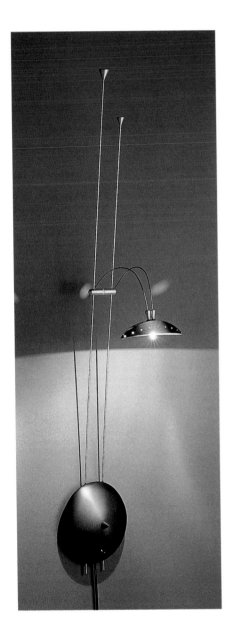

PLATE 95
Greg Healey (b. 1963)
Jumpy (wall light), 1996
Aluminium, stainless steel,
12 volt electrics
110 x 25 cm
Photo: Grant Hancock

the pre-historic, the mathematical, hi-tech, the Memphis school, as well as various organic life-forms. Closer observation shows these meticulously crafted hollow-ware vessels to have lids, spouts and handles, and are therefore designed to function as teapots or kettles. However, as sculptural interpretations of usually mundane domestic objects, it is just as likely that they would be collected by connoisseurs and museums as used in the domestic kitchen.

Apart from the striking originality of his designs, Foster's hollow-ware may also be admired from the point of view of the technical virtuosity evident in the burnished and vibrantly coloured, powder-coated finishes, and in the overall craftsmanship of each piece. Consider his Dolphin coffee set where the pot form evokes a leaping dolphin caught in the act of breaking through the water's surface, its arching deep-blue body complemented by aubergine fins and a smooth, jet-black face, the latter ingeniously forming the lid. Another favourite form, the teapot, has a backwards bending cylindrical soft-grey body, capped by a canary yellow lid and sporting a long, red spout, the elongated grass green handle arching confidently over the front of the body, finishing with the flourish of a pea sprout curl. A wide palette of intense colour contrasts is heightened by the use of powder-coated surfaces or anodised aluminium.

Other forms are derived with a precision that has mathematical deliberation, but shaped in a way that suggests their distortion through some imaginary time–space equations. These teapot series are finished in a raw grey stainless steel, the delicately hammered and heat burnished surfaces sensuously reflecting and contrasting against the smoother aluminium lids or handles; this is evident in the body of one work, a teapot designed as a symmetrical, turtle-like shell, with two spouts and a polished twin handle arching over the lid.

Aside from these one-off, exhibition pieces, Foster also designs a line of limited production hollow-ware marketed under the name Fink! Design, whilst also designing and making metal furniture. In this he is one of an increasing number of crafts practitioner/entrepreneurs who are successfully linking industrial approaches with studio design and creativity.

Foster's innovative work is at once brash and unconventional, confident and striking, full of verve and creativity, colourful and substantial, practical yet sensually stimulating — and elegant with a touch of humour.

Mark Edgoose (b. 1960) produces highly abstracted vessels and objects whose obtuse forms and exquisite finishes elicit considerable admiration. These sleek, sometimes aerodynamic and always futuristic forms extend beyond the sculptural to the functional, specifically underscoring the notion of containment. Engineered with intelligence and precision, his works are often brilliant, lateral design solutions of volume, shape, surface and function.

Using these parameters as a pure vocabulary, he generates a dialogue of subtleties articulating planes, surfaces, corners, lines, colours, shadows and sheens. Edgoose often stacks his box-like units in vertical or horizontal dimensions to create primal sculptural forms of repeat motifs which further enhance this play of craft qualities, as seen in *Stack III*. Aluminium, titanium, silver, gold,

PLATE 96
Patrick Hall (b. 1962)
Pillars of Society, 1995
Chest of drawers/filing cabinet
MFD, aluminium, screen printing inks
180 x 90 x 65 cm

and titanium nitride, these and other materials are engaged with advanced and innovative fabricating, welding, colouring, finishing, and other technological processes and skills.

His exploration of the qualities of metals and their surfaces is especially alluring, while the combination of this impetus with that of practical function, especially as his works are often food containers or vessels used at the dining table, elevates their presence beyond that of mere use. On another level, Edgoose's fabrications become metaphors for deconstruction, suggesting a review of our notions of function and form, while engaging our senses with the pleasures of the handmade, yet abstracted, form.

Mari Funaki (b. 1950) has a distinctive design sense that is undoubtedly influenced by her Japanese background, yet is clearly informed by a strong personal vision. The former is evident in the startling degree of reduction she creates in her forms. But she also imbues these with an organic suggestion, the praying mantis or other insect types, acting as points of inspiration for generating innovative vessel forms. The hard-edge of the insect's exterior skeleton has seemingly suggested her own hard-edged works, while overlapping planes or etiolated legs and antenna-like spouts suggest other parts of arthropod anatomy. On the other hand, her candle and other containers alternatively suggest the Japanese craft of origami as yet another design source.

Working in mild steel which is finished in a chemically blackened, matt surface, Funaki's *Container* series contrast strongly against the intense colour or reflective surfaces popular with other Australian metalsmiths. This is in part due to her homeland cultural background whereby the strong visual principles seen in her work are largely influenced by Zen aesthetics.

> I like objects that convey both a symbolic value for the individual and a ritual
> value in everyday life. My main interest is the creation of dynamism in objects,
> through the careful manipulation of space.

Beatrice Schlabowsky's design approach (b. 1958) centres on balance, harmony, repetition and the use of colour. She endeavours to juxtapose the contemporary with the historic in respect to the materials and techniques she employs. Her work demonstrates a close attention to detail and finish and is visually alluring in the manner with which she articulates a diversity of materials in her sculpturally conceived hollow-ware. Her use of gilded metal and cast glass appears to be specific to her approach, the combination of textures and colour creating opulent objects.

These are often architectonic in reference, although they also exhibit strong structural lines which blend futuristic and archaic models. In this respect, the work is post-modernist as its sources range across the historic and the geographic. Schlabowsky also suggests that her 'work relates to forms and symbols that infer the feminine and, on a more specific level, personal concepts'. Her work includes domestic tablewares such as fruit baskets, dessert beakers, trays, salt and pepper shakers and decorative vessels. Their iconic forms evoke elements of permanence, preciousness, and the ritualistic, which are evident in the set *Oil and Vinegar*.

Prior to studying jewellery, Peter Coombs's (b. 1965) background in the surveying industry honed his attention to accuracy and detail. He is particularly well known for his idiosyncratic spectacles, although he also makes hip flasks, goblets, perfume bottles, jewellery and a variety of commissioned requests, created predominantly from sterling anodised aluminium, gold and ebony. His works source many styles, including Celtic, Art Deco, Art Nouveau and Japanese design, although he insists that this is rarely the result of a conscious design decision.

> I am inspired by anything and everything — construction of any type always
> catches my eye. Indeed, I once described my work as 'constructionist', mostly out
> of frustration from people constantly wanting to impose categories.

This is possibly the best clue to Coombs's approach, one which exposes the methodology which suggests an engineering logic behind his designs. His work emphasises the functional as well as decorative aspects, the latter emerging from the apparent construction details and from the mixtures of materials used in any one piece. His spectacles, including the design titled *Sangraal*, exhibit a strong architectonic styling, but the work is best described as 'off-beat', as it usually includes quirky or unexpected details as well as innovative combinations of materials.

Wayne Guest (b. 1956) is a silversmith specialising in handcrafted one-off and limited edition domestic tablewares. Unlike most of the practitioners in this text, his design approach is less centred on the innovative than the traditional. Indeed, Guest's work is personally developmental of neo-classical through to early twentieth-century silver forms. An identifying feature is his use of a small amount of copper as a circle or cylinder; this creates contrasts of copper against the whiteness of the silver. In some works, copper becomes the predominant metal, silver being delegated to highlighting decorative detail in the overall design. His use of copper is also symbolic in so far as the intention is to evoke a hint of the red central Australian desert. Guest's work is mostly smooth, reflective and curvilinear, the geometry of his rounded forms, jugs, bowls, ladles and vases, creating a gentle imagery. Always functional, the work is essentially modernist in its reduction of decorative detail as described above, while the use of copper and classical elements hint at the work of decorative metalwork of French artists of the early twentieth century such as Jean Dunand or Jean Despres.

Metal and Furniture

As noted in the introductory chapter, the cooperative is currently a particularly dynamic area of contemporary craft practice. Mark Douglass (b. 1964) was one of six practitioners in metal and glass who established the Whitehall Enterprises in 1988 — a cooperative workshop which became celebrated for its quirky and original designs in furniture, lighting and other architectural fittings and objects for cafes, boutiques and other commercial and domestic settings. Since 1990, Douglass has been working independently within his own workshop (Mark Douglass Design), and is recognised as one of Australia's most successful designer-makers. His current approach is flexible combining his own hands-on skills in glass and metal; implementation of his designs within his factory workshop by a team of craftspeople ranging from five up to ten; and subcontracting work to industry. As expected, Douglass's output consists of a wide range of furnishings for commercial and domestic commissions (offices, shops, boutiques and restaurants), as well as work for exhibitions.

The style of Douglass's furniture, light fittings, chandeliers, doors, balustrades, display cabinets, signage and screens demonstrates a fertile imagination, yet retains an identifying set of features that are the hallmark of this designer-maker. These include a sense of the irreverent in his designs which rarely conform to the conventional; a fondness for rich textural effects; a vibrant fusion of glass and metal; and a sense of exuberance which verges on the baroque. Sometimes his light fittings, chairs or tables suggest a Victorian science fiction setting, while other works have a rococo boldness, or even an aggressive élan. Douglass demonstrates a willingness to constantly explore his favourite materials, glass and metal, embracing and hybridising a very wide range of techniques, materials and design sources. Art Deco, Art Nouveau, neo-classicism, retro-1950s and 1960s, hi-tech, craft and fashion are creatively sourced and intertwined to produce a personal aesthetic which varies from the cool and energetic to the engaging and playful. These qualities are variously seen in *Bullet Table and Chairs*, a startling, hi-tech work of cast and polished aluminium and timber seats, and in *Chaise Lounge*, an eccentric piece which especially typifies his irreverent approach to design. Douglass's juxtapositions of seemingly incongruous styles and materials result in highly individual, unreserved visual statements, and a vitality that ensues that one can never tire of his work.

> In the mid-1980s craft witnessed a dilemma. The role of the craftsperson was to produce a range of goods to sell in craft shops or galleries; craft was always considered the poor cousin of the fine arts. Unable to fit comfortably into this scene I decided to create interior environments. Mood and detail within otherwise commercial fittings could become artworks in themselves, an idea which seems to have been lost since the 1900s. A chair, for example, may occupy one's living room where one may view it more than ten times a day, yet sit in it only once. For me, the aesthetics and subliminal joy such a piece may give outweighs its function.

Marc Pascal (b. 1959) has moved even further from the studio model than Douglass, to focus on the design of furniture and lighting for mass production or for limited editions. As such, he typifies another contemporary trend in which the craft practitioner acts as a bridge between industry, design and craft. His skills include industrial design, crafting, furniture-making, print-making and painting. In his own words he 'ricochets from art to craft to product design and back again, aiming to create objects to use and look at, objects that have some kind of dialogue or interaction with the user.'

PLATE 98
Daniel Jenkins (b. 1947)
Transit Transition Icon: Memory, 1995
Repoussé copper, patinated
450 x 320 cm

His so-called *Mimi Chairs*, for example, combine powder-coated or chrome steel with thermo-formed plastics in a wide range and combination of colours. Although clearly the products of industrial techniques and processes, their colours and restrained yet playful and stylish forms have imbued them with a sense of exuberance which suggests an influence from the Italian Memphis school. Pascal's simple though elegant design solutions demonstrate the vigour which may be expressed through such successful metalsmithing, fine art and craft hybridisations.

Greg Healey (b. 1963) is a also a designer-maker who is working across a broad range of practices to make works which he categorises into three groups: architectural commissions, product design and exhibition work. The scale is similarly broad, ranging from wearable jewellery to large, site-specific architectural works. He is particularly drawn to the possibilities of metal and its integration with other materials, 'aiming to achieve design simplicity with added highlights and focal points'. The sources for his thematic content are diverse and include landscape, or personal events, as well as subjects of cultural interest. Healey uses jewellery as a starting point to

explore various themes; his mourning brooch series, for example, investigate death as a metaphor for the sanitisation of life within contemporary society. These ritual brooches are precise, geometric boat-like shapes which combine anodised aluminium with silk and imagery from laminated photographs. Various colours act as codes symbolising emotional states or human rituals. Indeed, Healey's specific use of colour as a signifier is a distinctive feature of his work.

Healey's furniture and light fittings especially demonstrate a lucid and singular design sense which favours simplicity and directness, but always includes a highlight of some kind or another, such as a quirky motif or unusual textural or colour surface treatment. Aside from steel and aluminium, Healey is also fond of working with iron as a 'contemporary metalworker', but after shaping the metal, he extends his treatment by adding surface effects for texture or colour using plate or powder-coating or other industrial techniques.

Furniture-maker, Patrick Hall (b. 1962) also typifies the multi-skilling trend of the contemporary designer-maker, although he works more within the guidelines of the studio-craftsman approach. His characteristic pieces are personal visual statements derived through a vigorous fusion of printmaking with metal and woodworking skills and techniques. Hall transforms the notion of furniture from its sole and mundane function of holding things into colourful, stylish and surreal forms which mock or lampoon society. These also enliven our domestic settings with their decorative richness, but whatever their appearance, they are crafted to be eminently suited to contemporary urban living.

Brushed aluminium is his preferred surface, as it provides a contrast for bright enamel surfaces, as well as a suitable texture on which he silk-screens magnified lino-cut compositions. It is a winning combination of approaches which combines luminous, bold imagery with crisp architectonic forms. His furniture often displays *trompe l'oeil* effects so that it doubles as sculptural artwork as well as being useful. Hall also enjoys distorting perspective so that full-length mirrors and filing cabinets double as towering, teetering skyscrapers (as in *Pillars of Society*) and the surfaces are richly decorated with images such as his favourite stars against a black enamel background. Sheep are not generally the most obvious images for ornamental purposes, but on his furniture they look perfectly at ease: several of his aluminium chests are embellished with personable sheep, peacefully grazing on the drawers and set, somewhat boldly, against a mauve surface speckled with orange.

His monochrome etching skills similarly embellish other works, such as sideboard chests decorated with etchings in the nineteenth-century style with large fish, another of his identifiable motifs.

Hall's work is steadfastly post-modernist in extending the useful into the realm of the symbolic and sensual, gathering a grab-bag of influences and imagery from past and present, urban and rural.

> I want to make the experience of opening a cabinet a mysterious, wonderful adventure. I want to make our domestic environment places that are inspiring, places that encourage humour and creativity. I want to make objects that, through their use, make the ritual of living richer and more enjoyable.

PLATE 99 (opposite)
Rachel Bowak (b. 1964)
Illume 4, 1995
Forged and constructed mild steel
230 x 65 cm
Photo: Penny Boyer

A New Iron Age

Until recently, iron has had a relatively minor place in the pantheon of the traditional decorative and applied arts media of clay, glass, wood and fibre. Today, hot-forged iron, hammered and beaten, assembled and finished and often combined with other metals or materials, is coming to the fore in the contemporary crafts as artist blacksmiths around Australia strike new directions with this base metal. After the relentless explorations by contemporary craftworkers of 'traditional' materials — ceramics, glass, fibre and wood — forged iron (or steel) still presents a relatively unexplored medium.

Yet, unlike glass, clay, wood or fibre, iron does not appear to have their universal or immediate impact as a medium. So why do individuals choose to interact with such a demanding craft? There are its sensual and dramatic attractions: the ringing of a dull piece of iron as it is hammered, and the bright yellow glow it takes on when put into the forge where it becomes transformed from its solid, unyielding state into a plastic medium, like molten glass or clay: in this state it can be manipulated into almost any shape. Finished forged iron (as opposed to welded steel), retains a unique and alluring hand-beaten patina, as seen in its lustrous sheen and faceted surface.

Once the preserve of the village smithy who hammered and repaired horseshoes, waggon rims, agricultural implements and other functional objects essential for nineteenth-century everyday life, the industrial revolution and the advent of the automobile saw the gradual demise of this craft. That is, until the beginning of the revival of ironwork in the late 1970s and early 1980s. Contemporary 1990s ironwork has not only reached a considerable level of activity and acceptance, but in some respects it is surpassing other crafts as it continues to attract adherents, including silver or goldsmiths, who have come to recognise the expressive potential of iron, and who have become enchanted with the material and its demanding but immensely satisfying challenges.

And while the contemporary edge of blacksmithing has inevitably seen the alignment of the medium with the fine arts, this has not necessarily been at the expense of its age-old traditions. Although the latter are inherent in the use of the metal, practitioners have demonstrated a willingness to acknowledge the depth of social and cultural associations contemporary ironworking embodies.

Yet another reason for the ascendancy of iron is its inherent primitivism, a characteristic

PLATE 100
Coral Lowry (b. 1951)
Play, 1993
Galvanised mild steel,
Ferrador charcoal wash
Photo: Victor France

increasingly seen as relevant to contemporary expression in this post-industrial age. Iron, steel and other metals, when treated to reveal their raw, literally, 'metallic', surfaces, can have an alluring quality which, to the jaded modern consumerist's eye, seem fresh, powerful, romantic, and even esoteric or erotic.

Not unexpectedly, practitioners have not restricted their range to the traditional metal of the blacksmith — iron or steel. Instead, their work embraces and often combines metals as disparate as copper, cast bronze, sterling silver, gold leaf, lead, aluminium, tin and zinc — as well as glass and wood. Once the traditional forge, hammer, bellows and tongs were all that was necessary for the blacksmith; today, although a proportion of art blacksmiths prefer this purist approach, most contemporary practitioners have embraced technology, exploiting casting, welding, rivetting, anodising, and the use of power tools.

Steve Weis (b. 1952) is an art blacksmith who established a large workshop and business, Weis Iron in 1988, where he employs up to twelve people. He has since designed and made numerous large-scale interior and exterior fittings, furniture and sculptural works for domestic and commercial settings. Weis aims particularly to integrate the forms and qualities of iron into the domestic setting, using a 'themed' approach to design which emphasises particular stylistic elements.

And while there is always a call for traditional design, Weis prefers to develop his own styles which source the traditional, but are innovative and often strongly sculptural. Not surprisingly, rococo and neo-baroque curls, post-modernist gestures, Art Nouveau and neo-Gothic styles inform his work. Weis strives to express the manifold characteristics of iron, beyond its functional ability, into the realm of the historic, the ritualistic and the primitive. He achieves this by retaining traditional techniques and treatments, albeit with contemporary improvements which make the execution of work more efficient. Hence, forging the iron and texturing it by hammering the surface provides the base form, while finishing processes include zinc copper sprayed patination, sprayed verdigris, zinc with gold and rust lustre, and painting. The latter enhance the decorative appeal of his spontaneous, flowing forms, and allow him to achieve alluring, aged effects.

Although much contemporary ironwork is still centred on the functional, one of its strengths, its application within a wide sphere of domestic, architectural and public areas, has seen a broadening of the diversity of approaches to its creation, as well as the forms and styles it can assume. On the cutting-edge of metalwork, Daniel Jenkins (b. 1947) works mainly from commissions. Some of his past work has included public art works such as four whimsical and ornamental (2.5 metre) repoussé copper weathervanes for Swanston Walk, in central Melbourne in 1992. Lately, he has been specialising in large sculptural forms. A master of repoussé, forged iron and other metalsmithing techniques and processes, Jenkins imbues his work with a reverence and powerful symbolism which is extended into the spiritual as:

> a journey of a level of conscience which links my own past to a perceived future. I have worked with the bowl as a starting point which has evolved into boat forms; both represent a containment of a personal life force. My materials, gold inlaid forged steel and repoussé copper are from the earth, formed by fist and fire for an assumed function, to be coloured by the minerals of the earth, and patinated with time. Their journey and my journey are icons of transitions, both transporting the immortal spirit.

In this Jenkins considers craft to be 'the means, the skill of the soul, in itself an icon of transition, to the spirit of the form'. His *Transit Transition Icon* series reflect this ideology, the lyrical bowls singular explorations of the vessel, orchestrating iron with delicate inserts of gold; his large forged and copper repoussé hollow sculptural forms employ kinetics as a key visual. These articulate selected symbols and motifs as dream-like images or metaphors which evoke a sense of transition and search.

Rachel Bowak's (b. 1964) intense passion for blacksmithing and steel expresses itself through her minimal, though intricate and organic, sculptural works. In her first body of work she

PLATE 101 (opposite)
Elizabeth Tulip (b. 1966)
Bird House, 1994
Forged and fabricated steel,
interior gilded with electric globe
140 x 60 cm
Photo: Tony Flint

achieved an extraordinary sense of lightness and movement using forged mild steel which she manipulated into open vessel forms. She works on an exceptionally large scale using long lengths of steel and minimal joins, creating a play of balance which gives a physical movement to the work when touched. These explorations are lyrical works which demonstrate the fluidity and sensitivity which iron may be coaxed to assume under the craft practitioners hand.

Bowak recently developed these concepts into a second major body of work where the scale has been increased even further, and where the vessel and other forms have achieved a greater spontaneity in their fluid lines. These heroic 'intertanglements' of long strands of steel seem woven by organic forces, or ordered by underlying physical resonances. Bowak refers to this second group as *Illume* (short for illumine), linking the forms to the aftermath of a bushfire when the blackened trunks of trees seem to stand frozen in a moment of time, yet contain the power to regenerate following the first rains. So too, do Bowak's trunk-like, feather or bowl forms which evoke a mixture of vulnerability and potential life. The *Spod* series, essentially seed forms, similarly explore these concepts, their shapes acting as metaphors of potential life.

> The linear work plays with the concept of heavy, dark steel transformed into a light, floating and uplifting form which responds to touch with movement, hence generating a visual and tactile dialogue — to illume each work exists on the edge of balance, relying entirely on the strength of its material and the forces of gravity.

Coral Lowry (b. 1951) similarly specialises in producing purely sculptural work, although she also works on public commissions to make artworks for public spaces — as well as the occasional functional piece. She works chiefly in metal, although it is difficult to classify her simply as a metalworker, given her forays into furniture and sculpture. Following her earlier work in ceramics and fibre, her present practice sees her working with mild steel which she finishes with rusted surfaces. *Dancing With Yourself*, is a sculptural work which deals with the issues relating to mental illness, and is one of two created for a 1993 exhibition entitled 'Advantage of Isolation'. It took the form of a chair with one leg raised, the supporting back a serpentine spine: it is a pose which projects a sense of dissonance, together with a feeling for the humanity of the subject in question, while the rusted finish enhances the notion of pathos in the form.

Lowry is also proficient in public artworks. Her recent galvanised steel child profiles, a part of the *Play* series of sculptures, adorn the galvanised fence of a Western Australian primary school, their jaunty poses animating and enhancing an otherwise sterile setting.

This combination of iron and craft with a sculptural approach is also descriptive of Elizabeth Tulip's (b. 1966) approach. Her diverse training and background in blacksmithing and design, visual arts and restoration crafts, guarantees a similar spread of application of skills: she not only makes purely sculptural, exhibition work and artworks for public spaces, but also carries out ornamental and decorative commissions.

Tulip's work is graphic in its visual imagery: a large forged and graphite-painted coffee cup complete with tendrils of metal representing steam functions as a sign for a cafe; a three-leaved dressing screen combines Gothic-shaped panels with tendricular supports, the red calico fabric contrasting against the grey, forged steel; *Bird House*, a steel sculpture lampooning the backyard garden bird house, is constructed as a pair of elongated bird legs with massive claws, the body substituted by a model house with a peaked roof. The raw qualities of the steel are permitted to make their own statement which is underscored by the gilded interior.

Her purely sculptural works are conceived with a sharp eye: four sentinel-like figures make up the installation of *Before Sleep*, the towering box-bodied giants with jesters' hats leering in anticipation of nightmares to come. *Twenty-four Dancing Slippers*, another installation, consisted of twelve pairs of life-sized slippers made of forged and fabricated steel, and arranged in a casual manner along a corridor where they seemingly mocked or challenged their recently absent owners.

> My work is an exploration of narrative as a state of mind; humour is
> used as an entry point for the viewer. Imagined images sometimes
> contain contradictions, developing their own logic when made real.
> Forged steel brings resonance to these images through alchemical
> processes.
>
> The physicality of forging draws maker and viewer into the
> object's realm of time and space.

Tulip's work stresses symbolic and emotive expressiveness which she achieves by combining an aggressive edge with an element of wit. Sharp, dangerous edges abound in her work which is often conceived on a scale which towers above the viewer, a further intimidating gesture. Her clear intent, coupled with an affinity for the qualities of the medium, results in works where the primitivism and strength of steel underscores a powerful, often dark, metaphoric imagery.

Is this contemporary iron renaissance simply a revival of particular techniques and the creation of objects? It appears to embody much more: it suggests a return to the original values of craftsmanship and the handmade such as truth-to-materials, function and integrity, values which have tended to be relegated to the wayside in the rush of post-industrial society and its consumer obsessions. Considering that as well as heat, forging iron requires strength of mind and body, then the qualities of strength and honesty, implicit in forged iron and in those processes necessary for its creation, may be seen to represent a stand against mediocrity, or even to satisfy a nostalgic craving for simplicity in life. Perhaps too, on a more personal level, the malleability inherent in forged iron may suggest the retraining of the senses and the recovery of lost values for both practitioner and user alike.

CHAPTER FIVE:
FIBRE – WEAVING STORIES

Whether they are pushing the boundaries or replicating traditional techniques and forms, making functional or non-functional work, contemporary textile and fibre practitioners are creating a richness of patterns, textures, colours, forms and images which delight and challenge audiences, and which are spinning yarns and telling stories of themselves, their society — and especially of women.

The link between textile and fibre skills, feminine creativity and storytelling, is a perennial theme in human history; literary metaphors concerning the weaving, spinning, plaiting and embroidery processes, often used to enrich our spoken language, and literary texts which include phrases such as 'unravelling complexity', 'spinning yarns', and 'fabric of society'. In their practice, textile and fibre artists are effectively involved in an activity in which story and memory is captured in stitch — currently one of the strongest themes.

While our notion of language utilises the spoken or written word for the expression of thoughts and feelings, the richness of metaphorical allusions possible through the practice of weaving can communicate specific cultural associations, moods and ideas. In effect, textile and fibre practitioners are replacing the grammatical arrangement of words and rules of our written and spoken language with the vertical warp and horizontal weft of interwoven yarn; in this manner, the structures of twinned fibre become a metaphorical syntax of the spun, woven, embroidered or whatever other textile or non-textile techniques are used for manipulating fibres. The concept of intertextuality is therefore especially fertile in the field of textile and fibre works, with a focus on its links with the continuity of social practices, feminist issues, as well as with the broader cultural setting.

Out of this activity emerges a diversity of fabrics and fibreworks which include the functional or non-functional, the decorative, abstract or symbolic, embodying biography or encoding narratives and texts.

Textile and fibre art today communicates through the common ground of woven fibre with its rich history of social tradition and cultural content, and through its physical characteristics of texture, visual patterning and tactility. Practitioners in this field also exploit and extend the vocabulary of their medium through its juxtapositions with the body, the domestic or the public environment, or the exhibition space. Indeed, the sensual qualities of this medium, the fact that

PLATE 102
Pat Davidson (b. 1950)
Letter to my Daughter, 1993
Appliqué and machine embroidery;
acid dyed silk, commercial threads
35 x 25 cm
Photo: Michael Van Ewijk

PLATE 103
Marie Larkin (b. 1958)
Icon Image: The Circle of Motherhood,
(central panel), 1995
Petit point embroidered rayon on linen,
stranded cotton,
braid and tokens on velvet
25 x 30 cm
Photo: Marie Larkin

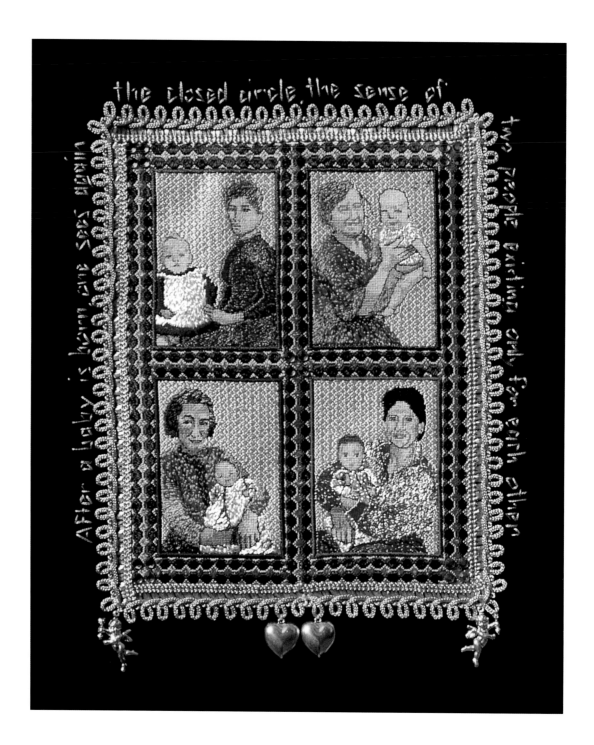

its original chief function was to be wrapped or draped about the body, to be protective, tactile, signifying and alluring in its presence, has similarly become a critical focus of exploration.

Practitioners have at hand many strategies: they may choose deconstruction, perhaps exposing and fraying edges to evoke the process of fabrication or deterioration and hence allude to an activity which is essentially analytical; they might investigate the fundamental nature of the interlocking grid of the medium, the horizontal and vertical threads and the repetitive structures exaggerating its scale or its cohesive ability, its regular or irregular geometry to evoke allusions to

PLATE 104
Alvena Hall (b. 1941)
Carcase In The Sand, Lake Eyre series, 1992
Hand-dyed cotton, linens,
synthetics, pieced, embroidered and
quilted over polyester batting
90 x 60 cm
Photo: Eric Algra

cross-referencing; or, like ceramists, jewellers or other craft practitioners, they may take the approach of bricolage, gathering together discarded fragments and reassembling these into arresting constructions which signify ideas or explore cultural issues; Diana Wood-Conroy, for example, is one such practitioner whose work centres about the investigation of archaeological metaphors in the medium. On the other hand practitioners may chose to avoid representation — graphic, abstract or symbolic — and be seduced by the physicality of the medium, making works which celebrate textile's sensuous qualities, colours and textures.

This is a far cry from the textiles of the past: throughout the history of this activity, the mother passed on her skills in the time-honoured method of the family sewing group or embroidery circle, the daughter emulating the mother, and friends and neighbours sharing food recipes, swapping community gossip and enjoying each other's company linked through creative activity. Change was gradual despite being accelerated by the Industrial Revolution but, by the 1940s, the plethora of sample books and correspondence lessons broadened the repertoire of the creative housewife: examples of sewing samplers, hooked rag rugs (or Waggas), doyleys, knitted lace, mantle runners, wall tapestries, embroidered homilies, tea towels, curtains, crochet work and tea cosies, were perhaps the most popular articles, mostly mundane forms for use around the home.

The postwar period saw renewed creativity in the area, especially during the first two decades of the crafts movement in the 1960s and 1970s. During these years through to the present, the International Biennial of Tapestry in Lausanne, Switzerland, was especially instrumental in stimulating innovative and experimental directions in textile and fibre art. These biennials

PLATE 105
Janine Boyd (b. 1965)
Quilt for Helen, 1995
Free machine embroidery
onto cotton base,
procion-dyed rayon thread,
cotton fabric,
cotton printed fabric,
free machine quilting
64 x 47 cm
Photo: Grant Hancock

(initiated in 1963), together with a proliferation of magazines, including *Textile Fibre Forum* in Australia, as well as other influences, encouraged the breakdown of boundaries and the exploration of work within the sphere of the fine arts. Large-scale work, installations, sculptural directions, and the use of a wide range of materials, aside from artificial and natural fibres, were especially favoured by these influences. The investigation of the interaction of textile and fibre forms, creative processes and structure, with space, light and history came to the fore during the 1980s. Other directions became prominent as post-modernist ideas took hold, especially deconstruction which encouraged the exploration of the basic units and processes of construction of textile and fibre art — an enduring tendency. The essence of various fibre cultural traditions also became sources for exploration, especially as interest in the origins, traditions and meaning of the crafts expanded.

Hence, over the 1980s and 1990s, as with the other areas of the contemporary crafts, various approaches and ideologies passed in and out of fashion: the medium as the message, links to various art movements, on the wall then off the wall, traditional or non-traditional, deconstructionist, bricolage, technical finesse or primitive finish, and so on.

The essential point that endured is that, just as in clay, glass, wood and metal, the prime medium of choice — in this case fibre — is investigated for its inherent characteristics as a creative, expressive language.

From the functional and traditional to the decorative, narrative and conceptual, the humble stitch has certainly come a long way from its origins as a domestic craft of necessity. Now textile and fibre practitioners not only seek the translation of textile or fibre into functional, representational or abstract forms, but also explore and utilise the material and its skills basis as an essential aspect of its being, as well as the layered cultural meanings and social traditions and constructions of the medium. Personal, narrative, historical, social or political content is combined with aesthetic expression, and traditional or innovative techniques are applied as tools in numerous approaches. Works may simply be decorative or practical, but more often than not, they are sculptural or visual art presentations, or ever complex, multilayered, conceptual or metaphorical works designed to tell personal stories, or to make statements or question various issues or themes as broad as environmental concerns, past ideals of feminine workmanship, or urban domestic violence; on the other hand, the works may evoke psychological moods, and more generally, explore the condition of everyday life.

Fibre and textile arts today embrace an extraordinary range of techniques, approaches and practices, including tapestry, hand and machine embroidery, knotted lace, stumpwork, appliqué, collage, lace-making, quilting, goldwork, knitting, patchwork, millinery, three-dimensional sculpture, felting, batik, and beading, to name just a few. It is not unusual too, for practitioners to combine two or more techniques in one work.

The trend for fibre and textile practitioners to borrow ideas from visual arts practices to extend traditional work into three-dimensional sculpture, blurring the boundaries between art and function, which was initiated in the 1960s, has shown no signs of abating in the late 1990s. Such an emphasis on the artistic concept in a work sometimes comes with a tendency more typical of the earlier decades, but is still persistent, to negate technique and medium: it has even been manifested in the approach of some textile artists who do not even use fibre in their work! This perspective is not pervasive, and the centrality and celebration of process, medium and skill in fibre remains a central attraction.

Exhibitions of textile and fibre art are frequent, but the Tamworth Fibre and Textile Biennial is the one major event which regularly surveys and exposes the experimental and cutting edge of fibre and textile practices to a wide audience in this country. As a consequence, this is not a show where one would expect to see traditional tapestries or woven baskets: instead, recent surveys have

PLATE 106 (opposite)
Cheryl Bridgart (b. 1956)
Dreamtime '96, 1996
Free machine embroidery attached
to billy can
18.5 x Diam 18 cm
Photo: Carmel Bridgart

invariably focused on the innovative edge, on craft-as-art or, visual art working with craft, categories.

But the diversity of approaches typical of contemporary Australian fibre and textile practice extends beyond these to encompass other categories. Fibre and textile artists may certainly take a course which privileges iconographic, conceptual or other fine art or sculptural approaches over medium and process; a middle stream tends to hybridise traditional craft with fine art whereby, in successful work, the one reinforces and references the other; or else practitioners may prefer the attempt to achieve a dynamic interplay between aesthetic elements with craft skills, process and medium, while not ignoring the traditional, social and cultural realms of the craft.

Not surprisingly, we are back at the art-versus-craft debate. But defining boundaries is always risky, and it would seem more instructive to suggest an opening up of categories and blurring of edges in an acceptance of today's eclecticism with its diversity of approaches, yet acknowledging or maintaining a sense of the traditional social and cultural values inherent in the craft — that is its essential human qualities and identity. It may be that this is the means by which textile and fibre artists might avoid finding themselves in a phase of their craft whereby a lack of vitality and originality characterises the work; after all, when every possible material, technique, scale, formal expression, and novelty of approach have been investigated and expressed, what will remain?

Embroidery

The strength of embroidery as an art form often comes to the fore in the biographical or narrative approach. It is, after all, the intimate links between the thread, home, memory and the feminine realm, that endows embroidery with the means to effectively tell stories of a personal nature. And because storytelling, whether in a visual or literary medium, has the power to closely engage an audience, embroidered works are invariably inspiring and familiar.

For these and other reasons, embroidery continues to be a quintessential feminine craft, and a popular one, often applied to create snapshots of the maker's experiences of family life, intimate or universal, the images freezing memories in stitch.

Some practitioners still prefer to use traditional techniques such as the timeless nature of the sampler, for example, applying it in a contemporary manner to exploit its strong historical associations. Yet others employ embroidery as a form of 'painting' to create pictorial representation, itself sometimes extended into photorealism, with technique often overtaking the subject matter.

Colour is often liberally applied, but restraint and the use of monochromatic techniques such as goldwork is always present in a small proportion of works. Line embroidery, for example, can be used to literally sketch out a composition using black thread on a white background, simulating a fine-line etched print. Multi-varied approaches combine various techniques such as air-brushed and dyed silk, appliqué and feather handstitching.

The biennial Dame Nancy Buttfield Embroidery Exhibition (held in Adelaide), permits a comprehensive sampling of the varied approaches to making an embroidery where 'the majority of the work is created with the threaded needle', by hand, machine or both. Certain themes are perennial favourites — such as the landscape study or personal narrative within the domestic realm, and other social or personal issues; most embroiderers appear to have the ability to explore the subject afresh each year.

Textile artist and educator Janine Boyd (b. 1965) is one such practitioner who has participated in the national embroidery exhibition at least three times, the most recent was in 1995 when she won the first prize for her evocative work *Quilt for Helen*. Constructed from layered surfaces of dyed rayon thread with free machine embroidery onto a cotton base thread with cotton printed fabric and quilting, Boyd captures a snatch of childhood memory that is ethereal and dream-like in its quality. The image depicts the artist as a child 'who loves and trusts without judgment'. Intimate and universal, the seemingly time faded central image is surrounded by quotes of embroidered text which accentuates the sense of the innocence of childhood.

> My work develops over a period of months. I begin with an inspiration, words I
> have written, or an old family photograph, and develop a series of tonal studies
> and drawings. Next, I work on colour, as swatches and experiments abound.
> When the final composition and planned method is complete, I transfer it to a
> fabric base. Areas of light and dark are identified. The stitching begins.

Boyd continually changes the threads, sometimes using as many as sixty different shades, tints and colours on one piece, thereby achieving the semblance of a time-faded photograph. Through this intensive process, she translates, and celebrates, her personal histories.

Autobiography is also Marie Larkin's (b. 1958) concern, although her approach employs *petit point* and other techniques to create almost jewel-like images of her chosen subjects or narrative themes. *The Dream We Share*, for example, is a series which explores the continuity between generations, using a photorealism achieved with extraordinarily detailed and delicate, *petit point* work on linen.

Larkin strives for a mastery of technique, endeavouring to imbue her work with meaning. To this end she sources her home setting creating images from her experiences of day-to-day life: thus she captures the clutter, textures and colour of her desk or embroiders self-portraits. These extraordinary works effectively capture a sense of immediacy and liveliness. Other works include her vibrant *Icon, Circle of Motherhood* series: these are jewel-like images which symbolise the enduring relationship between mother and child.

Pat Davidson (b. 1950) uses appliqué and machine embroidery to translate familiar ideas into decorative and challenging works. Her textile pieces have recognisable images and intricate surfaces designed to seduce and entice the viewer into a closer examination. The work then 'delivers a contradiction to the initially more obvious stereotype'. Political and social values

PLATE 107 (opposite)
Kay Lawrence (b. 1947)
Mother, 1994
Woven tapestry: cotton warp,
wool, cotton, linen weft
180 x 132 cm
Photo: Michal Kluvanek

relating to feminist issues, linguistic variations and other cultural implications are conveyed through an imagery which is sometimes complex, and other times disarmingly simple. Through this approach, Davidson attempts to generate 'an alternate frame of cultural reference' as a means of interrogating her subjects and stimulating the viewer to partake of a dialogue with the work.

> I enjoy the twists and illogicalities of social structures. Concepts within each work explore the narrow line between public domains and the intimacy of personal spaces.

Letter to my Daughter is a work which is exemplary of the latter aim and utilises acid-dyed silks, appliqué and machine embroidery to combine image and text. Another work, *Eve and Adam*, uses the familiar graphic image of this couple, but reverses the Biblical narrative to shift the woman out of her traditionally submissive role and assign responsibility for the 'ultimate act' to the man.

Alvena Hall (b. 1941) similarly combines a variety of techniques, in this case specialising in machine embroidery, photo imagery, cyanotype, dyes and piecing, to create graphic textiles which focus on the environment and 'the human context of technology'.

She is especially interested in exploring the idea of the 'edge': between water and land, the horizon and the arid landscape, as well as the boundary between technology and nature. By transferring photo images onto textile and combining these with a layered approach to produce the effect of multiple horizons, she creates painterly images with a stark, hyper-realism reminiscent of the work of Australian painter Jeffrey Smart. *The Fragile Zone, Lake Eyre* series explore this idea of boundaries and horizons, the clash between technology and the fragile quality of this environment; through its stark juxtapositions and crisp edges, the image has a haunting stillness which heightens the notion of dissonance. Another work, *Carcase In The Sand*, is an image which locates the rusting hulk of an abandoned vehicle in the middle-ground of the ageless panorama of Lake Eyre: it suggests the conquest of nature over the artificial, and once more, evokes the idea of a dissonance between the pristine environment and the cluttering proclivities of humanity.

Hall's *Littoral Zone* series also explore this fragility theme, although in these works she uses machine-embroidered lace, gauze and found beach objects to create multi-media, sculptural works.

Cheryl Bridgart (b. 1956) stitches surreal images which are infused with a sense of play and humour. Her detailed, painterly images are first drafted in a series of drawings, the subject matter being derived from life or her imagination. Eschewing the use of paint or dye, she applies the sewing machine as a paint brush and thread as her palette. In this manner she creates her fantasy works on a blank fabric, achieving a free-hand drawn quality which is vibrant with colour and joyous in its celebration of life. The detailed images are usually figurative and draw from Bridgart's experiences, dreams and emotions, 'things felt rather than seen in the form of personal symbols'.

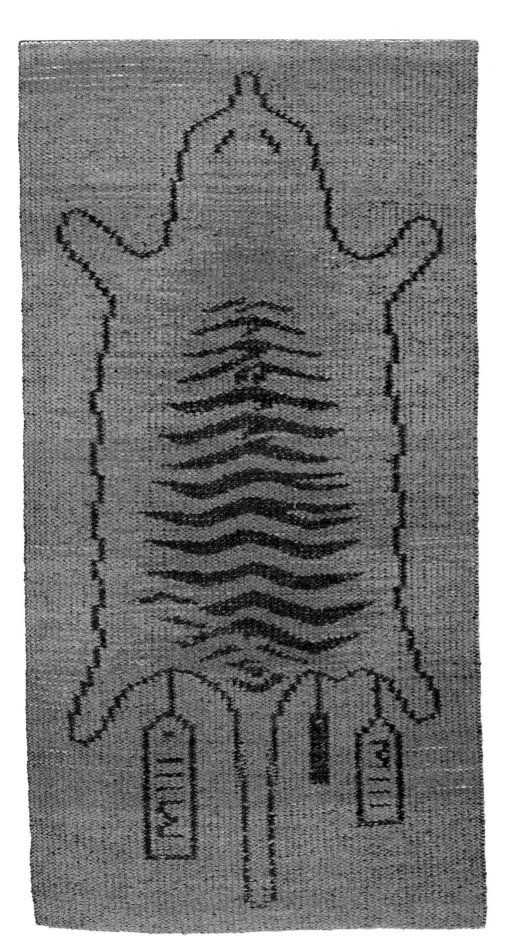

PLATE 108
Beth Hatton (b. 1943)
Tasmanian Tiger Rug
(Endangered Species — Second series), 1995
Tapestry: dyed wools woven on a cotton warp
90 x 160 cm
Photo: Ian Hobbs

PLATE 109
Sue Rosenthal (b. 1950)
Women's Work: Which Weapon, 1996
Tapestry diptych: linen warp,
cotton and wool weft,
supplementary weft technique
Each diptych: 112 x 63 cm

Bridgart also views her works as 'colourful and tactile diaries' and has mastered a style which translates her inner visions into the reality of thread, yet retaining the illusionary quality of memories, dreams and fantasies. Faces and eyes are a perennial motif, freely embroidered with numerous overlapping stitches of flesh-coloured threads to create the considerable degree of realism she aims for, the imagery suffused with mystery and intrigue. In *Dreamtime '96*, an embroidery made for the National Billy Can Art Competition, Bridgart's first prize winning work lyrically combines a number of Australian images including an Aboriginal portrait and a parrot, as well as icons such as Ayers Rock and the Sydney Opera House: strands of the tune of 'Waltzing Matilda' seemingly meanders through the image which is a delightful riot of colour, texture and stitched line.

Tapestry

Tapestry is currently enjoying an international resurgence of popularity with works often being confronting and subversive. Reinterpreting Europe's tapestry traditions, the current wave of contemporary tapestry practices provide a window into personal, social and psychological issues, often feminist orientated. Tapestry may remain traditional in its construction whilst actively

PLATE 110
Sara Lindsay (b. 1951)
Throw Away Your Dahlias, 1994
Tapestry weaving using torn fabrics
of cotton, silk, rayon and wool
with fine yarn
130 x 220 cm
Photo: Terence Bogue

drawing elements from diverse sources such as psychological notions of identity, aesthetics, archaeology, popular culture, literature, comic strips and mass advertising imagery.

The new tapestry is an especially vibrant artform which demonstrates a keen concern for materials and process and their relationship to traditional notions of this genre which extend beyond the image.

Perennial themes include the tapestry as narrative, text, gender or identity. Tapestry as a metaphor pervades our language, but it is the medium which has a double message, both read and unread, and set into thread. From this perspective, tapestry is a woven language which signifies particular traditions, histories and meanings. These include its past restriction to the wealthy classes, its function as a decorative wall hanging, its close associations to fine art, and of course, the extraordinary labour and skill required to complete examples of this genre of work.

Traditionally, the labour intensive nature of tapestry-making restricted it to the upper classes and linked it to the grandeur of the palace and baronial hall. Once dependant on highly organised workshops where designers and weavers collaborated to translate an image, usually of allegorical or mythological nature and often of an original painting into the woven texture of the cloth, contemporary practitioners subvert its historical role by reducing its conventionally large scale and by creating images of a more individual and usually, domestic nature. The control of tapestry making has also shifted from a patriarchal system to become a feminine and even, at times, a feminist activity.

There are exceptions, and the Victorian Tapestry Workshop in Melbourne would seem to have developed the historical Renaissance model into a contemporary version whereby artists and

PLATE 111
Jan Irvine (b. 1950)
Out Of Gondwana, 1995
Quilt: Air-brushed dyed silf,
woolfilled, handstitched
90 x 150 cm
Photo: Ian Hobbs

PLATE 112 (opposite)
Sarah Crowest (b. 1957)
Edith, 1996
Quilt made from dyed and screen-printed
and painted linen pieces,
hand-stitched with cotton embroidery
threads on cotton damask backing
207 x 201 cm
Photo: Grant Hancock

designers are engaged in interpreting paintings or other sources for weaving by a team of practitioners into large-scale tapestries, mostly for public spaces.

Given this cultural matrix, tapestry can only remain true to its type if it remains on the wall as a hanging and makes references to its social and traditional functions and forms. Whereas embroidery and the other textile arts, because of their historical links and functions with the body or domestic spaces, may be crumpled and articulated into three-dimensional or other forms. Nevertheless, contemporary tapestry practitioners have taken its classic woven processes to the extreme, oscillating from hard-edge French Gobelin techniques to considerably more freely worked surfaces which appear as sketches or more abstract patterning, bringing out the essence of the being of tapestry in structure and image.

There is a polarity of perspectives in the way tapestry is defined: on the one hand there is the textural, hand processes, structure dictating design approach which underpinned Bauhaus teaching. The other view prefers to stress the mimicry of tapestry with painting: image into woven thread. Post-modernism and its encouragement of plurality has seemingly reconciled the dilemma, although debate on the seeming contradictory relationship between these extreme views continues.

PLATE 114
Sylvia Parr (b. 1937)
Scarf, 1995
Handwoven fine wool with dyed warps
150 x 45 cm
Photo: Concept Hobart

Kay Lawrence (b. 1947) is a tapestry artist whose work has spear-headed much of this contemporary genre in Australia. Her celebrated work is invariably a sensitive interpretation in the medium of tapestry of her chosen theme or subject matter. The latter has varied over the years of her practice, but certain themes are prominent, including studies which capture the sense of the Australian landscape, its timelessness and the patterns and colours of its unique flora and fauna. Other tapestries, such as her *Women's Suffrage Centenary Community* tapestry series, have centred on women's studies, interpreting the historical events within the contemporary setting. She is also adept at translating gender issues or psychological ideas into this medium.

Mother, a tapestry woven by Lawrence using linen, wool and cotton as well as standard techniques, is an example of the way she produces images of considerable power. As with all of her tapestries, Lawrence first completes numerous drawings, selecting the one which has the most potency or 'emotional intensity' for her. The work was a response to her own ideas which were initiated by observations of her daughter drawing stick figures; these suggested to her that gender identity was not fixed at birth but was a fluid concept. When Lawrence began to draw her own images based on these observations, she recalled Sigmund Freud's concept of the 'phallic mother', and at first, as she worked on the tapestry she titled *Mother*, she intended to represent gender identity. Certainly, the tapestry's visual portrayal of a child's drawing whose undifferentiated world has bequeathed the larger adult background figure with both phallus and breast, evokes a psychological state suggesting a diffuse gender identity.

Weaving images in tapestry takes considerable time, and while sitting at the loom unconscious ideas, which were 'caught' in the original drawing, began to emerge in the warp and weft of the tapestry as Lawrence progressed. At this point, constructing tapestry became a means of deconstructing past lives. Lawrence now interprets the image as a means of coming to terms

PLATE 113 (opposite)
Liz Williamson (b. 1949)
Gold Textiles 2, (detail), 1993
Handwoven wool, wool blend,
wool lycra, copper wire,
nylon mono-filament, and gold threads
40 x 163 cm
Photo: Ian Hobbs

PLATE 115
Elsje King (b. 1947)
Transformation, 1995
Handstitched and felted silk
and cotton fabrics
with recycled and decayed fabrics
and vegetable dyes
103 x 170 cm
Photo: Victor France

with the earlier loss or separation of her mother, through her life experiences with her own child.

In *Mother*, the weave evokes the naivety of the child's drawing, the textural quality of the process eminently matching and projecting the potent image.

> My practice in woven tapestry and drawing is on the edge of both the Visual Arts
> and Crafts, informed by the long tradition of woven tapestry in Western culture,
> yet engaged in negotiating some of the issues that characterise contemporary
> Visual Arts. Issues such as feminism, representation and questions of identity. The
> contradictions and tensions that arise from working at this edge invite questions
> rather than answers. It is these uncertainties that activate my work.

Beth Hatton (b. 1943) weaves functional tapestries which combine fine art statements with specific subject matter of current social concern. Her ongoing *Endangered Species* series consist of woven woollen rugs which centre about the theme of humanity's destructive effect on the natural environment and particularly, the cogent issue of biological diversity.

The impact of European settlement on the Australian environment has been especially damaging, given the fragile nature of this land and the vulnerability of its unique marsupial fauna to exotic mammalian feral species, land clearance and degradation. And given the fact that numerous native species are already extinct, and that the rate at which remaining species are edging towards this fate is accelerating, this issue has become highlighted in the public mind.

Hatton's series of rugs feature endangered native animals such as the hairy nosed wombat, the quoll and the Tasmanian tiger: the latter is almost certainly extinct, although 'sightings' are still reported by hopeful individuals who venture into the dense forests of Tasmania. Because Hatton's rugs actually depict the pelts of these animals, laid out and tagged with identifying

PLATE 116
Christopher and Jennifer Robertson
(b. 1957 and 1962)
Succulentus Oos, 1995
Merino wool/cotton doublecloth,
handwoven on sixteen shafts to produce
raised surface; steel, plywood,
feathers, foam, nylon;
back rotates from central pivot
69 x 115 x 820 cm
Photo: Daniel Bruyn

museum labels, the finality of the process of extinction is underscored. Her *Tasmanian Tiger Rug* and other works are all the more effective in their visual potency given the fact that humanity once relied entirely on animal pelts to provide surface covering, that is, to act as rugs. Although technological know-how may have led to the discovery and use of weaving which has essentially replaced the material culture need to use animal pelts with woven rugs, human activity continues to pose a threat. Hatton's work weaves a narrative of this process, the grey and brown tones and jagged outlines of the wool weft accentuating the insubstantial nature of the once-living 'remains'.

> I am attracted to the expressive qualities of the weaving process, its muted subtle
> language which speaks of time, steady patient accumulation, and the integrating
> of disparate elements into a new order. The weaving of functional textiles such as
> rugs imposes a further discipline which is that of balance, a useful quality to
> cultivate at the end of the twentieth century as we try to reconcile competing needs
> within a deteriorating environment.

We may view Hatton's rugs in the exhibition setting hung on walls, but their practical use is to act as floor coverings which we walk over, and in this sense she endeavours to raise awareness of our ongoing abuse of endangered species. But then there are also the labels she weaves into her rugs, tags which identify once living creatures now represented by their sole remains as pelts in our cultural museums. It is through these various layered meanings and stories that Hatton's tapestry-works relate the seemingly inevitable narrative of extinction.

Textile artist Sue Rosenthal (b. 1950) specialises in weaving tapestries which challenge our everyday perceptions of our social being and lives. Specifically, she seeks, through her tapestry work, to turn our scrutiny inwards to consider the manner in which our perceptions of and attitudes to world events are manipulated by the media, particularly photo-journalism.

My interest is in exploring issues such as the sense of dissociation from world affairs and the different realities that their media presentation engenders, as well as the subliminal attitudes that some powerful images can initiate.

Selecting cogent images reproduced in the daily press or from television, Rosenthal has adapted a traditional loom weaving pattern, exploiting its graphic rendition of the half tone dot form of appropriated images; supplementary weft processes also further reflect the media from which the images are sourced. In this manner, the tapestry technique and the resultant textural and visual qualities of the finished work enhance the communication of intended meaning beyond the surface graphics.

In her diptych tapestry *War and Peace, A Piece of War*, Rosenthal depicts in black and grey tones an African (Somalian) child soldier smoking a cigarette while resting with a rifle; alongside this image is the depiction of a sitting room with a vase of poppies rendered in bright orange and red tones decorating the television whose screen shows a news scene of the boy soldier. The technique is powerful: our eyes are drawn to the bright bunch of flowers decorating the domestic setting as a reality more palatable than the disturbing image of the child soldier. As a result, Rosenthal succeeds in stimulating awareness of the dissonance between the reality of the two images, and of our desire to dwell with one but 'pass' on the other.

In another work, *Women's Work: Which Weapon?* Rosenthal uses the same techniques to juxtapose a masked women with an assault weapon on a lipstick pink background, alongside a contrasting image of a smartly dressed business woman carrying a briefcase; a row of bullets accompanying the first image is ingeniously counterbalanced by a row of pink tipped lipsticks. Once more, the powerful imagery creates a dissonance, the work raising the issue of perceptions and alternatives, in this case in regard to political action, posing the choice — violence or the subtle means of corporate business?

Sara Lindsay (b. 1951) works at the cutting edge of tapestry techniques, combining unusual materials and designs with the innovative use of computers. Lately, she has been creating tapestries using a selection of black and white gingham fabrics which, when torn up and re-woven, are transformed into rich, visual textures. Lindsay then scans these textures into a computer, manipulating these images to explore ideas relating to the migrant experience of journey, settlement and return whereby 'the gingham acts as a metaphor for home and various dualities and contrasts such as north and south, today and the past, and of hope and despair.'

Lindsay's approach to tapestry is relentlessly post-modernist as it subverts and opens up conventional attitudes to the practice. A senior weaver at the Victorian Tapestry Workshop during the 1980s, she has reversed the traditional methodology whereby an artist designed then prepared cartoons which were interpreted and translated into the warp and weft of the tapestry process; some five or more years on, and Lindsay now either works entirely from start to finish using the preceding innovative techniques, or else she occasionally works with others on collaborative

PLATE 117 (opposite)
Tori de Mestre (b. 1951)
Taming the Land, 1994
Collage: eucalypt sticks with photo image and oil painting
167 x 76 cm
Photo: Ralph Silva-Lindsey

projects where specialised skills are pooled to produce explorative and ground-breaking works.

Lindsay's tapestries centre on the dialogues generated between the use of black and white gingham and the transformation of these 'first' images into subsequent series which intensify the cross-links between colour, texture, image and pattern — as seen in *Throw Away Your Dahlias*. The resultant works are richly layered with metaphor and visual interest whereby process is effectively captured in the surface complexities of warp and weft.

Quilting and Patchwork

Collecting, salvaging and recycling textile fragments and assembling and stitching these to create new objects, images, functions and meanings, has a powerful allure for many artists, and quilting and patchwork are popular activities for these reasons. Bricolage aside, they are also popular for other reasons, and like other defined genres of textile practice such as embroidery and tapestry, they carry their own set of connotations or cultural allusions.

Of the latter point we may consider the intensity of feeling or the store of memories that a family heirloom such as a quilt engenders or arouses. Quilts act to reaffirm bonds of affection between family members or friends — consider the 'friendship quilt'. This folk craft has deep roots in old traditions whereby rural European communities each maintained their own set of design, pattern and colour rules and their particular symbolisms. The folk processes associated with quilts cannot be denied, and today, the elite category of contemporary quiltmaking may access and interpret these rich associations extending tradition to produce innovative work.

Quilts are, of course, still made to cover and decorate the bed, but contemporary reappraisal of this activity has seen the quilt leave the confines of the bed to become repositioned and displayed on the wall as an art object. Quiltmakers essentially manipulate the textile medium, designing and articulating elements such as surface texture, image, pattern, colour and form to produce visually complex and lyrical compositions.

Repetition remains an important element in quilting where traditional techniques and patterns may be one basis for contemporary explorations. The traditional Log Cabin and other block approaches to assembling quilt patterns generally strived to achieve symmetry which conferred a strong visual impact. Today, the bringing together of fragments can be utilised consciously as a metaphor to convey or intensify various meanings or moods, and this process need not follow traditional paths but may take inventive and alternative directions. Landscape themes, for example, may be explored by balancing textural qualities with three-dimensional arrangements, emphasising the attachment of segments, or through appliqué, embroidery and other stitching techniques which may accentuate or represent various elements of the landscape such as the horizon.

Pictorial representation, abstract patterns, colourfield work, the range of compositions is unlimited and may freely borrow from specific fine art movements such as Op Art, Pop Art and

PLATE 118
Patricia Black (b. 1956)
Fauve, 1995
Body sculpture
commissioned by
Art Gallery of NSW
Silk organza, pleated
and discharged Shibori
technique
Photo: Ricardo Martin

PLATE 119
Keiko Amenomori Schmeisser (b. 1949)
Lightning (Diptych), 1995
Shibori, dye and paint on linen
180 x 76 cm
Photo: David Paterson

Expressionism. Contemporary quilt-makers may also incorporate patches of textile which have been independently worked with many of a number of techniques including painting, dying, and printing, as well as the use of multi-media.

Jan Irvine (b. 1950) is the family descendant and inheritor of the once humble stitch as represented by the work of her mother Grace Irvine (b. 1924), her grandmother Linda Averay (b. 1900), and her great-grandmother Ida Toop (1865–1942). These four generations cover some one hundred and twenty years of textile activity, beginning with the traditional tatting of Ida Toop in the late nineteenth century, through to the symbolic and vibrantly expressionistic works of contemporary textile and quilt artist Jan Irvine.

Irvine is renowned and celebrated as a textile artist very much on the cutting edge. Her extraordinary work shimmers and lifts the viewer into new heights of sensual pleasure and intellectual appreciation. Invariably pictorial, and always charged with symbolic meanings, her textiles are created through multi-varied techniques combining air-brushed and dyed silk, appliqué and feather handstitching. Influences include landscape, tradition and Aboriginal themes and political issues: *All Australian*, for example, is presented as a gigantic postcard which combines many nations' flags, a new Australian flag, a map of the Asian region, and an out of control bushfire, its billowing smoke and flames heading towards Canberra. Irvine has the skill to convey the drama of the image: the viewer feels the fear of the raging fire, and realises the vulnerability of the capital city so dwarfed by this natural menace which emerges from the undulating landscape. *Summer Storm, Electra,* and *Land and Meanings* are some of the other series that command attention through their luscious colour-impregnated and richly textured, stitched renditions of visual evocations of the Australian landscape, its events and its inhabitants.

As well as communicating her own personal, deep sense of appreciation and belonging to the landscape, Irvine's works also effectively interpret and express the Aboriginal people's Dreamtime spiritual unity of nature, land, sky and stars. In the work, *Out of Gondwana*, a pre-dawn illuminated distant mountain range looms over a desert plain dominated by a massive spiral mound, an Aboriginal symbol seemingly linking the earth with the heavens. Irvine's masterful airbrushing and stitching has created a powerful and expressive image which transfixes the viewer with awe and admiration.

Sarah Crowest (b. 1957) makes quilts as wall hangings which glow with a symbolist patina of colour and age. She developed her practice from a base of industrial textile design and the production of functional printed fabrics; currently, her pieced cloth work creates personal narratives, the fragments of cloth and the images they carry are at once concealing and revealing, evoking 'memories of passions, conceits, distractions, and the detritus of personal history.'

Crowest's quilts are contemporary in their conception, although strongly historical in their allusions: they are based on linen squares on which she dyes and handscreens with textured imagery and colour. Her work sometimes includes figurative imagery which relates to feminist issues or her own stories, but more often than not the designs are strongly geometric, the compositions of arranged squares and colours creating decorative schemes. Techniques which enhance her decorative patterns include a multi-printed approach which generates a layered effect, while her dominant colours tend to be ochres and warm tints. Bold handstitching adds further decorative detail, while her use of linen fabrics complements the textured surfaces.

Crowest also recycles fabrics she created some years ago, cutting and arranging these to produce further layers of interest or to generate particular symbolic or geometric patterns as in the accomplished work, *Edith*.

Creating Structures

Liz Williamson (b. 1949) handweaves wraps, scarfs, lengths of blankets, each piece being individually designed, woven on a floor loom and finished by hand. Her preferred yarn is a fine, pure Australian worsted wool, dyed to selected colours, but she sometimes includes wool lycra, copper wire, nylon mono-filament, and gold threads in her woven forms.

Her predominant concern is in the process of making and creating these forms as 'structures', and in this way, creating deceptively simple patterns which are luminescent with colour and extraordinary in their textures. This interest has resulted in unusual structures — intricate double plain weave cloth, scarfs with three, four or six selvedges, pieced blankets and layered wraps alongside flat surfaced, plain weave wraps and scarfs. Some of her larger exhibition work has referred to traditional West African strip weaving for its source of design construction, but the cultural traditions of a number of countries have also inspired her work. Other sources seem to be organic, and yet others have a painterly or abstract colourfield imagery suggestive of oil paintings.

Textured surfaces, seersucker effects, crinkled and crushed, all of these approaches accentuate the interest in surface design through the combining of fibres and particular finishes. Indeed, Williamson often exhibits her works in horizontal arrangements to enhance their three-dimensional qualities, often evoking the lie of land, its contours, folds, fields or hills. *Gold Textiles 2* is one such work which, when viewed from above, becomes imbued with a sense of landscape.

> My work revolves around the notion of 'coverings' — coverings for body and soul.
>
> My interest lies in functional objects created using traditional weaving techniques
>
> — objects made in a contemporary way — by the materials, by the finish, the feel,
>
> colouration and decoration.

Through their rich colours and complex textures, Williamson's textiles are exuberant and joyous in their celebration of the sensual qualities of fibre and its interwoven structures, giving much pleasure and satisfaction to the wearer.

Sylvia Parr (b. 1937) is similarly interested in structures and their relationship to pattern and colour. Her handwoven fabrics are mostly wearable and include jackets, scarfs, shawls, stoles and tablerunners, although she also makes wall hangings. She uses fine Tasmanian wool or silk to handweave her textile pieces which often have a dual purpose — they may be used as decorative wall hangings or worn as fashion garments. The fibres she uses are dyed in either rich glowing colours or soft, pastel tones.

Parr's study of computer-assisted weaving led her to master various software programs linked to industrial design processes; her abstract designs are therefore created with the use of a computer, the main focus being to produce a decorative effect by emphasising the structural basis and colour contrasts of the weave. Simplicity and function combine to produce compositions of colour and weave which are pleasing and direct in their communication of an aesthetic which is modernist-based.

PLATE 120
Cindy South Czabania (b. 1961)
Phillipe-Louis Mentroux: (heart-smith), 1995
Hand-carved wood, hand-coloured cloth,
dyed hemp threads, hemp threads, wire,
perspex, found objects
56 cm
Photo: Michal Kluvanek

Unlike the 'pure' approach whereby a single technique is honed and applied to create a genre of work, Elsje King (b. 1947) explores a wide range of textile traditions, using whatever processes or techniques are available to develop and produce the images she seeks: nevertheless, similarly to Liz Williamson, her main aim is to construct 'structures'. She considers this eclecticism as an Australian trait, pointing to our lack of traditions as an advantage in freely sourcing those of other nations.

Much of King's current work is utilising piecing and an 'all-over' stitching approach similar to quilting. However, she does not consider herself a quilter or embroiderer. On the other hand, she considers that her use of various techniques to construct textiles allies her work with tapestry. Indeed, King's work accentuates the interleaved structures found at the core of most textiles, her interest being the exploration of the creative processes which create these structures. Her works often combine Oriental and Western fibre and textile cultural traditions including Batik, indigo dying, block printing, hand-stitching and quilting; vegetable dyes and decayed or recycled fabrics are also incorporated in some works.

The resultant works meld contemporary and traditional processes to create rich abstract patterns or bold colourfield images. King's textiles are not only characteristic because of the particular combinations of technique she selects and melds, but also in the manner in which she organises these into harmonious compositions which are always revealing of their structural and traditional sources. In the work *Transformation*, vegetable-dyed silk and cotton fabrics are combined with recycled and decayed fabrics and handstitched and felted to produce a layered image of gentle tones, with crisp, jagged and disintegrating edges: is the transformation creating a defined image, or is the image wearing away?

Christopher and Jennifer Robertson (b. 1957 and 1962 respectively) are particularly keen to develop professional practices which are 'intelligent and sustainable'. Their collaborative work could easily have been located in the chapter on metal as it results in furniture, although it is presented here as the main visual component is the outcome of Jennifer's weaving processes, and less so of Christopher's metalwork. Their partnership exemplifies the trend towards multi-skilling and collaboration: Christopher is trained and experienced in metalwork, woodwork and design, while Jennifer focuses on woven textiles and art.

Their furniture forms fuse a free-form, though disciplined, organic approach to produce curvaceous lounges and chairs (such as *Succulentus Oos*) which are subtle yet lively in their profile and textural look, inviting interaction with the human form.

> Our interests involve the wider dimensions of craft whilst maintaining a very strong commitment to skills and technique. Working independently and collaboratively we carefully research and propose practical and inventive works through semiotic, metaphoric and cultural analysis, exploring the potential 'depth' of their relationship.

PLATE 121 (opposite)
Greg Leong (b. 1946)
Twin Carp Codpiece, 1995
Codpiece: condom, fishing hooks, sequins, beads, rhinestones, metal coils, metallic thread on screen-printed silk satin and hand-dyed silk; Tray: screen-printed acetate satin, polyester crepe, mirror, card
40.5 x 40.5 x 12 cm
Photo: Ian Hobbs

PLATE 122
Agnieszka Golda (b. 1969)
To Wish for a Peasant, 1995
Body of soft sculpture: stitched calico
filled with loose wadding;
Costume: stitched and screen-printed
hessian and cotton lace;
Face: hand-painted,
collaged and laminated fabric
130 x 52 x 40 cm
Photo: Martin Johnson

Alternative Practices

Tori de Mestre (b. 1951) is a textile artist whose principal work consists of creative collages which combine a wide variety of materials and which explore personal interests and concerns such as landscape, the idea of contradictions, and the fragility of nature.

Her innovative work melds fabrics, natural and artificial fibres and objects as diverse as echidna quills, paperbark from native melaleucas, wire, and indeed, whatever is necessary to produce the image or effect she seeks. Her ordering of these diverse materials is disciplined and thoughtful: each work projects a distinctive character according to its make up and artistic intent. The themes of fragmentation, manipulation, layering and stitching are employed as symbolic gestures to communicate 'expressions of time, invasion, erosion and healing.' She acknowledges the structural and decorative signs of the stitch and its implications of the feminine.

De Mestre's current work focuses on land, settlers and the impact of introduced plants and animals; these subjects are also investigated as a means to express her interest in contradictions: fragility and strength, delicacy and harshness, constancy and change. De Mestre has always been interested in the collection and ordering of natural materials such as sticks, leaves and feathers: *Taming the Land*, consists of a large blacked board as a backing which is covered by eucalyptus sticks attached by thread; a central small photo-image panel depicts a bearded settler axing a massive tree, the text below is a four-lined ditty from Cohen's 'Ned Kelly: Man of Iron' — 'To clear the land as needs we must Oh! Oh! Oh!' The collage evokes the wilderness cleared into a wasteland, while the representative hero myth, Ned Kelly, is satirised and subverted as a metaphor for the nineteenth-century attitude of man's supposed superiority of nature.

Figurative elements are generally rare in de Mestre's work; they are mostly abstracted collages which layer materials to create patterns of repeat motifs or combine collage and oil-painted works which speak of personal feelings and concern for the Australian environment, simultaneously conveying a quality of the feminine.

Patricia Black's (b. 1956) studio practice has focused on developing her own variations of an ancient and traditional Japanese set of resist-dyeing processes whose collective name is 'Shibori'. Today, Shibori provides practitioners with the challenge of blending traditional processes with contemporary approaches and ideas. Black, one of Australia's leading practitioners in this specialty, is particularly captivated by the three-dimensional possibilities it creates with fabrics. She uses Shibori to produce works as sculptures that are free-standing or wrapped around the body. For Black, her practice is a way of 'realising the value of any hands-on manipulation, as it communicates to the maker the nature of physical reality.'

Black's most frequently used fabric is silk organza which is particularly resonant to the subtleties of the Shibori technique. The latter involves the binding, dying and steam-pressing of cloth to produce textures and patterns; it includes four main approaches to the process, each producing its own characteristic pattern such as the *Kumo* or 'spider web', and *Arashi* or 'storm'.

PLATE 123
Tony Dyer (b. 1942)
Federal Fools, 1994
Wool, dye, wood, paint
120 x 100 x 10 cm
Photo: Werner Hammerstingl

Not surprisingly, given physical and chemical vagaries, the outcome is unpredictable, although the practitioner accepts this as part of the process. Indeed, there is a parallel here with the Japanese ceramic raku technique which relies on serendipity for unexpected effects to enhance the practitioner's intent (see Chapter Two).

Colour is not the only effect created by this process which also shapes the flat cloth into folds which are retained by the chemical changes. Shibori represents, as Yoshiko Wada commented at the 'New Tools, No Limits Conference' in Portland, Oregon, USA, in 1995: the 'effect of tension and energy on fabric resulting in imprint or memory [and] offering a poetic narrative of cloth'.

Black's works are dramatic, almost theatrical, in their sculptural conception; she generally favours brilliant colours combined with folds and swirls, the luscious cloths or costumes intimately wrapping and interacting with their respective human figures. *Fauve*, is one of a series of 'body sculptures' commissioned by the Art Gallery of New South Wales as an extension of the Fauves

PLATE 124
Brett Alexander (b. 1963)
Souvenir (Installation), 1994
Handmade cotton fishing net,
wooden shoe last, nylon filament;
Combined process/mixed media
techniques
150 x 120 x 120 cm

painting exhibition (1995–96). In this work, Black appropriated the bold juxtapositioning of brilliant colours as seen in the work of painters such as Derain, Cezanne and Gauguin, and recreated their vibrancy and explosive energy in pleated and otherwise textured silk organza costumes worn by dancers.

Keiko Amenomori Schmeisser (b. 1949) creates printed and painted fabrics which reveal a process of fusion between her Japanese homeland heritage and her observations and visions of the Australian landscape. She also has a strong background in European textile design which has modified her inherent Japanese perspective in conjunction with the additional influence of her present-day Australian homeland.

PLATE 125
Adele Outteridge (b. 1946)
Heart Books, 1994
Left: Monoprints, shellac, thread;
Right: Paper, Indian ink, thread;
Double needle binding
9 x 5 cm
Photo: Rick Harper

> Much of my work originates from sketches of natural landscape elements and also from the observation of natural forces such as storm, fire and the powerful calmness of the Australian landscape. These visual memories are developed into abstract forms and compositions.

Schmeisser absorbs then expresses the various colour combinations, textures and forms of Australia's natural environment. In recent works the tie-dye technique (Shibori) further enhances the textural qualities of the work which has its basis in both Japanese tradition and international contemporary design. Schmeisser translates her observations of nature's textural elements into the medium of textile design; specifically, she interprets selected qualities which appeal to her refined eye, condensing these into subtle colours and patterns, usually on drops of various fabrics (often diptyches) including cotton, linen, voile or chintz.

The textures of bark, smooth rounded pebbles, the eroded surfaces of granite rocks, the marks left by foraging beach fauna or the layered effects of fallen leaves, these and other natural outcomes of the interaction of time, nature and the physical environment, form the basis for her work. From this richness of observations, and through a process of multiplication of particular motifs or calligraphic 'signs', Schmeisser produces screen-printed, graphic patterns which express a characteristic and personal aesthetic. On the other hand other works, such as *Lightning*, have a restrained visual imagery made up of combined motifs which represent elements of the landscape and which utilise additional techniques to Shibori such as dying and painting on textile drops.

Cindy South Czabania (b. 1961) combines her skills as a textile artist and woodcarver to make puppets which express her fascination for archaeology, the medieval era and a personal mythology. The art of the puppetmaker is an intriguing one as it attempts to extend the visual representation of the human figure into a simulation of movement and character. Czabania's puppets are extraordinary on two accounts: the detailing of their carved heads and their costumes.

Czabania is especially skilled at fabric manipulation and costume-making, and it is in the finished, dressed puppets where her attention to detail brings them to life. Over a number of years of experimentation, she has become especially skilled in the unique Japanese Shibori technique of colouring and adding texture to cloth, particularly silk; Czabania follows up this application with 'aging' techniques to create a roughened, worn look. These Shibori textiles are combined with other torn, faded and aged textile pieces to be cut and finely stitched into miniature costumes complete with hats, chains, purses and other details.

Utilising her wood-carving skills, Czabania creates heads, hands, legs and feet which are not only articulated, but also have expressive sculptural qualities which enhance the gestural and facial features of the finished, large-scale puppets. Each has his or her own personality and vocation: there is the *Shaman* striding with the help of his crooked staff, his fantastic robe woven through with talismans of foxes' teeth and Tibetan bells, his leathery long-lobed ears sporting beaded earrings. *Liam and Aurora* are a partnership of street musicians, playing tambourine and flute. *Phillipe Louis Metreaux, The Broken Heart Repairer*, peers through spectacles as he holds and mends a wooden cracked heart with thread and needle — his robe embroidered with homilies of love. Then there is the eccentric *Dr Reinhard Von Stinberg: The Time Traveller*, standing somewhat apprehensively beside his time machine, a padded chair embellished with intricate wiring and electronic devices. *Portrait in Black*, another puppet, appears as an aristocratic woman dressed in black antique velvet who holds and gazes at a miniature naked puppet — this may well be a self-portrait of the artist.

> Most of my inspiration comes from the child inside, itself fashioned by my love of archaeological digs, shipwrecks and found objects. I seldom draw up designs before beginning my pieces, preferring to work spontaneously with my materials in much the same way as I paint. The carving is done first, then the materials added to create puppets of character and integrity, and as latent expressions of the personality of the inner child.

There are a number of craft practitioners and artists in Australia who use their craftwork as a means of investigating and exposing to a wider audience aspects of gay and lesbian subculture, including their interpretations of HIV/AIDS, the closet, sexual identity, recognition, tolerance and other homosexual subculture issues, codes and the various, familiar homosexual icons or signifiers. Greg Leong (b. 1946) is a textile artist whose work explores personal and social concerns related to gay life, simultaneously challenging conventional notions of textile design. A self-professed gay and middle-aged Asian, Leong is acutely aware of the inherent racism and homophobia to be found in some segments of Australian culture. This is the content of his textile work which is usually presented as a sculptural or art object that entices the viewer through its luscious combinations of innovative and richly worked surfaces.

PLATE 126 (opposite)
Penny Carey Wells (b. 1950)
New Cross for NLC, 1995
Boxed work: sandcasting, handmade paper, dyes, shellac, photocopies, gesso
60 x 50 x 10 cm
Photo: John Farrow

PLATE 127
Inga Hunter (b. 1938)
Searcher's Robe: Iboriis, 1996
Handmade paper, wood, fabric,
bones, paint, pastel and thread
36 x 36 x 4 cm

I believe in craft's subversive marriage to art. I sometimes make 'pure' craft —
such as the decorative silk scarf — but my more serious work, always
painstakingly crafted, takes on the political agenda of a gay Asian living in a
homophobic and racist environment. While I celebrate the seductive beauty of
cloth, culture-specific costume becomes a metaphor for the disguise and display of
the entrapped physical/spiritual body.

Leong's textile work accesses the intimate relationship between craft and daily life, exploiting its
practical and symbolic qualities as a means of expressing his particular political, cultural and
personal ideas and concerns. His *Twin Carp Codpiece* is a major, autobiographical work which
exemplifies his aesthetic and conceptual approach. It is presented as two carp which represent
codpieces, but which also represent himself and a deceased partner. These textile fish are
intricately embroidered and beaded multi-media forms which combine sequins, beads, screen-
dyed and hand-printed silk, a torn condom, rhinestones, metallic thread on screen-printed silk

satin and hand-dyed silk. The sparkling, bejewelled fish are laid out on a dark triangle of cloth and set within a mirror-lined, clear plastic box. Leong has identified the latter as a 'glory box', one which remains unopened as a symbol of his unattached or 'unmarried' status.

There are other signifiers in this work: the carp are an Oriental symbol for, among a number of things, perseverance, while twin carp signify lovers; the fishing hooks act as scales, presenting a rather vulnerable and painful image, as does the torn condom. These also suggest gay, fetishistic elements, and act as metaphors for Leong's own sexual identity and self-image. The base, made up by a dark triangle of cloth, acts as both a reminder of the original homosexual sign, as well as the Chinese bridal gown, yet another reference to his ethnic origins.

There are a multiplicity of signs and symbols which are used to construct and delineate gay and lesbian life as a valid minority culture within the desired diversity of mainstream Australian society. Leong's work appropriates and recontextualises these within the medium of the textile. His work has a full-in-the-face flamboyance coupled with a powerful subversiveness whose ironical images are layered with meaning, narrative and feeling. As such, they can confront those who are not prepared to accept the diversity of lifestyles which make up our post-modern, multicultural society.

Agnieszka Golda (b. 1969) is a textile artist whose versatile multi-skilling abilities permit her to move freely from furniture-making to textiles, painting and sculptural works. She often combines the latter three to create life-sized, saint-like figures which are masked and garbed in a variety of costumes. These draw from and represent various aspects of her European upbringing, and specifically from Polish folklore. Superstitions that came from her homeland were the principal means of inspiration of her female figures and portraits.

These mixed media collage works are portraits derived from the female figure, their painted, beaded and cloth faces are combined with textural, patterned textile panels to reveal aspects of her childhood. *To Wish for Comfort* is a figure whose metaphoric representation of this desire is symbolised by the richness of the embroidered velvets, lace and beaded mask. Whereas, *To Wish for the Messenger*, is a similarly life-sized figure which symbolises the Christmas folklore tradition which involved the ritual of children being dressed as angels, as in Poland, angels are referred to as messengers. Golda's angel is dressed in quilted cotton, stitched and collaged with fur trimming, and has wings of duck feathers, and a mask of clay: its imagery cogently revives the memory of the artist's childhood.

Another work, *To Wish for a Peasant*, is dressed in screen-printed hessian, patterned with images of women's faces, the mask of cloth painted red with intense staring blue eyes. Golda uses textiles in an imaginative and creative structuring, employing the materials to emphasise or signal aspects of the figure's intended portrayal, in the latter case, peasant or folk qualities. Ultimately, despite these representations of Polish folklore, contemporary imagery underscores the artist's autobiographical intentions for these masked female figures.

At once folksy, primitive, and painterly, Golda's works embody an invigorating fusion of

European culture with Australian make-do traditions and contemporary fine art approaches: above all, the process is driven by her inventive and personal vision.

Tony Dyer's (b. 1942) sculptural or decorative work has its foundations in the traditional techniques of batik and handmade felt, which he exploits for a quality of directness of expression as evident in their inherent nature and character.

> These materials act as vehicles and inspiration to support my visual images and forms. My textiles and text, generated for several recent curated exhibitions, have forged a more lively dialogue about the strong and positive links, on a variety of levels, between theory and practice.

Dyer's recent work explores forms which integrate surface and image, acting, in turn, as metaphors for personal reactions and reflections about change within himself and his immediate environment. His technique employs multi-layered felt and dyed silk forms which 'reveal images and personal statements of self and surroundings'. Batik and felt are quite different mediums, and Dyer's work reflects this contrast: when batik is the technique, the works are colourful and lively, as well as figurative and patterned representations; when felt is the principal means of expression, they are generally dark and textural, suffused with sombre, symbolic meanings. Both approaches retain a strong narrative sensibility.

Federal Fools, a mixed-media work which combines felt and painted wood, lines up a series of political caricatures, the heads emerging from black felt stockings: the puppet imagery effectively lampoons the political subject. The conjunction of materials is artful, the heads gold-painted in the style of his batik figurative work, while the felt's fuzzy edges accentuates the humorous aspects of the work.

Brett Alexander (b. 1963) is a fibre artist whose work explores complex concepts through installations or sculptural forms at the boundaries of textile art.

> My work contains dual elements of juxtaposition/antithesis between male/female metaphors specifically in relating to fibre/textiles tradition and technique. I am targeting the boundaries and perimeters of craft and how gender experience manifests itself relative to this. I install constructed, manipulated and readymade objects, acknowledging, yet challenging the nature of process in craftwork and its value in a western context, disputing sedate definitions of fibre and textile activity.

Alexander's work is an example of how far textile and fibre art can be pushed to its expressive limits, so much so that, in the recent past, he has used laser beams as threads to weave patterns on gallery walls. Less ethereal and grounded in the actual medium recognised as fibre, a recent installation titled *Souvenir*, consisted in part of a handmade cotton fishing net hanging from its four corners attached to the ceiling, its centre weighed down with a cobbler's wooden shoe-last (the other component consisted of displays of groups of cotton and polyester shirtsleeves). The gallery lighting picked out the detailed woven structure of the net, especially the regularity of its fine patterning which was also repeated as shadows on the floor. The sculptural folds and textures of the net suggested the ephemeral qualities of the net, and by association, of the tenuous nature of existence.

Souvenir is a typical work by Alexander in that it challenges our ideas of the nature of fibre and textile craftwork. In this instance, his focus was on the notion of the grid and multiples, and of structure and repetition as the heart of fibre and textile work. Idea, in this approach has been privileged over skill, but the references are there, and it is in pondering these that a return to the essences of the traditional core of craft becomes, perhaps, more cogent.

Paper

Contemporary handmade paper and baskets have been catapulted from their functional origins to become mediums in their own right; today, the paper or basket form may retain, avoid or minimise its functional aspects to be presented solely as a decorative or sculptural 'art object'.

The tactile pleasure of paper, its historical continuity, and its intimate relationship to writing, books and literature, presents a rich field of investigation for the paper and book-making practitioner. As well, industrialisation and the mechanical manufacture of paper and books, as well as the expansion of the use of the computer in everyday life, has enhanced the unique qualities of the handmade paper artefact.

A particular development in this area has been the use of handmade paper in combination with other skills to produce the 'artist's book', a sculptural or decoratively conceived artefact. Adele Outteridge (b. 1946) is one of a number of fibre artists who conceives and constructs books as sculptural forms, while still retaining and honouring their conventional function as a collection of pages which can be 'sequentially turned'. Outteridge considers that successful books are those 'which bring together the container (the pages) with contents (text and imagery), into a unified whole.'

A perennial theme in her work is the physical fibre form that paper entails, as a metaphor for the 'spiritual threads that tie, support and dictate so many of our actions and thoughts'. Outteridge also explores the sculptural potential of handmade paper and its articulation into the book, as a means of expressing landscape form: when opened, her *Mountain Books* feature elongated three-dimensional tableaus evoking the blue haze of distant mountain ranges. Other paper and book creations include fan-shaped paper sculptures and callographs which combine a number of skills including cover design, book-binding, and paper-making. One work entitled *Heart Books*, presents two heart-shaped books which combine these and other elements including monoprints, shellac, thread, handmade paper, Indian ink and double needle binding. Their contrasting visual and textural qualities entice a tactile, interactive response, their potent imagery accentuating this sensual resonance.

The work of Penny Carey Wells (b. 1950) is also concerned with the concept of the 'book as

PLATE 128
Marlene Thiele (b. 1936)
Pier Dreaming, 1993
Palm bark, bark fibre,
New Zealand Flax, *Cordyline Australia*,
leaves, beads and apple seeds
48 x 30 x 40 cm
Photo: Grant Hancock

PLATE 129 (opposite)
Virginia Kaiser (b. 1945)
Through The Core, 1991
Pine needles stitched in open spiral,
coiling technique with linen
30 cm
Photo: Grant Hancock

sculptural object'. Her use of paper and paper pulp is considerably imaginative and diverse, and ranges from paper as flat sheets either bound or unbound, textured, coloured, containing forms, images and perhaps text. Paper pulp is similarly used as a sculptural material which Wells views as 'endlessly malleable, non-toxic, lightweight, warm and forgiving'.

Books have always held a considerable allure for Wells who recollects childhood memories of the 'texture and suppleness of rag books, the bright, bold picture books, and being allowed to gently turn the pages of a huge, mystical encyclopaedia and marvelling at the tiny detailed drawings…' She also recalls the 'lingering sadness' following the completion of a good story, and of the 'reluctance to leave the characters who have entered our lives…' It is precisely this sense of wonder, delight and mystery that Wells succeeds in recalling and presenting for us in her contemporary paper and book works.

Wells is concerned with the recreation of a gestalt of this experience of the book, and has become a master at constructing artist books which generate a sensuous and intellectual aura, that is, the physical presence of the book, its feel and the accompanying psychological effects on the reader. The smell of ink, the touch of paper, its weight, the mechanical sensation of turning pages, the visual elements, the intellectual content, and the unique quality of the one-off or limited edition work — are all details of concern.

Wells links the contemporary artist's book with the illuminated manuscript of the Renaissance: 'The making of the book as with the making of paper, the weaving of a rug or dying of yarn can restore to the artist the human qualities of their activity.' In this way, 'the power and mystery traditionally associated with books is retained and enlarged'.

The thematic concerns for her work are also diverse, being derived from political, social, environmental and personal sources. The forms her work assume include the expanding file whereby in one specific work she examines wage relations, industrial safety and equal pay for women; installation work such as *22 Cases for Hobart* which refers to a number of unresolved cases of sexual harassment in Tasmania; artist's books such as *Not Flowing, Draining* which underscores the deplorable state of rivers in Tasmania; and finally, her boxed works, a format which presents a tableau made up of dyed and cast handmade papers: *New Cross for NLC*, an example which deals with the issue of lost soldiers and unmarked graves, is a strongly textural and visual work which cogently explores this subject.

Wells considers that it is 'essential to have a close and respectful relationship with one's chosen material and working methods'. In this manner she creates works which 'extend the power of the artist to communicate ideas, inviting the 'reader' to linger through both the written language and the language of imagery'.

Inga Hunter (b. 1938) is an Afro-Australian whose practice covers a wide area, from drawing to painting, embroidery and sculpture, although paper and fibre generally are favourite, and sometimes predominant, elements in her mixed-media works.

PLATE 130
Marion Gaemers (b. 1958)
Casement I, 1993
Coiled basketry: coconut fibre,
palm flowering stems,
sticks and string
120 cm
Photo: Marion Gaemers

My sculptural work is based on my African-Jamaican background and the fact

that I am descended both from African slaves and those who enslaved millions,

over a period of three centuries. I am alien in all of the cultures of my heritage,

a fact which has profoundly affected my life, and now, at last — my work.

This background, in combination with a study of anthropology, suffuses Hunter's vigorous works with an exotic blend of African and European elements. Her works are often difficult to categorise as either craft or art, although the extensive use of fibre and handmade paper can strongly link her sculptural pieces to the former. *Searcher's Robe: Iboriis*, is one such sculptural piece based on handmade paper, yet combines the fibre with other media including paint, wood, pastel and thread to produce a multilayered work of rich textures. It contains references to African material culture and the notion of 'making do' with what is at hand — hence the folksy and ritualistic imagery. 'I am like many of the other artists of the African Diaspora and work with everything'.

Basketry

Last but not least, let us celebrate basket-making, a craft which parallels human evolution and represents the earliest use of fibre, and indeed, the oldest craft. The rich tactile and visual qualities of this medium, its repetitive processes, its mesmeric and therapeutic effects on the maker, its blatant functionalism, not to mention the close links to nature through the direct use of plant fibres, are among the reasons fibre basketry and related fibre work continue to attract a considerable numbers of adherents.

Much of what is called the 'new basketry' aims for the expression and exploration of the nature of fibre-weaving processes with the physical and cultural qualities of the medium to express the functional, aesthetic and/or sculptural potential of this craft. The finished article may therefore be viewed for its aesthetic and conceptual qualities whilst still highlighting links with the traditional utilitarian basis and age-old historical associations of this activity.

As well as these historical origins, the practical and ceremonial functions of baskets and other woven forms in the everyday life of numerous world-wide cultures, deepens the well-spring of metaphorical or symbolic allusions that may be accessed by the imaginative fibre weaver. They may address numerous themes or issues, particularly of an ethnological nature, but applicable to the contemporary area: migration, the social relations of production, the cultural transmission of skills, regionalism, the relationship between design and status within community, and folk expression.

Another important characteristic of fibre work is the derivation of materials from the natural environment: practitioners may gather plant or animal fibres. These materials may be the stems or leaves or other parts of plants which have been naturally discarded or harvested and treated, if necessary, for use. Recycling fibres from discarded artefacts sometimes also occurs, linking the resultant object with environmental issues.

Contemporary fibre work is also producing baskets and other articles, sculptural or functional, often imbued with an Australia flavour, or at least a 'sense of place'.

The fibre material culture traditions of the Australian Aboriginal and New Zealand Maori peoples, are among the many sources Marlene Thiele (b. 1936) has investigated in her fibre basketry practice.

A new dimension was added to my life since discovering natural basketry in 1985.

To capture that moment of experience and discovery by weaving a material into a basket, creates an almost spiritual sense of time and place. None of the previous mediums that I worked in has appealed so strongly to the senses, and yet has been so sympathetic to pushing the boundaries of creation and form.

Thiele's materials are gathered from the urban and rural landscapes: from gardens of the former she collects the familiar long, strap-like leaves of *Cordyline Australis* and New Zealand flax, philadendron sheaths and ivy stems; from the beach she finds seaweeds; and from the bush, the paperbark of melaleucas. These materials and others are treated then woven into a variety of forms, almost always these retain their basket origins but are sculptural, organic explorations of space, surface and volume. As such they closely relate to similar explorative concerns which ceramists, and some glass and wood practitioners, seek in their work. *Pier Dreaming* is a particularly characteristic work by Thiele, and is based on the vessel form, two palm bark pieces forming a strongly bilateral shape which seemingly thrusts upwards with its own vigorous energy. Coiled and applied surface fibres add a textural and decorative surface element which seemingly accentuate the organic aspects of the form.

Virginia Kaiser (b. 1945) similarly focuses her work on vessel forms and the use of natural fibres, the distinguishing characteristics of her work being the extraordinary degree of finesse and craftsmanship she brings to the work. Using traditional basketry techniques and simple geometric forms, her work explores an aesthetic which centres about the finely wrought surface textures and the subtle colour contrasts created by the differing plant materials she employs. Especially notable in her work is the precision of woven fibre which creates a decorative pattern through repetition. Because Kaiser's refined basket forms overtly display the traditional techniques and processes through which they were created, the textures they generate enhance the interaction of action and medium, that is the very fibres and the manner in which they are interwoven and transformed.

I am inspired by the plants that create the Australian landscape, and continually experiment and explore natural plant materials, forms and traditional techniques. Through this means I express concerns for environmental issues, and hopefully, raise awareness of the need to protect our surroundings.

Through The Core, is one work which demonstrates her meticulous technique and mastery of the skills of basket-weaving, the seeming perfection of the rhythmical and symmetrical vessel transforming natural fibre to functional and contemplative form.

PLATE 132
Charlotte Drake-Brockman (b. 1933)
Painted Basket, 1996
Traditional willow frame,
painted cardboard
50 x 20 cm
Photo: Alister Jones

Marion Gaemers (b. 1958) gathers discarded, natural plant fibres and recycles these through traditional basketry techniques to create woven forms which extend beyond the functional into the sculptural. The tropical setting of northern Queensland provides an abundance of natural plant materials which are constantly shed by the rainforest trees, while the shoreline is littered with driftwood and stranded seaweed, flowering palm stems, palm and coconut fibre, and grass: these are transformed through the technique of coiled basketry into large vessels or forms which resemble or allude to the human figure.

> My sculptural baskets are modelled on things I see in nature, whereas the use of ancient female forms maintains the tradition started by women thousands of years ago. My work will not last forever: it has a built-in obsolescence. Once the work deteriorates, it will return to the garden.

With their exaggerated, pendulous breasts made from woven coconut fibre and trunks represented by flowering palm stems, Gaemers's large, free-standing, female figurative forms (*Casement* series) evoke the fecund imagery of the earth goddess. Other works she refers to as 'Venus' figures are more closely modelled after the human female form, their smooth-coiled, coconut fibre bodies usually shown hung from trees, or lie on the ground, split open as if the form has given birth. Given their origins in such a quintessential female craft as basketry, these works evoke metaphors of the feminine and the construction of a timeless sense of identity.

By photographing her work in the context of the landscape, open settings on beaches or in rainforests, Gaemers also underscores the origins of these forms, places of their inevitable return through decay and their rebirth, as their nutrients are released to sustain new plant growth. In this manner she also emphasises the links between nature and our necessary physical interaction with it. Basketry, fertility, rebirth and sense of place, may seem unlikely conjunctions, but these concepts are clearly implicit in the forms and metaphors of her work, in the materials and techniques she uses, and in the locations her installations or one-off works are presented — and sacrificed.

Nalda Searles (b. 1945) is a fibre artist whose work centres about the making of baskets which retain an intimate link to their natural bush and landscape origins. Closely woven with grasses, feathers, banksia leaves and other materials, these baskets seem inseparable from their cultural and physical environment: her *Bush Baskets*, for example, made of spinnifex grass, paper fragments, and linen threads, are reminiscent of the meticulously woven nests of certain birds.

With the addition of galah feathers to this combination, Searles coils a lidded basket, emu feathers and some dyed wool results in *Emu Basket*. It is this blend of mostly indigenous bush materials gathered from dry regions of Western Australia, which give Searles's baskets their organic, natural appearance. Lately, she has also begun to move into more sculptural forms using materials such as xanthorrhoea grass tree scales, silk dyed with mallee leaves and even mallee flower buds netted with linen threads.

But it is her gently conceived, nest-like woven bowls and lidded baskets with their intricate textures and soft tones, which evoke a sense of the bush in its natural and unassuming appearances.

Unlike the former, Charlotte Drake-Brockman (b. 1933) produces fibre work which is more sculptural or painterly in expression, and more closely allied to the urban rather than bush environment. Drake-Brockman, together with Virginia Kaiser, founded the Sydney Basket Weavers to promote the craft following their exposure to the techniques and innovative work of visiting fibre artist American Douglas Fuchs in 1981. Drake-Brockman's work is also influenced by a background in surface design, Batik, painting and drawing.

Drake-Brockman's baskets reflect these eclectic sources through their painterly surfaces and the fusion of artificial with natural materials. Her baskets mix traditional cane weaving with painted cardboard, plastic tape and even recycled plastic bag strips. The result is basketry which departs considerably from the former: it retains its functional form, yet eschews the idea of naturalness. On the other hand, the use of recycled plastic and cardboard establish these baskets as metaphors for environmental issues.

CHAPTER SIX:
WOOD – THE TACTILE REALM

Wood and humanity have a special relationship which derives from the organic origins of wood, the lore of the tree and the forest, and from the history of its use. This epoch of intimate association has resulted in an extensive material culture heritage which intimately records and mirrors our life on earth. It is this background which continues to infuse present-day woodcraft practices with a singular vitality.

The longest living of all of this planet's higher life-forms — deriving its energy from the sun, cloaking the earth in a green protective mantle — the tree manufactures its own living structure: wood. Wood transports water and other materials about the tree, it records its life events, the seasonal changes and long-term climatic developments — and it supplies us with a remarkable material whose range of qualities and versatile capabilities seduce and draw the crafts practitioner into a creative union.

Wood's multifarious uses underpin and infuse many of the concepts and approaches to woodcraft today, so it is useful to reiterate these. Wood was once the only material used to build vessels, for plying rivers, lakes and oceans, for voyages of discovery and the transport of other materials; it continues to be a prime material used to construct homes and other buildings; to make furniture; to carve architectural decoration; it was once the prime material for wheels and transport vehicles; for tools; bridges and railways; forms and patterns; musical instruments; sculpture; treen; toys; and, of course, to make paper.

Beyond these numerous historical, traditional and ongoing uses, another factor which influences the output of contemporary woodcraft is the mysterious power, lore, legend and beliefs associated with wood. Spirituality and wood are inextricably linked: just consider the many objects fashioned from wood which were once used in ceremonies or rituals to control or communicate with the mystical forces of the world: masks, cult vessels, wooden grave effigies, ancestor figures, spirit boats, house posts, and totemic poles. These are objects fashioned from wood and which symbolise, contain, focus or somehow influence spiritual forces. Little wonder certain enduring superstitions such as 'touch wood' are evoked when protection from the fates is sought.

To these beliefs we may add the mythology which has grown about the tree: as the tree of life symbolising human life; the tree of knowledge; and the tree as a symbol of the cosmos.

So wood is set apart from the other craft media through this background and unique

PLATE 133 (opposite)
Geoffrey Hannah (b.1948)
Australiana Collectors' Cabinet, 1993
Marquetry and inlay, forty-seven Australian and exotic timbers, gilding and petrified wood and emu-egg inlay
218 x 171.5 x 58 cm

PLATE 134
George Ingham (b. 1940)
Boxes, 1995
Macadamia,
Medium Density Fibreboard,
leather, glass
15 x 15 cm

relationship to humanity. Add to its symbolic and mythological aura the practical, craft qualities of wood: versatility, durability, texture, colour, grain, and figure, and even, scent. The totality of these features — history, familiarity, tradition, mythology, and physical features — gives each wood its unique character.

In addition, the actual manipulation or working of wood further sets it apart from the majority of the other craft media. Unlike clay, glass and metal which require the application of heat to effect substantial changes, the wood practitioner works directly with the timber, and is concerned with design and construction details, as well as surface finish considerations. The lustre of freshly planed wood, the paper-thin curls of shavings, the release of delicate, distinctive scent, its colour, grain, and tactility (and sometimes its rarity) — these add to the pleasure and seductiveness of the medium. Indeed, that vexing question of the 'seduction' of the material, which we saw was especially applicable to glass, and which similarly applies to this medium, is generally not an issue.

Wood is also a prime material in the making of domestic furnishings, objects of considerable intimacy about which we negotiate personal space, providing the setting for the basic body, cultural and social activities of our daily lives. Wood practitioners may therefore access this relationship, making artefacts which challenge these traditional and symbolic functions.

The diversity of approaches and applications of wood provides contemporary professional practitioners with a number of specialist niches: furniture making, turning, carving, and alternative

PLATE 135
Leon Sadubin (b. 1948)
Church Furniture (altar, lectern,
side-table, president's chair),
Cabrini Hospital Chapel, Melbourne,
1994
Coopered curve construction,
silver ash, stainless steel
Altar: 99 x 180 x 70 cm
Photo: Robert Colvin
[Note: David Wright glass window,
and Helge Larsen and Darani Lewers
metalwork]

activities including sculptural work. Furniture making itself comprises a number of distinctive approaches as elaborated later in this text. The four basic approaches to woodcraft are not only united by common influences and links, as well as a long continuity attached to this particular medium, but through the contemporary practitioner's urge to find his or her own particular way of working with their chosen medium, exploring its inherent mythological power, and its alluring physical qualities in the universal quest for meaning and expression.

In terms of its more recent applications, craftsmanship in wood has never faltered, so that the 1960s crafts revival appears more pronounced in the other media than wood for this reason. Today, professional cutting-edge woodcraft flows with and against the grain of creative diversity. Practitioners may selectively choose particular qualities they wish to express in wood, using these to develop their own vocabulary to convey ideas or emotive states, to make functional and/or decorative articles, to evoke the depth of cultural memory or reinterpret the traditional ritualistic uses wood embodies.

These may take the approach of fine craftsmanship where the smoothly planed wood surface invites the caress of the hand, or where one may cast the eye and marvel at the precision of perfectly fitting dovetail joins. Or else the practitioner may take the approach which favours rough

finishes and assemblies which bring out the primitive qualities of the medium and its associated technical processes. Or the practitioner may take items of wood which once had a life as crates or other pieces of furniture, or salvage driftwood, or even recycle railway sleepers, reassembling these into new forms with new meanings and values. Yet other practitioners may take the once living material and imbue it with another, metaphorical life by carving figurative or other metaphorical representations in wood. Such pieces cannot fail to resonate with the organic basis of the medium, its past and its present life in relation to maker and viewer.

The approaches are as numerous as the practitioners themselves. Of course, post-modernism encourages this diversity as well as the use of a mixture of materials with wood: paint, metal, plastics — whatever is at hand, and whatever is needed to convey a particular visual look or meaning; each category of contemporary woodcraft has its own set of guidelines or conventions. Post-modernism also encourages the expression of the vernacular, imbuing woodcraft with a sense of local identity and place. This may be imbued by the practitioner through the use of local, endemic timbers and other historical or cultural motifs or elements that are specific to the particular locale. And in this period of heightened environmental awareness, of greenhouse effects and their relationship to forests and sustainable resources, wood practitioners are among those in the forefront who are addressing these issues in their work.

PLATE 136
Matthew Harding (b. 1964)
Vice Versa, 1996
English elm, upholstery
100 x 52 x 49 cm
Photo: David Paterson

Furniture Making

Although it is difficult and sometimes preferable not to place practitioners into particular categories, doing so facilitates any presentation of the diversity of approaches encountered in this area. Within the field of furniture making, there are a number of approaches which tend to define practitioner's work: the traditional, modern, post-modernist or avant-garde, and recycled or 'making do' work.

Inspiration from the historical in combination with what may be considered the ultimate in craftsmanship is represented here by the work of Geoffrey Hannah (b. 1948). The traditional category refers to that activity which seeks to maintain time-honoured cabinetmaking techniques and styles.

The making of presentation pieces of furniture was a long-established European tradition at the time it was transferred to Australia. Colonial cabinetmakers would produce special pieces on the occasion of their wife's birthday or wedding anniversary, or otherwise design and make the work as a commission. Migrant German cabinetmakers working in the Barossa Valley in the nineteenth century, for example, were especially faithful in this respect: for them, the making of a presentation piece was an opportunity for showmanship, to create a work which displayed the highest standards of the craftsman, his skills in design, inlay and cabinetmaking.

This is how we respond to the high quality of Hannah's work which combines the traditionalist's singular attention to detail and finish with an Australian idiom. This approach is exemplified by a recent masterpiece he calls *Australiana Collectors' Cabinet*. This neo-renaissance styled cabinet, which took Hannah two years to complete, is decorated in marquetry with Australian flora in a naturalistic style using forty-seven types of Australian and exotic timber; it also features the floral emblems of each Australian State and the Northern Territory.

Hannah's virtuoso work invites us to marvel his showmanship, at the intricate craftsmanship as demonstrated by the fine inlay, the exuberant design and richness of the wood, as well as the rich traditions it recalls, reaffirms and celebrates.

Modernist

The modernist-based mainstream approach revels in the pure and simple, in clean lines and functionalist approaches to solutions and forms; it focuses on the geometric and is essentially restrained to using wood as the principal material. In this category, sometimes also referred to as the moderate approach, craftsmanship is made evident in the quality of the timber used and in the exposed construction processes, as well as in the preference for natural finishes.

Strong influences on this group include the British Arts and Crafts Movement, the Bauhaus and the Scandinavian modernist schools of craft: all infuse the moderate approach with a respect for truth-to-materials where wood is exalted. As well, there is an acceptance of sculptural form as defined by functionalist notions. These well-defined aesthetics are a reminder of those of the Anglo-Oriental School of Ceramics (Chapter Two), and although they place certain restraints on the maker, they also set up considerable challenges to create furniture within these tenets, yet allowing a considerable degree of expression of the individual in the work.

As would be expected of an activity grounded in modernism, ornament is generally subdued but not eliminated in this approach. Instead, the grain and textural finishes of the timber, together with colour contrasts, generally suffice. The latter is achieved through the use of staining; other ornamental details may include minimal, if any, carving details; the use of large unrelieved surfaces and veneers; contrasting timbers; and the discrete, functional combination of other materials such as leather, stone and metal.

Not unexpectedly, the directness of approach to the design and crafting of this category of furniture lends itself to limited edition industrial production, and designer-makers in this field often produce prototypes for industry.

George Ingham (b. 1940) is one such designer-maker whose work expresses the craftsman's delight in material and traditional processes. Although strongly informed by the British Arts and Crafts Movement, his work has a characteristic, individual imagery which sources modernist, functional ideals. The former is no doubt a consequence of Ingham's background, his education and work as a lecturer of furniture and environmental design in Britain, prior to his arrival in Australia.

The identifying characteristics of Ingham's furniture include his penchant to expose and even highlight structural techniques, especially joins; functional, pleasing forms; simple yet elegant design solutions; an emphasis on wood, but the inclusion of other materials as visual counterpoints such as steel, glass, nylon or leather.

> I see my work as a series of points in time, there to be re-examined as new wisdom supplants that which has informed past decisions. I hold strong opinions on the rightness or wrongness of my chosen craft, but I am aware that opinions evolve and change, sometimes imperceptibly. However, I do not discard those constants that have informed, challenged and excited me through my development as a designer and maker: my craft, my enjoyment of structure, my responsibility to my material and my pleasure in beautiful objects. The best, if there is such a definable thing, is yet to come.

Designer-maker Leon Sadubin (b. 1948) similarly creates refined, elegant furniture which extols the medium of wood and wood-working traditions. He specialises in one-off items of furniture, but is particularly well known for his public commissions for the benches in New Parliament House. These and his other works invariably use local timbers in an understated modernist style which includes references to organic lines, masses and the natural qualities of the medium. The almost disarming functional and aesthetic directness of his work relates strongly to the Danish and Scandinavian furniture ethos, although Sadubin informs his work with an Australian sensibility.

Sadubin expresses or hints at this characteristic through the use of endemic Australian timbers which, through the simplicity and practical functionality of the work almost become paeans to the medium. This praiseworthiness is evident in his *Church Furniture*: an altar, lectern and side-table he constructed for the Cabrini Hospital Chapel in Victoria. There, collaboration with a group of other practitioners including David Wright (Chapter Three) and Helge Larsen and Darani Lewers (Chapter Four), resulted in an integrated symbolic fusion of timber, glass and metal furnishings.

Post-modernist Influences

Post-modernist or avant-garde furniture and woodcraft generally depart from the gentler visions of the moderates. Within this category rules may be jettisoned, and the 'anything goes' attitude seen in the other craft media become the only guide, or else, the practitioner may simply bend the rules slightly, maintaining traditional elements but presenting a new perspective or element into

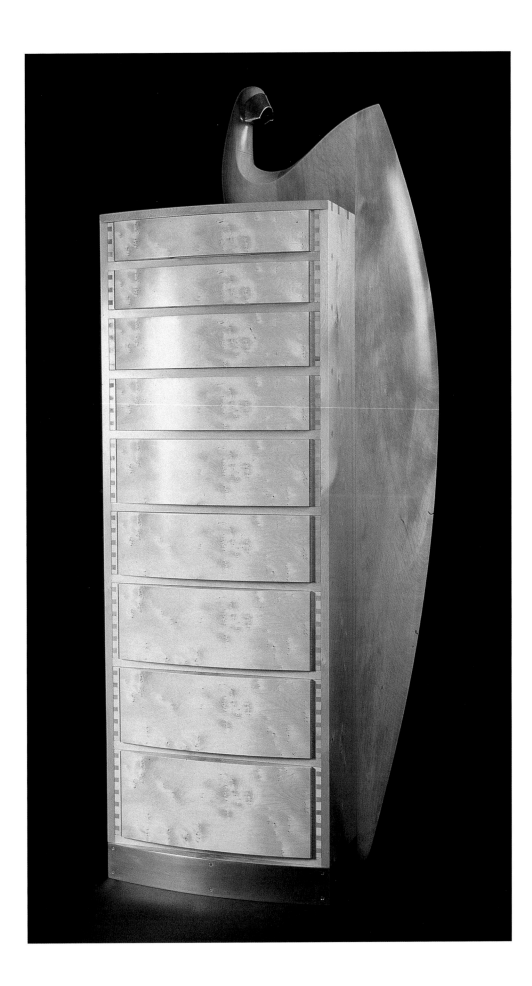

PLATE 137
Kevin Perkins (b. 1945)
Cape Barren Goose, 1994
Chest of drawers, Huon pine, east coast
peppermint, ebony, silver and glass
164 x 64 x 50 cm
Photo: Simon Cuthbert

the design. Wood also may become transformed and freely combined with other materials, especially steel, glass, stone and cloth. As with the other media, this approach also brings in the ambiguity, vigour, perplexity, narrative and eclecticism favoured by the post-modernist attitude.

As a consequence, post-modernist furniture is not necessarily rational or straightforward in appearance, and may even tend towards the theatrical, often combining dramatic, architectural, colourful and ornamental elements — with a twist of irony or a touch of humour.

Kevin Perkins (b. 1945) may be positioned somewhere between the moderates and the avant-garde: his furniture combines fine craftsmanship with respect for material, yet departs from the more conventional design ideas to explore more sculpturally conceived directions. Some of his recent work included the fusion of stylised figurative sculpture with functional furniture forms: his *Cape Barren Goose* chest of drawers, for example, appears as a winged, sensually curvaceous chest, the bird's neck and head crowning the immaculately finished carcase of solid Huon pine. The curved drawer fronts are faced with Huon pine bird's-eye sliced veneer, with their dovetails left exposed as an additional decorative feature. The wing, neck and head of the Cape Barren Goose (a native bird of Tasmania) were carved from solid Huon pine, with ebony and silver detailing on the head.

The attention to detail, the cabinetry and the celebration of timber's natural qualities, suggest Perkins is more strongly allied to the moderates; while this may be arguable, his departure into expressive, sculptural, figurative — and symbolic — explorations suggest a freer interpretation of his craftsmanship. It is also interesting to compare the aforementioned work by Perkins with the Biedermeier furniture of the 1930s, whereby swans and other animals of the classical period were appropriated and applied as stylised motifs or figurative forms by German cabinetmakers to provide strong decorative and symbolic design elements in their neo-classical work.

The focus of Matthew Harding's (b. 1964) wood practice is transformation, whether it be the self, or ideas and materials into objects. As a versatile wood practitioner, his work is infused with a strong philosophical stance, and includes carved sculptures as well as furniture. The former work consists of naturalistic figurative sculptures ranging from his favourite animal, the frog, through to sensitively human studies. These exhibit his masterly skills at carving out form from wood, and imbuing the figures with a strong sense of vitality.

Harding's furniture is similarly imaginatively conceived and follows lateral design approaches: his *Pelican Chair*, for example, evolved from a brief to incorporate zoomorphic characteristics into a piece of furniture. He approached this 'in a linear, rather than depicting manner, with the structure providing the support for a compound weave that creates the functional surface'. Another chair, *Circumstance*, was designed from the view that 'I take a seat, not to resign myself to it, but to integrate. It is my legs that provide the stability'. Constructed from laminated hoop pine, Harding's striking circular chair embodies 'evolution and revolution, the imposition of the cross on the world, Leonardo's *homo universalis…*'

PLATE 138 (opposite)
Stuart Montague (b. 1962)
Curved Gum Cabinet, 1994
Turpentine, laminated cedar, and silky oak
1400 x 100 x 400 cm
Photo: Wayne Grant

PLATE 139 (opposite)
Donald Fortescue (b. 1957)
Assay (low table), 1995
Tasmanian myrtle, patinated,
cast bronze
60 x Diam 50 cm

Harding's furniture is invariably rich with metaphorical allusions: his *Cube Chair* (a cube with a superimposed image of a conventional chair), is a 'parody of all thrones that seek to dispossess their origins, a metaphor of modernity, the good, the bad and the totalitarian.' Yet another chair entitled *Vice Versa*, is a 'perspective chair' which plays with the boundaries of materiality. In this work which presents an object that is familiar yet distorted to read as a frontal perspective from either direction, Harding poses the question: 'where does the object stop and where does its shadow begin?' Not surprisingly, its construction involved a number of complex angles and sections designed to create the illusion.

> Everything is subject to change and transformation, if not physically, then by our perceptions; my choices inform and shape my experience of reality. As a designer I choose ideas and materials then transform them into objects. Once removed from my hands and vocabulary, an object's persona carries my inspirations, intentions and identity, or may take on other personal, social, cultural or historical significance.

Although Stuart Montague (b. 1962) has a traditional training in furniture making through his apprenticeship, and later, tertiary design education, his furniture departs from the usual to gently bend our notions of conventional forms. He designs and constructs furniture which is both sculptural and functional, investigating a wide range of sources for inspiration. The latter includes the styles of periods ranging from the early nineteenth century through to the early and postwar years of this century. Design elements derived from Georgian, Biedermeier, neoclassical, Australiana, and especially, of the 1930s and 1950s, are to be seen in his works.

Montague's design skills imbue his forms with a distinctive character immediately recognisable as his work. He achieves this by reinterpreting historical and conventional forms into contemporary designs. Much of his output has strong surreal imagery: *Twisted Tallboy*, is literally just that, a tallboy of conventional rectilinear form, seemingly twisted on its vertical axis; *Curved Gum Cabinet* has an unlikely semi-arching form; *Bat Cabinet* has a flaring waisted form; *Bent Boy* is another tallboy which tilts to the side from its upper portion. These seemingly unlikely curves are achieved through structural laminations of cedar on ply; visually the effect is illusionary, intriguing and stimulating.

These and other works utilise Australian timbers with a consummate craftsmanship which accentuates their natural qualities. Other works such as chairs and lounges have cast aluminium legs or arms which when combined with upholstery of vibrant textiles, create stimulating stylish forms with a strong visual appeal.

As a practitioner, Montague is essentially a designer-maker who produces his work within a commercial workshop setting which employs a staff of fifteen consisting of skilled cabinetmakers, French polishers and apprentices. Montague's designs and work may be compared to those of Kevin Perkins in that they are located somewhere between the moderates and the avant-garde,

combining traditional fine craftsmanship and techniques with designs which explore the sculptural, visual and emotive potential of furniture.

The tendency for furniture to take on the appearance of sculptural, architectural and other forms not usually associated with it, can become innovative to the point of being extreme. Yet there are practitioners who have specifically embarked on a quest to explore crafting processes, as well as the cultural and functional relationships of the applied arts in order to achieve such an outcome which pushes processes, boundaries and the medium. Donald Fortescue (b. 1957) is one such designer-maker who revels in exploring the fundamentals of furniture, what it is, its sources and the process of its design and making. He often constructs forms which investigate the personal space of domestic interiors through the shape and arrangement of various furniture elements. Aside from commissions, and design for small-scale production, his practice has always embraced speculative exhibition work.

> I have increasingly moved away from media-based craft approaches, and now design and work with metals, paper, glass, textiles and even sand-casting — in short, any material which serves my intent. Although mostly handmade, I also collaborate with other designer-makers and manufacturers. The understanding of material culture which comes from these collaborations is essential for quality, nuanced design.

Fortescue's sensitive and intelligent use of materials and form results in visually stimulating objects infused with charm and allure, and which often make references to historical processes in building and furniture making.

Designed to challenge notions of what furniture is, his exhibition works have often appeared as intriguing sculptures: consider two large elongated and delicate pods illuminated internally; or, three wooden lattice screens tilted vertically on bases of dark-stained wooden domes; and finally, *Assay*, a low table with a top of laminated timber and base of fissured blue metal, the precise geometry of the piece resembling a stylised mushroom. The textural richness and formal boldness of the latter especially reveals his virtuosity in combining disparate materials such as metal and wood, and the attention he applies to their finishes.

These objects are pleasing in terms of the visual harmony derived from their meticulous crafting, their minimalised forms and the seemingly unadulterated material surfaces — wood, clay, bronze, paper, glass; they are united by a design approach which fuses a strong geometry with an added twist, or an historic or cultural element. One work, *Crossing Table*, consists of a lattice and earth installation and combines pioneer building and furniture techniques, reconfiguring these into an evocative form. His works often emerge from or allude to Australian landscape elements: seed pods, termite mounds, adobe walls, colonial verandahs, or a stand of saplings. Part of the strategy Fortescue utilises in his efforts to evoke particular memories and associations, in turn, transform the external setting into an internalised mental landscape. Gradually, through this methodology, he creates distinctive Australian interiors.

Philip Monaghan's (b. 1960) work similarly challenges the boundaries of contemporary art and craft, in this case by reinserting rich decorative images 'in an era of ornamental depravation', as he refers to it. His sculptural furniture generally defies categorisation, although its elaborate wood carving suggests ethnic folk influences, in part an outcome of his travel and work in Nigeria, southern India and Pakistan, countries which have strong indigenous cultural traditions in art and sculpture (in stone, bronze and wood), and in part from the richness of art he was exposed to in the myriad of museums in London. He designs his furniture as 'intense wood carving derived from multiple sources, such as industrial urban images and the rich organic Australian flora'.

As a result of his bold, vigorous style of high-relief carving, Monaghan's work, which ranges from chairs, tables, beds and bowls, has a distinctive, characteristic imagery which accentuates the rich colours and graining qualities of the timbers he uses. As well as the floral forms, certain motifs such as whorls and spirals — which are derived from industrial sources including the components of trains — appear regularly; while his penchant to selectively stain particular components or aspects of his carving, further highlights the sculptural and decorative qualities of his work.

PLATE 141
David Ralph (b. 1946)
Chair, 1996
Horizontal scrub tree
(*Anodopetalum biglandulosum*)
96 x 52 x 52 cm

Recycling, Making Do, and Bricolage Approaches

The recycled, bricolage or 'making do' approaches comprise a fourth category of furniture. Also called the 'bush' style, this latter term tends to omit the variety of approaches encompassed by a philosophy which favours the use of reclaimed timbers, old furniture, found objects, driftwood, or endemic timbers. This is a fertile area of creativity which extends the boundaries of craft, and which permits a fusion of personal, as well as broader social concerns in its expressive form or imagery. As an approach to crafting it is best comprehended from the anthropological notion of the post-modernist bricoleur or junk collector as a modern-day culture maker.

'Making do' is considered today an endemic, vernacular Australian craft style. Its roots lie in the pioneering years when essential bushcraft skills for furniture and tool-making were primarily exercised out of necessity. As the rigours of the pioneering period diminished, and as the appreciation of handcraft skills as instilled by the British Arts and Crafts Movement had its influence in Australia from the 1890s, pioneering woodcraft skills became increasingly applied to the creation of decorative furniture or for other leisure or hobby purposes. During the years of the

PLATE 142
Peter Hart (b. 1939)
Bookcase, 1996
Joinery, packing cases
(surplus army ammunition boxes),
Australian cedar, Huon pine
and found objects
170 x 60 cm
Photo: Michal Kluvanek

Great Depression necessity once more stimulated make-do activity: the country inhabitants' prudence and bent towards improvisation saw the salvaging of materials from the products of the industrial age, especially old packing boxes and kerosene tins, to be recycled into domestic folk furniture.

Out of this emerged an Australian bush vernacular which has inspired contemporary practitioners to work within a similar context, salvaging and recycling timber from any of a number of sources, and using these to construct a modern version of bushcraft or 'make-do' furniture.

Informal folk furniture making was driven by various motivating factors, so a number of kinds of bushcraft furniture styles emerged in country regions around Australia. For example, there is the contribution of ethnically specific bushcraft forms which came from cultural regions such as the Barossa Valley and Adelaide Hills where Prussians had formed close-knit settlements in the nineteenth century. The pioneer tradition of improvisation using natural resources at hand, resulted in 'slab and stick', primitive furniture designed for entirely functional ends — hence the familiar modernist maxim of 'form follows function' is representative of surviving examples. Because shelter and food requirements were prerequisite, aesthetic considerations were rarely involved in the making of this category of furniture and superfluous embellishments were usually avoided.

Primitive furniture such as the stick chair appears to have evolved from the English Windsor chair, itself derived from the basic rural cottage stick chair of the seventeenth century. A similar design and construction progression occurred in Tasmania where the cottage chair evolved into a regionally identifiable form known as the 'Jimmy Possum chair'. This Tasmanian vernacular chair had rounded stick components shaped with simple tools to fit the slab seat; five back-rest sticks joined a straight top-rail, while the extended legs passed via the seat to protrude through the simple straight-stick arm rests.

David Ralph (b. 1946) is a contemporary wood craftsman who is perhaps working as closely as might be possible in the original mode of the make-do pioneer. Since the mid-1970s, he has lived in Tasmania where the free availability of wood exists alongside critical concerns for the survival of the primeval forests of the region. In the 1970s he made the first of what became an immutable series of stick chairs and tables which show a strong affinity to the work of Jimmy Possum. Ralph's work, however, is not driven by pioneering necessity, but by a contemporary urge for artistic expression, and perhaps even more so, by a desire to raise the awareness of the uniqueness of Tasmania's forest heritage and the need for its conservation.

Ralph's chairs (and tables), are always made according to the model he first developed. These consist of naturally round branches of a particular diameter cut from an endemic rainforest species commonly known as 'Horizontal'. Selecting branches with natural bends which conform to the shape of the intended chair's armrests, he trims them of any sideshoots but retains their bark. The appeal of *Chair* and other simple forms derive from their primitive yet functional

PLATE 143
Gay Hawkes (b. 1942)
Newell Beach (Chair), 1993
Mangrove and found objects
12.7 x 10.1 x 10 cm
(see also Plate 5)

simplicity. And although they differ from the historical antecedents made by Jimmy Possum, in terms of their construction details and the retention of their natural bark covering, they are otherwise closely comparable.

By maintaining a particular style, unchanged for over eighteen years, Ralph's practice conforms to and accentuates the production ethos and basis of craft, more so than the prevalent contemporary emphasis given to innovation. His chairs speak of a rustic aesthetic which evokes those aspects of the past now long-gone: they echo the pioneering necessities and spirit of Jimmy Possum, they point to a need for the conservation of forest resources, and they celebrate the qualities of wood in its almost natural state.

Although Peter Hart (b. 1939) makes furniture which is still linked to the colonial 'make-do' bush tradition, his work has also moved into a bricolage genre to exhibit a singular character. Unlike the pioneer farmer and 1930s depression householder who were forced by necessity to reuse old fence palings, boxes and other discards to make tools or furniture, Hart deliberately seeks out such discards for his work. This penchant to gather found objects and assemble them into alternative constructions started at an early age during the time he assisted his father in his metal workshop. Perhaps because of this early influence, Hart considers his present-day work as autobiographical.

Hart's 'make-do' approach to furniture uses wood recycled from surplus army ammunition boxes into items of furniture such as tables, cupboards or dressers. The form of some of these pieces is, in part, influenced from Hart's knowledge of early Barossa furniture of the same category; in 1993, these dressers often featured a traditional moustache-shaped pediment; the boxes are a drab army green, over-painted with bright-yellow stencilled lettering. Currently, *Bookcase* and other works have become less influenced by this regional heritage and appear more generally as colonial Australian pieces. Metal beer-bottle tops have lately become a part of the applied, found object, layering which acts as both on a decorative, as well as symbolic level.

In reconstituting these boxes into other articles, this lettering remains visible, but is supplemented with Hart's own stencilling of quotes taken from the Bible, or text from other sources. In this context the lettering is both decorative and symbolic, acting to intensify the impact of form and individuality of the work: it is also deliberately cryptic, so that the viewer of any piece may project his or her own personal meaning; yet other, wider, interpretations are possible. The essential point here is that, in our society, this type of overt and calculated symbolism is as relevant as the practical use the item may have. And it is through these works that Hart reveals to us something of his inner life and past.

Revealing more overt self-motivation, Gay Hawkes (b. 1942) makes functional furniture as art objects which express personal, political and social commentary, as well as embodying aspects of the natural and man-made environment to generate narratives of Australia's historical past and cultural present.

PLATE 144 (opposite)
Andrew Munn (b. 1947)
Driftwood Screen, 1996
Recycled driftwood, rusted iron cut-outs, and metal hinges
200 x 200 cm
Photo: Michal Kluvanek

In Hawkes's practice, making do is not an activity indulged out of necessity, although her chairs, cupboards and other furniture items utilise found timber to function in the intended practical manner of their genre; but rather, making do is embodied as a cultural or historical reference. Her preference for making sculptural items which retain their function emphasises this facet, even if Hawkes's chairs do not especially invite one to sit and rest in them. Her works are assembled and constructed from pieces of driftwood, old planks and even eroded metal objects such as tin cans — whatever may be scavenged along the seashore or from the bush.

In this respect, Hawkes is (inadvertently) involved in that perennial bricolage strategy we have already encountered. Her discards are recontextualised into functional and sculptural forms to tell stories of their prior lives, their journeys and the processes, natural and artificial, which led them to their present revival.

> I am not interested in contemporary craft; I am interested in innovative practices
> of the past and the ideas of the present: chicken coops are my biggest challenge!
> Most of my past works are pure landscape.

This embodiment of landscape is both literal and metaphoric: we see it in her work *Newell Beach* where a chair is constructed from the mangrove branches and found objects salvaged from this far North Queensland site. Throne-like in its imposing form, this armchair may appear too rickety for support, yet its construction has given life to the materials of past manufacture and growth.

Andrew Munn (b. 1947) is a wood-carver and furniture maker who is less concerned with the embodiment of personal, political and social aspects in his work than with the direct expression of the decorative, sculptural and functional. Using driftwood and other materials gathered from the sea-shore, he constructs a genre of make-do furniture which embodies stories of sand, sea, sun and time.

Munn's affinity with the sea has already led to a body of work which, although essentially decorative, relies on his imagination, sense of play, and his wood-carving skills. Carved and painted fish presented as candle holders in clustered groups he calls schools, carved figures such as clowns, and mantelpiece seashore changing-sheds in brightly-painted patterns and colours, have been a part of his output for some time. Lately, he has developed the work into the *Beachcomber* series, whereby he has focused less on carved and painted decoration than on making functional furniture 'which allows the use of natural shape, form and line, as well as retaining the raw beauty and feeling of the timber'. Through the judicious selection and placement of driftwood pieces, side boards, tables, mirror frames and cupboards assume spontaneous, jagged-edged forms according 'to nature's own sculptural patterns'.

The action of sand, saltwater and sunshine on wood is abrasive, but it results in a particular medium, weathered wood, which as we have already seen, is avidly collected and used as a starting point for creative work by various practitioners. This is Munn's medium: he cherishes these raw qualities — the bleached colour, the sanded, tactile surfaces and other signs of the forces of nature. Rusted hinges, tin cut-outs, carefully preserved old painted surfaces, worn seashells, and the

PLATE 145
Martin Corbin (b. 1949)
Bushfire Shrine, 1994
Reconstruction from original, old blackwood
dining chair, with photograph, perspex,
brass hinges; original paintwork sanded back
100 x 48 cm
Photo: Michal Kluvanek

PLATE 146 (above)
Ondrej Mares (b. 1949)
Console For Liba, 1995
European ash, blackwood and paint
45 x 140 x 130 cm
Photo: Michal Kluvanek

occasional brushstroke as additional, minimal surface decoration, complete the works. Removed from the detritus of the beach, Munn's driftwood furniture-making not only acts to clear the shoreline, but also gives a second lease of life to the remains of tree branches and the timber of crates, fences and other discarded objects; as such his make-do articles evoke our concerns of the need for forest conservation — this is their social function.

The *Beachcomber* series is also considerably restrained compared to Munn's former work, at least in respect to its decorative surfaces, although whimsical elements are still to be found in the applied cut-out tin imagery or in painted motifs; mostly, however, Munn has allowed the material to make its own visual statement, to quietly tell its story of the shoreline, to gently suggest metaphors regarding the boundary of sea and land, as well as to make references to the making-do tradition which he sustains as relevant within our contemporary setting.

The flotsam and jetsam of society does not necessarily begin at the seashore, but can originate on our very doorsteps. Martin Corbin (b. 1949) transforms the ubiquitous and humble, postwar kitchen, slatback chair into a myriad of alternative sculptural and exotic forms — shrines, cabinets, bowls, tables and stands. In doing so, Corbin explores certain themes fundamental to craft practice, including its definition, the identity and role of the craftsman in contemporary society, and the meaning of function.

The journey for this extraordinary transformation, one which changes our perceptions of what was once ordinary and mundane, begins in garage sales, second-hand shops, and even rubbish dumps. From these locations, Corbin 'rescues' jettisoned and the unwanted wooden kitchen chairs. This bricoleur relishes their multi-painted and worn-out surfaces. After all, these are documents representing and recalling the evidence of the drama of past lives, of family meals, of restless children, of momentous decisions, and of sad and happy occasions.

But first, Corbin disassembles the various components that make up the original chairs: the slightly curved rail backs, the flat lathes or slat supports, the moulded seats and the square-form, splayed legs and stretches. These components are cut and reassembled, their original curves and forms suggesting sometimes the intended finished article. The sparse construction of curvilinear slats and chair legs often give these works a strong Japanese stylistic imagery which is accentuated when the form's (ostensible) function is intended as a shrine.

My work is created within a predetermined philosophical framework in which I'm commenting on aspects of contemporary culture from a strongly personal perspective. It's important that the work is more than aesthetically pleasing, and I like to think it is distinctly Australian in character. Within this framework, I design as I make, working with intuition, deliberation and serendipity in an attempt to achieve something beyond the ordinary.

PLATE 147 (opposite)
Martin Johnson (b. 1970)
Pink Women Cupboard, 1996
Recycled wood, tin, with acrylic paint
1198 x 48 x 40 cm

With these materials and through this methodology, Corbin creates tables as xylophones, zoomorphic forms which act as rocking 'horses', shrines and wall cupboards. In these, one can always detect an echo of the former object, the chair, and it is this and the process of patination which Corbin utilises to give his works an additional voice or edge. Using judicious sanding he selectively exposes the multi-coloured paint layers, creating a new patina. In part a decorative effect, the process is similar to an archaeological investigation which reveals the aesthetic preferences of the original chair's previous owners.

In metamorphosing form, so too has function also been rearranged from one of seating to one of storage or perhaps prayer. In regard to the latter, Corbin's shrines pay homage not only to specified subjects, such as his *Bushfire Shrine*, but also, and with a strong sense of irony, to the ideals of craftsmanship, function and meaning. For in directing his craft skills to recycle functional, everyday articles into what are art objects to be primarily appreciated for their sensual and intellectual contents, Corbin suggests a re-evaluation of craft which, in this instance, appears to be redirected to the service of art — not utility!

Combining a sense of wit with strong visual imagery, Ondrej Mares (b. 1949) has created a distinctive, contemporary style of furniture using recycled timber and other materials from various sources. Mares's work skilfully articulates a sculptural and decorative vocabulary which elevates recycled timber and galvanised iron into fine furniture forms which fuse ceremonial intent, metaphoric allusion, and a touch of humour.

Decorative and sculptural in form, Mares's works have a surreal feel due to his penchant for adding unusual appendages to his mostly functional forms. These include foliar or aveolar outgrowths which sprout from the sides of consoles, bookshelves and cupboards. Mares reveals that these forms are derived from European custom and are an abstracted figurative representation of the cuckold. Large wooden, trolley-like wheels transform his minimalist forms into giant toy-like modular works, giving them a visually mobile appearance; because these wheels are fixed and cannot function, they become an ironical touch; they are an influence derived from a friend, a Spanish sculptor, and are acknowledged in the title to one of Mares's works, *Homage to Gonzales*.

Brightly-painted, dual or three-tone colour schemes of red and white, yellow and red, or black, blue and red, accentuate this playful imagery. Mares heightens the decorative surfaces by sanding the paint back to reveal the timber surface, and contrasting this with highly-polished surfaces to produce strong textural and patterned effects. More recent work continues the use of raw solid timbers with the painted surfaces dominated by black tops and white theatre-like prop outlines. Another innovation is the use of corrugated legs with perforated edges as a decorative wavy-fringe, 'like a dancer's legs' to support the consoles or tables. Salvaged and painted, corrugated, galvanised iron sheets are an occasional additional, vernacular element.

Mares does more than create attractive and useful furniture from discards, and his works are often inspired and made as a gesture of devotion or as offerings to honour family members or friends. The sum total of these construction approaches and surface treatments and influences are characteristic furniture forms which are not only sculptural and functional, but also playful and symbolic.

Further along the developmental line deriving from the original bush making-do genre of furniture, is the folk art furniture of Martin Johnson (b. 1970). Combining enterprise, imagination and ingenuity, Johnson uses recycled materials to make furniture in a very contemporary style of the Australian depression era, make-do tradition. The difference between his approach and that of the past is his combination of this spirit of improvisation with painterly, decorative and humorous elements.

Although his background training was in photography and painting, Johnson exemplifies the versatility of the contemporary practitioner to successfully apply his skills to the unrelated area of furniture making, although he views this furniture as 'an extension of my sculpture and painting'.

Johnson's furniture is especially distinguished by preceding or other Australian craft practitioner's work in this genre in its unique combination of a strong folk art sensibility with a contemporary, primitive appearance. The European folk streak is undoubtedly an influence from his textiles practitioner partner Agnieszka Golda (see Chapter Five). Typical depression-revival furniture of the 1920s and 1930s was always functional and displayed ingenious adaptations of the use of the recycled materials; it also frequently revealed the maker's wish to imbue his or her work with some semblance of design, the latter usually borrowing stylistic elements from commercial or professionally made furniture of the time. This sometimes included boldly painted patterns or broad areas using whatever was at hand to give the make-do constructions an imaginative finish.

Johnson's furniture is also constructed from recycled wood and tin, but the extent of his decorative finishes surpasses earlier work. As well as being functional, his work is always highly decorated with hand-carved, decorative motifs which are applied to brightly painted surfaces. Designs are always quirky and catchy: *Letterbox*, for example, features a roughly carved nude male figure sitting astride a peaked box; while the aptly named *Pink Women Cupboard* eschews the usual rectilinear approach to making a storage space to begin with a figurative form which incorporates cupboard spaces in the face, neck, legs and chest. Here, recycled, pressed-tin pieces which have their own moulded patterns are used to make the surface of the torso, while the painted head is hand-carved from a solid piece of wood: this is decorative and applied art approached in a fresh, non-conventional manner.

Much contemporary craft is represented by the international design trend in finely-crafted materials, sophisticated sleek lines, innovative design, and links with industry — a kind of 'designer chic'; Johnson on the other hand, is among those practitioners who are defying this trend, presenting work with strong, bright imagery as a type of 'grunge craft', that is, off-beat, folksy, and always imbued with symbolic qualities.

PLATE 148
Norman Peterson (b. 1946)
Hollow Form, 1996
Turned, grooved and sandblasted
redgum
23 x 29 cm

Woodturning

Woodturning is an area of woodcraft with an especially large following of makers and collectors. As a craft, woodturning has a surprisingly long history beginning with the Egyptians who used lathes to produce decorative turned wood for chair legs and other uses. Today, turning is used to hollow out wooden vessels from solid pieces of timber. It is a remarkably active area of exploration which seeks the unique expression of this timeless form in the medium of wood. Woodturners are interested in the decorative and metaphorical potential of wood, and achieve this through the articulation of textural and other physical qualities, usually in combination with an expression of wood's inherent cultural or emotional content.

The woodturned bowl embodies a unique harmony of form, texture and colour which can exemplify the characteristics of the medium in a very alluring manner. Formed from either native or exotic timbers, woodturned bowls can make striking or subtle statements which often express the heart or soul of timber more eloquently than other forms in the medium. The woodturned bowl also acts to expose the life of the tree, combining bark, heartwood, burl and pattern into a sensuously tactile and visual artefact for decorative or contemplative purposes.

The derivation of the wooden bowl from a spinning tool, the lathe, suggests the use of another

spinning tool, the potter's wheel which is similarly used to produce a vessel. However, the similarity stops there, for, while the latter has the plasticity of clay, timber is rigid and therefore demands its own set of skills and sensibilities. Techniques for texturing, shaping, carving, staining and otherwise treating the surface range from traditional approaches such as chainsaw carving, scorching, painting, pokerwork, and bleaching to the use of more modern processes including the exposure of surface to ammonia fumes or wax resist, fuming and sanding. Metal, metallic leaf, fibre, glass and other materials are sometimes also combined with the basic forms. Forms may be classically inspired or else they may take their precedence from African or Pacific cultures, from ceramic or cast iron models, or from any source the turner chooses to explore.

There appear to be three mainstream approaches to woodturning which may, for the purposes of convenience, be termed the natural, the painterly and the conceptual, although like most categories, these merge into one another, while practitioners often practise more than one approach. The natural stream is relatively straightforward in that it seeks to express the intrinsic qualities of wood, its grain, burls, knots, and colours, often accentuated through the use of strongly defined, though generally, conventional vessel forms. And aside from polishing or other minimal finishes, the turned wooden form, symmetrical or otherwise free-flowing, receives little other treatment. This moderate approach is not without its challenges to the craftsman: selecting a piece of wood and treating it to bring out a form which artfully integrates it with the natural qualities of the medium requires considerable skill. People will always be attracted to this genre, for the simple, tactile pleasures of handling and viewing a vessel turned in wood, to appreciate the quality of the craftsmanship, to enjoy the delicacy or drama of the characteristics of the particular timber used, to savour the visual balances of rim and body, and to engage with the specific dialogue of wood, line and volume.

Seemingly more on the cutting edge of contemporary woodturning are the other two approaches. The surfaces of the turned form are treated as a canvas for further decorative treatment or embellishment, enhancing visual, highly decorative qualities over tactile and 'natural' finishes. Rims or whole surfaces may be exaggerated by being painted with designs, or decorated with metallic leaf, colour washes or staining and other painterly techniques. The conceptual approach seeks to enhance sculptural aspects of form, or else cultural, historical, narrative or other elements are introduced to produce more challenging work. The natural surface may be deliberately stressed, gouged and split to produce rough, primitive finishes; or else it may be combined with metal or other materials, generally opening up a spectrum of sculptural and metaphorical possibilities.

Redgum Odyssey

Among the numerous specialist niches professional contemporary craftspeople have opened up for themselves, that of redgum turning and carving is perhaps one of the more unusual. This is

PLATE 149 (opposite)
Terry Martin (b. 1947)
Hot Lips, 1992
Turned Celtis timber,
blow-torched surface, acrylic paint
30 cm
Photo: Russell Stokes

especially so when one considers the historical and cultural associations engendered by this quintessential Australian timber — such as its Aboriginal cultural significance, its pioneer roots, and its intimate links with the landscape.

Norman Peterson (b. 1946) redgum turner, carver and sculptor is one of these craftspeople who have taken specialisation to an extreme limit by concentrating on redgum as their sole medium of creative expression. His redgum vessels transcend the functional or decorative to embody elements of landscape, history and the natural and built environment; indeed, his works often illustrate a narrative of time, place and man, of origins and art.

The story of redgum and its crafted forms begins with the majestic tree, the river redgum: it dominates the Murrumbidgee river basin, spreading over dryland water courses, and lining the River Murray banks and its lagoons. For thousands of years, the Aboriginal people utilised the redgum to make bark canoes, wurleys, firewood, spears and shields, food and medicine, or simply sheltered beneath its mighty boughs and hollowed trunks.

European settlers similarly found many uses for this tree: the hollowed-out boles of some of the larger specimens provided temporary shelter; later, pioneers cut many trees down to use the durable and strong timber for building their homes, barns and flour mills. Throughout the nineteenth century too, migrant Prussian cabinetmakers in the Barossa Valley experimented with the timber, making a variety of formal forms which had their stylistic roots in Biedermeier and other historic Germanic furniture practices.

Peterson is a contemporary practitioner who applies his skills to redgum, not out of necessity, as was the driving force of the pioneer craftsman, but in a spirit of artistic exploration: this primeval wood is now manipulated to express its inner essence and historical connotations. The main interest in his work is in coaxing memories and creating beauty from the remains of ancient trees.

Peterson is one such craftsman who salvages old fence posts, old tree stumps, or discarded timber. His century or older timber comes in a weathered grey skin which covers a rich brown to blood-red timber: 'The grain is extraordinary and gutsy, varying from a fine fiddleback (wavy), through to basketweave or a checkerboard pattern. The textural qualities are therefore rich and variable'.

The density and irregularities of redgum make it a notoriously difficult timber to work, yet Peterson works the hard wood with a surprisingly limited range of tools. Burnishing, Swedish oil and wax finishes revitalise the timber bringing out its characteristic graining, and adding a warm glow to accentuate its sensuous surface. The surrounding rural, semi-arid landscape has a marked influence on his work: after shaping a piece he may decide to leave it outside for up to two years, allowing a natural weathering action to form a silver-grey surface. He may also then turn the inside of the vessel to reveal the rich red grain, creating a strong contrast against the grey toning of the outer surface.

His formal repertoire centres on the turned vessel — usually bowls and vases — which vary

PLATE 150
Stephen Hughes (b. 1958)
Something Fishy Going On, 1992
Turned and fretworked,
inlayed and leaf: Huon pine,
antique glass mirror, mother-of-pearl,
opal triplets, 24-ct gold
54 x 4 cm

from a modest mantle size to huge, one metre jars. Intriguingly, although he sketches and draws, this craftsman states that 'nothing is planned, it's always a spontaneous action of the blade on the wood ... the wood determining, as much as myself, the form which emerges.' These forms often have some affinity with pottery, and Peterson admits to an influence from pre-Columbian and early African pottery — as is evident in the larger vessels and their rounded bodies or well-formed rims.

Recently, the exposed layered beds of creek banks suggested to him the application of bands of grooves; while barbed wire unravelled from old fence posts is sometimes coiled about a vessel, endowing these pieces with a palatable sense of place and history. Other vessels which have ruptured rims or veins, have snippets of rusted fencing wire inserted to seemingly repair them — although this is essentially a decorative device. In these works, the unique and contrasting qualities of metal and timber — grey and red, tensile and smooth, cold and warm — simultaneously reinforce and contrast, creating tensions and harmonies.

PLATE 151
Andrew Gittoes (b. 1959)
Slatted Bowl, 1994
Turned, shaped and assembled
silver ash and black bean
24 x 39 cm
Photo: Brenton McGeachie

Norman Peterson's redgum vessels conjure up a richness of images and associations: of Aborigines venerating an essential part of their environment; of pioneer farmers fencing their land, of sawyers splitting railway sleepers from fallen giants; of migrant Prussians crafting ethnic furniture forms. And through forms of grace and strength they excel in rousing an appreciation for our endemic timbers.

Terry Martin (b. 1947) is another practitioner who is also sensitive to environmental concerns and holds the view that 'wood turning allows the use of limited timber resources for maximum effect'. And similarly to the former practitioner, much of the wood Martin uses is recycled from fence posts or felled suburban trees. He retains and enhances the natural faults and features of the timber through treatments which range from the minimal to retain intrinsic qualities, through to painterly and sculptural approaches.

In his work *Sum and Substance*, for example, an acacia burl was first turned and hollowed, then assembled with a bronze cast to create an illusion of flow. Another work, *Hot Lips*, consists of a turned, baluster-form, timber vessel whose external surface has been blow-torched until a split occurred along a determined fault; rubbed back and sealed, the thin walled edges or 'lips' were then painted with a pink-red acrylic, creating a strong contrast against the blackened body. The work has a fired clay or ceramic feel, yet its timber origins are revealed through the grained texture which shows against the blackened surface, while the 'hot lip' edges seemingly parody the medium.

In a radical departure from this preceding approach, one which demonstrates Martin's versatility in wood, *Huon Dream* is a powerful, meditative sculptural work which consists of a hollowed, depressed central vessel flanked by two triangular forms: the vessel's surface is textured to resemble undressed sandstone, while the ends are water-stained in a soft blush: the object is reminiscent of an Oriental ritual vessel carved in stone, yet closer examination reveals the timber's natural grain.

> People always cup a wooden vessel in their hands and caress it, sensuously feeling
> its surface and, almost invariably, lift it to their faces to smell it. Wood talks to
> humans and in the form of a vessel it takes on a new meaning. The turner works
> by sight, feel, sound and instinct; the viewer's response reflects the relationship the
> turner has with the material.

Stephen Hughes (b. 1958) uses wood crafting 'as a means to both challenge and satisfy myself in a quest for personal expression and technical excellence'. As with the preceding practitioners, he also demonstrates a considerable versatility in his approaches and skills. His work ranges from the naturalistic to the sculptural and the painterly. He often combines turning, carving and painting techniques in one piece to create complex though lyrical works. *Talisman Seed* is one of a series which explores a combination of turning and carving with enhanced naturalistic timber finishes: these large vessels of smooth, ovoid form have gently parted lips carved with fretwork: in these works Hughes pays homage to timber and the intimate relationship of woodcraftsman and his medium. Entitled *The Protector* or *The Keeper*, works in this series are always gracefully presented on delicate stands.

This filigree or delicate fretwork carving, which suggests the Celtic knot style, is also executed on wide rims as a decorative and sculptural feature on Hughes's turned shallow bowls. But perhaps

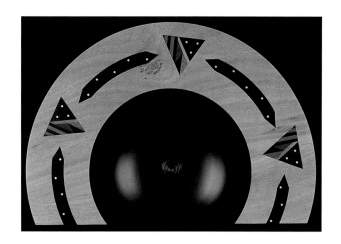

PLATE 152
Greg Collins (b. 1952)
Inlaid Bowl, 1996
Turned blackbutt; inlaid with
Osage orange, ebony, purple heart
(timbers), pink ivory and silver
Diam: 50 x 10 cm
photo: Wayne Beames

his most luminous works are similar bowls which also combine his skill in painting wood. *Something Fishy Going On* combines expressionist painting with antique glass mirror, with mother-of-pearl and opal triplets insets, to create an opulence which alludes to a folk medieval, magical imagery.

Andrew Gittoes (b. 1959) is a designer-maker of functional and decorative woodwork, who proclaims that he is governed by two rules: 'a concern for pure form and the use of only reclaimed timbers'. He designs and makes pure, simple forms which he considers 'can equal, even surpass, the inherent beauty of timber'.

Like his fellow craftsmen in wood, Gittoes is 'very conscious' of the environmental significance of trees and only uses timbers salvaged from roadside or other clearing projects to make 'beautiful and useful items from timber that would be otherwise destroyed'. His geometrical forms are sublime in their simplicity and in the manner that his minimal treatment accentuates the timber's rich graining, colour and texture.

Although some forms are turned in one timber then polished without further applications, other works articulate two or more timbers to create lyrical sculptural forms which rely on their colour and shape combinations: the rim of a red rosewood vase is inlaid with small dots of ebony; a 'rocking' bowl is created by carving creamy silver ash into curved coasters as a base for a brown myrtle burl bowl; the illusionary piece, *Slatted Bowl*, is formed by turning, shaping and assembling silver ash and black bean.

Greg Collins (b. 1952) is proficient in both furniture making and woodturning. He has a craftsmanly and imaginative approach to design, and enjoys blending various timbers and other materials to produce decorative work which has a strong contemporary feel. He uses mainly native timbers salvaged from farm or roadside clearances, but he also utilises exotic woods.

Although Collins's furniture falls within the category of the moderate school, the innovative decorative treatment shifts it towards the avant-garde. His tables, desks and other forms are decorated with inlaid, geometric motifs which lend the furniture an architectonic imagery. Lately, his turned-work has also taken on this decorative direction, the wide rims turned from various eucalypt species enriched with inlaid patterns made up of contrasting timbers such as black ebony, Osage orange, purple heart and raspberry jam, which are further enhanced with materials such as sterling silver and pink ivory — as in *Inlaid Bowl*. Other works have lately taken on an even stronger geometric imagery as he has extended his decorative work with the use of spines of silver, and ebony border inlays and dots which create movement and interest.

Carving

Although William Matthysen's (b. 1954) wooden clockwork mechanisms are often identified within the sculpture and carving section of wood shows, they could well be classified as furniture given the joinery and other cabinetry techniques associated with this genre. An experienced architect, Matthysen turned to the development of woodcraft as a means of exploring the aesthetics of the mechanical timepiece within this medium and practice. To his mind, 'the quartz revolution has rendered the mechanical timepiece obsolete. Liberated now from servitude, its mechanism is now available for rediscovery and new interpretations'.

He has pursued this aim by borrowing techniques and design approaches from the crafts, integrating these into one object 'capable of sustained movement'. From woodcraft he applies the methods and equipment of precision engineering, modifying them as necessary to suit the materials in question. On the other hand, clockmaking has indicated the need to 'address issues of composition and narrative to what is essentially a utilitarian functioning object'.

Matthysen's fascination for the timepiece and his adaptation of woodworking skills has resulted in sculptural works which celebrate the qualities of wood as well as the intricate mechanisms and precision engineering associated with clocks. Wherever practical and adaptable most of the parts are constructed in wood, usually solid native timbers which are finished to exhibit their natural qualities. Typically, as in *Clock 0033*, the clock's case, plates, wheels, pendulum rod, hands, and dial are turned on the wheel or constructed using traditional joinery techniques.

But beyond these handskills and the idea of a clock constructed mostly from timber, Matthysen considers his elegant timepieces as narrative works which reveal more than the time of human existence.

> At a metaphorical level, no material has 'time' written over it as graphically as wood. Its growth rings not only speak of the passage of seasonal time, but the primordial forces that operate within it.

PLATE 154 (above)
John Wooller (b. 1939)
The Wheel Of Fire, 1994
Turned and carved jarrah
burl and bronze
110 cm
Photo: Photo-Foons Photographics

PLATE 153 (opposite)
William Matthysen (b. 1954)
Clock 0033, 1995
Joinery and turning techniques,
bulloak, rose sheoak, fiddleback
sycamore veneer, brass and steel
105 x 48 x 20 cm
photo: Robert Colvin

In yet another singular approach, John Wooller (b. 1939) uses turning and carving to create what he terms 'monolithic' sculptures. These are intriguing works which are based on the application of an extraordinary, indeed heroic, level of skill which results in intricate and complex, though quite lyrical, and at times, evocative imagery. His medium is almost exclusively Jarrah burl, a difficult timber to work, and which he sometimes integrates with metal.

> The most important part of my work is the content; the style is merely the means
> of expressing it. Working to a theme, often drawn from a literary source, I like to
> create a number of pieces of an interpretive nature.

Wooller's sculptures seemingly metamorphose text into symbolic images, or else freeze concept into tangible form and imagery. In the work, *My Intricate Image*, the reticulated, layered, horizontal and circular form suggests a sense of resolution from convolution. Another work, *The Wheel of Fire*, is evocative of ancient Hindu mantra imagery, the carved, flame-like and circular form seemingly evolving out of the heart of a shell of Jarrah burl, a metal teardrop emerging from its centre.

In these and other works we are constantly drawn to the complex though ingeniously resolved images; Wooller's specific use of Jarrah burl takes advantage of its inherent qualities, specifically the convolutions this timber is renowned for, its knots, deep colour and the grain structure. Hence, the development of these sculptures from this material underscores Wooller's focus on the notion of form emerging from chaos, an effect he achieves through manual virtuosity.

The idea of resolving sculptural form from special pieces of wood appears to intrigue and captivate a number of practitioners. Paul Noordanus (b. 1959) searches about clear felled forests in Tasmania, collecting discards of what he judges to be the most spectacular pieces of Tasmanian timber, to carve these into yet another distinctive genre of abstract sculptural forms.

As a European migrant, he is sensitive to what he perceives as Australia's search for identity, specifically as reflected in contemporary craft. Free of the constraints of European tradition, he feels that Australian craft has a chance to express 'the colours and shapes of the country … and the pioneering spirit of its people'. His contribution to this ideal is his work which stems from the carving of large pieces of his 'found' timber remnants such as eucalyptus burl, blackheart sassafras, Huon pine, Blackwood and native myrtle.

From these remnants of Tasmania's great forest trees, Noordanus uses a rotary chisel to carve out his designs, later sanding and finishing them for presentation. His designs focus on broad circular planes or shields with extended wing-like appendages or bulbous swellings, usually to one side. These large abstract forms are calculated to display and celebrate the inherent qualities of the timber; he combines these concerns with the metaphoric suggestions the form embodies. Entitled *Guardian*, *Silent Progress*, *Wings*, or *Aesculapian Snake*, Noordanus imbues the once-fallen timber with a new life, his sinuous works seemingly soaring with a sense of place, spirit and renewal.

PLATE 156
Michael Gill (b. 1953)
Brooch, 1996
Carved rose sheoak, 9 carat gold,
enamel paint
7.5 x 5 cm
Photo: HBW Productions

Michael Gill (b. 1953) is a carver and sculptor whose work usually relates to recognisable Australian icons such as our flora and fauna which he renders in wood with lyricism and a sense of wit. The scale of his work varies considerably, from over two-and-a-half metre high figurative work down to a few centimetres. The former is exemplified from his work *The Green Woman*, a life-sized figure, hand-carved in camphor laurel to the knees, the remainder of her body immersed in the remaining, uncarved cylindrical log; with her fingers and eyebrows carved as leaves, the figure appears to be metamorphosing from the forest tree.

Gill's other category of work consists of wearable jewellery, usually brooches carved from wood and combined with other materials. A typical work includes his rose sheoak *Brooch* carved as a sprig of eucalyptus leaves, buds, fruits and flowers, with the characteristic circular brush of delicate stamens that emerge from the flower cup, and effectively made from gold wire tipped with yellow resin. The work is naturalistically conceived, and although the design acknowledges the Art Nouveau whiplash style, it does so without descending into the excesses of the revival of this style as it emerged in the early twentieth-century Australian 'gum nut nouveau school'.

Silvio Apponyi (b. 1948) works in wood, stone, bronze and silver, his predominant inspiration being the endemic fauna of Australia, particularly its endangered animals, such as birds, fish, frogs and reptiles. Working as a sculptor, Apponyi first carves in wood or stone, then often follows these originals with casts of a limited edition in bronze or silver. His work spans the scale from the close to miniature, netsuke-style carving through to life-sized or larger works. Apponyi's stylistic expression is also diverse and includes the fusion of the realistic and abstract, but more often than not his work is exceptional for its naturalism.

He is particularly concerned in capturing the intrinsic spirit or nature of the animal he seeks to represent, and works from close observations of living or preserved specimens, as well as photographic images. Apponyi's sensitivity to materials is particularly evident in his wood carvings which take advantage of the grain, figure and other qualities of the wood, the texture of the represented animal being echoed in the level of detail as well as in the finish. This reaches extraordinary levels in works such as *Nautilus*, a carving in cedar and rosewood which not only contrasts these richly coloured and grained timbers, but also reveals his virtuoso work in the intricate details of the inlaid tentacles.

Platypus With Yabby, carved in English boxwood and inlaid with buffalo horn, is a netsuke figure of this monotreme shown in the traditional styling in a curled posture; it effectively captures a playful quality, while the conjunction of the finely textured surface, representing its hair, with smoother underbody and bill, creates tactile interest. Apponyi's forms embody a poise and inherent tension which acts to give the figure a sense of vitality. It is this sensibility that infuses his endangered animal series, placing them in an optimistic context.

Catherine Truman (b. 1957) began her professional life as a jeweller but now carves small objects in wood: these invariably have a strong visual imagery which evokes narrative and

PLATE 157
Silvio Apponyi (b. 1948)
Platypus With Yabby (netsuke), 1995
Carved in English boxwood,
inlaid with buffalo horn
5 x 3 x 4 cm

metaphoric associations: 'My work deals with a memory of the body rather than a direct concern with adornment'. Her work combines a disciplined approach to specialised craft skills with the intent of creating detailed and highly textured, carved objects replete with meaning.

Truman's practice has evolved from working in metal and other materials to detailed carving in wood, the latter focus being the result of an intensive study of netsuke carving in Japan. There she became inculcated with age-old traditional techniques of netsuke and its associated cultural attitude. This experience fostered the considerable degree of craftsmanship her work displays in its immaculately executed forms and surfaces, while her motivation to express personal and social concerns, as well as exploring particular concepts, has imbued her work with its contemporary imagery.

As Truman's work has evolved over the past five years or so, a handful of motifs have emerged as central elements, especially those of the boat and fish. These comprise much of the personal imagery she creates, and act as metaphors for multi layered meanings, but especially of lifelong journeys in growth, self-delusion, vulnerability, and aging. A recent exhibition of her carvings

entitled 'Lifeboat' displayed as sculptural assemblages exquisite carvings of wooden boats combined with similarly detailed carvings of fish in mother-of-pearl: a rowing boat filled to the rim with fish; another turned over onto its keel, the hull supporting impaled red herrings; in *Piecemeal*, yet another vessel with its inner surface painted an intense red is displayed alongside the portions of a quartered fish carved from mother-of-pearl. Other, non-exhibition works, such as *A Fish for the Fight*, are executed on a much larger scale.

Her crafting skills and the other processes are especially expressive and include the red colouring which is based on a traditional Japanese treatment; the use of English lime and local mangrove timbers with their particular fine grain and textures; and the opalescence and lustre of the mother-of-pearl. These qualities and their associated working techniques result in alluring, sensuous works.

In addition, these selected forms, their juxtapositions, their characteristic colouring, the contrasting materials and other minute details — all correspond to a conceptual vocabulary which signals Truman's personal concerns and conceptual explorations. The boat, with its bellying hull, supporting ribs and inner fleshy-red painted surface, represents the corporeal body; while the fish is utilised as a metaphor for our inner emotional lives, particularly our mortality. Truman's work does not simply present scaled-down representations of lifeboats or fish, but presents them, through her crafterly and refined surface treatments, as sculptural objects imbued with rich imagery and narrative evocations that entice the viewer through intellectual and emotional levels.

Human experience, our relationship to the natural world, our aspirations and our imagination, all may be mirrored or expressed by the works of the wood practitioner who shapes the medium according to the forces imbued in the past and still active in the present. Wood is pre-eminent in its ability to convey broader historical, or social issues, or else express more personal psychological tensions, narratives or concerns.

PLATE 158 (opposite)
Catherine Truman (b. 1957)
Piecemeal, 1992
Carved English lime wood,
Shu Niku ink, mother-of-pearl, paint
Boat: 20 x 6 x 3 cm
Photo: Grant Hancock

BIOGRAPHIES

BRETT ALEXANDER
East Maitland, New South Wales
Born: Newcastle, Australia, 1963
Studied: University of Wollongong, MA (Creative), and University of Newcastle, Graduate Diploma (Art), B.Ed. (Art), 1990–91
Exhibitions: (Selected Solo) 'Crossing Borders: History Culture and Identity in Australian Contemporary Textile Art', touring USA, 1995–96; 'Survey of Men Artists of the Hunter Region', Maitland City Art Gallery, NSW; 'Discerning Textiles', Goulburn Regional Art Gallery; Tamworth National Fibre Exhibition, 1989 and 1990
Collections: Rajbhat Institute Suan Dusit Collection, Bangkok, Thailand; University of Wollongong Union Collection, Sydney

LIENORS ALLEN
Canberra, Australian Capital Territory
Born: Canberra, 1972
Studied: Institute of the Arts, Australian National University, BA (Visual) Hons (Glass and Computer Animation), 1992–95; Crystalex Glass Factory School, Novy Bor, Czechoslovakia (glass engraving), funded through Queen Elizabeth II Silver Jubilee Grant, 1991; Anne Dybka Glass Engraving Studio, The Rocks, Sydney, 1988
Related Experience: Pilchuck Glass School, Seattle, USA (Teaching Assistant), 1996; Ausglass Conference Workshops (Technical Assistant), 1993
Exhibitions: (Selected) 'Handle Like Eggs', Beaver Galleries, Canberra, 1995; 'Life/Drawing', Singapore, 1995; Ausglass Student Exhibition, Adelaide, 1995; Ausglass Student Exhibition, Canberra, 1993

SILVIO APPONYI
Adelaide, South Australia
Born: Munich, Germany, 1948; in Australia from 1950
Studied: North Adelaide School of Art, 1967–71; Munich School of Art after winning the German Academic Exchange Scholarship, 1972–73; Working as a sculptor full-time from 1987
Awards: Winner of the 'Alice Prize', Alice Springs, 1987; National Endangered Species Exhibition, 1992; Award of Merit; RAIA with Rick Bzowy, 1993; Prize Winner, Working with Wood Show, Melbourne, 1990–94
Exhibitions: Holdsworth Galleries, Sydney, 1986, 1988, 1992, 1995; (Festival Show, March) Greenhill Galleries, SA, 1986, 1988, 1994, 1996; Greenhill Galleries, Perth, 1989; Flinders University Art Museum, SA, 1990; Beaver Galleries, Canberra, 1991; 'Framed', Darwin, 1991, 1993, 1995; Okayama Japan, Kongoso, Takeshi-Maya, 1993, 1994, 1995; The Mall Galleries, London, 1991
Collections: Flinders University, SA; Adelaide University, SA; Port Adelaide TAFE; State Bank; Tamworth City Park; Healesville Sanctuary; Adelaide Zoo

ROBERT BAINES
Melbourne, Victoria
Born: Melbourne, 1949
Studied: RMIT, Diploma of Gold and Silversmithing, 1969
Related Experience: Established Studio, 1973; Commenced as Lecturer in Goldsmithing, RMIT, 1980; Study of Etruscan and Nineteenth Century Revival Goldwork, Rome, London, Berlin, 1985 and 1991; Study of Ancient Goldwork, John Paul Getty Museum, LA, 1986; Editor *Lemel* Journal for Jewellers and Metalsmiths in Australia
Awards: (Selected) L Puzsar Award, RMIT, 1970; Winston Churchill Fellowship, 1979; Australia Council for the Arts Fellowship Grant, 1992
Exhibitions: Ten solo and over twenty group shows.
Collections: Represented in a number of major public collections in Australia including: National Gallery of Australia, Canberra; Victorian State Craft Collection, Melbourne, and overseas

RODERICK BAMFORD
Sydney, New South Wales
Born: Sydney, 1958
Studied: East Sydney Technical College, Ceramics Certificate
Related Experience: Artist-in-residence, John Michael Kohler Arts Industry Program, USA; (Other residencies include): International East/West symposium, University of Hawaii, USA, 1995; Ipswich Regional Art Gallery, Artist in residence, Place/Product, 1994; Australia Council Studio, Greene St New York, USA, 1993; Lecturing at various institutions; President, Craft Council, 1992–94

Awards: Newcastle Art Gallery Ceramic Purchase Award, 1995; Elected Member of the International Academy of Ceramics, Fletcher Challenge Ceramic Award, Commendation, 1994; VACB International Studio Award, 1993; National Ceramic Award, (Mayfair) Melbourne, 1987; Caltex Ceramic Award, Queensland; Purchase Award, Clay Statements Award Exhibition, Queensland, 1986; Purchase Award, Ballarat Fine Art Gallery
Exhibitions: (Solo) Greene St Studio, New York, USA, 1993; Roslyn Oxley Gallery 9, Sydney, 1986, 1989; Shepparton Regional Art Gallery, Victoria, 1985; (Group Exhibitions) Australian Ceramics, Museo Internazionale, Faenza, Italy, 1995; Ipswich Regional Gallery, Queensland, 1994; AETA Touring Exhibition, Montevideo, Sao Paulo, Santiago, 1994
Collections: Represented in major public collections in Australia and overseas, including major regional public collections in Australia

CLARE BELFRAGE
Perth, Western Australia
Born: Melbourne, 1966
Studied: Graduated from Chisolm Institute of Technology (now Monash University) with BA Ceramic Design (Hot Glass Major); Completed traineeship in glass at the Jam Factory Craft and Design Centre, Adelaide; (Related Experience) Associate Lecturer, School of Art, Curtin University, WA; Established Hot Glass Facility; Vice-President, Ausglass
Awards: (Include) Northern Territory Craft Acquisition Award and an Individual Project Grant from the Department for Arts and Cultural Heritage, SA
Exhibitions: Participated in numerous exhibitions throughout Australia including Perth Craft Award at Craftwest Gallery, WA; Alice Craft Acquisition, Alice Springs, NT; Jam Factory Craft and Design Centre Twenty-first Birthday, Adelaide; ACI Glass Award Collectors Exhibition, Meat Market Craft Centre, Melbourne; (Solo) Jam Factory Craft and Design Centre, Adelaide, 1993
Collections: (Include) Northern Territory Museum; Curtin University of Technology; City of Footscray Collection

STEPHEN BENWELL
Melbourne, Victoria
Born: Melbourne, 1953
Education: Victorian College of the Arts, Diploma of Art, 1971–74
Related Experience: Studied in USA and Mexico; Resident in Cité des Arts, Paris, 1984–85; Tutor in Ceramics, Preston Institute, Melbourne, 1978–79
Awards: (Selected) Fletcher Challenge, Judges Commendation, 1995; Bathurst Art Purchase Award, 1995; Sydney Meyer Award, 1995, 1994; Fellowship, Australia Council, 1993; Sydney Meyer Award, 1992; Mayfair Ceramic Award, 1980
Exhibitions: Twenty-one solo and over fifteen group exhibitions
Collections: Represented in major public collections in Australia and overseas, including major regional public collections in Australia

GILLES BETTISON
Canberra, Australian Capital Territory
Born: Canberra, 1966
Studied: Institute of the Arts, ANU, BA (Visual), 1995
Related Experience: Participant in Alessi Design Workshop, University of NSW, 1995; Technical Assistant for Bullseye Glass Workshops, Glass Studio, Canberra School of Arts; Participant in Dick Marquis Workshop, Canberra School of Arts
Awards: Finalist, Resource Finance Corporation Glass Prize
Selected Exhibitions: Bullseye 'Latitudes', Craft Space Gallery, Sydney, 1995; Ausglass Student Exhibition, University of SA

PATRICIA BLACK
Sydney, New South Wales
Born: South Australia, 1956
Studied: University of Adelaide, BA, Dip. Ed.
Related Experience: (Studio Workshops) International Shibori Symposium, Nagoya, Japan, 1993; 'New Tools, No Limits', Portland, Oregon, USA, 1995; Currently member of Steering Committee of World Shibori Network; Appointed on Board of TAFTA, 1992–95
Awards: Overall Design (NZ Wearable Art Awards), 1993; Winner Silk Section, 1994–95; Costume Commissions, Australian Museum, 1994–95; Powerhouse Museum, Sydney, 1995; (Public Collections)

International Shibori Society, Nagoya, Japan, 1993; Wearable Art Collection, LA, 1995; Studio Residency in Besozzo, Italy, VACB, 1996
Exhibitions: Newcastle Art Gallery, NSW, 1993; CCNSW Craftspace, Sydney, 1994; (Group Exhibitions) 'Contemporary Cloth', Craft Council ACT Gallery, 1995; 'Decoration and Diversity', CCNSW Craftspace, 1993; 'New Directions', OSAC, Portland, Oregon, 1995; 'Wearable Expressions', Palos Verdes Art Centre, LA, 1995

BENJAMIN BOOTH
Adelaide, South Australia
Born: Melbourne, 1969
Studied: North Adelaide School of Art, Diploma in Applied and Visual Arts, 1994
Related Experience: Technician to Ceramics Studio, Jam Factory Craft and Design Centre, Adelaide, 1994– present
Exhibitions: 'Beyond the Spiral Staircase', Jam Factory Craft and Design Centre, Adelaide, 1995; 'Groove Gallery', Crown and Sceptre Hotel, 1995; 'Myth Conception', Red Shed Gallery, 1995; 'Anim8', North Adelaide School of Art, 1994; 'Two Bens And A Dave', Carclew Youth Arts Centre, 1994

CLAUDIA BORELLA
Canberra, Australian Capital Territory
Born: Canberra, 1971
Studied: University of Canberra, Bachelor of Industrial Design, Final Year completed at European Institute of Design, Milan, Italy, 1989–93; Institute of the Arts, ANU, BA (Visual), First Class Hons, Major in Glass, 1992–95
Related Experience: Technical Assistant to Yumiko Noda, Institute of the Arts, ANU, 1994
Awards: Institute of the Arts Acquisition Award
Selected Exhibitions: 'Handle Like Eggs', Beaver Galleries, Canberra, 1995; 'Finish', Drill Hall Gallery, Canberra; 'Ideas to Function', Goulburn Regional Art Gallery, Goulburn, NSW; 'Ausglass Student Exhibition', Adelaide, SA; 'Compatibles', David Jones, Sydney and Canberra; 'Sunday Brunch', David Jones, Canberra, 1993
Public Collections: Institute of the Arts, ANU

RACHEL BOWAK
Canberra, Australian Capital Territory
Born: Perth, 1964
Studied: Canberra Institute of the Arts, ANU, BA in Gold and Silversmithing, 1993
Related Experience: Chicago Institute of the Arts Oxbow summer school Direct Metal Technique and Hollow Forming, 1994; Iron Corroboree, Blacksmithing Workshop, Braidwood, NSW, 1995; (Teaching) Enmore Technical College, CIT, Sydney, NSW Jewellery and Object, Design. Blacksmithing and Design Concepts, 1995; Canberra Institute of Technology (CIT), ACT, Design Studies Workshop Leader, 1995; ACT Education Department, Pilot Program for the Integration of the Arts and Technology in High schools, 1994; Canberra Institute of the Arts, Sculpture Workshop, Basic Blacksmithing Techniques, 1994
Awards: ACT Arts and Special Events, Individual Artist Grant, 1995
Exhibitions: (Mixed/Selected) 'International Women's Day', ANCA Gallery, Dickson, ACT, 1995; 'A Show of Hands', ANCA Gallery, Dickson, ACT, 1994; 'Passionate Obsessions', Craft Council Gallery, Watson, ACT, 1994; 'Roar', Double Bay, Sydney, 1994; 'Rustique', Fire Station Gallery, Sydney, 1994; 'Unanimous', ANCA Gallery, Dickson, ACT, 1993; (Solo) 'Intertwangled', Institute of the Arts, ANU, ACT Collections, 1993; 'Circle', Mr and Mrs Martin, 1994; 'Intertwangled 3', Buyer Unknown, 1994; 'Intertwangled 2', Jamie McCaddum, 1993; 'Intertwangled 4', Ruth Allen, 1994

STEPHEN BOWERS
Adelaide, South Australia
Born: Katoomba, NSW, 1952
Education: Trainee, Jam Factory Ceramics Workshop, Adelaide, 1982
Related Experience: Principle Designer, Jam Factory Ceramics Workshop, Adelaide
Awards: British Council Sponsored Study Tour in UK, 1995; Tenth National Ceramic Award, Gold Coast, Museum and Galleries National Acquisition Award, Darwin, 1991; SA Ceramic Inglewood

Award, 1990; Museum and Galleries National Acquisition Award, Darwin, 1986

Exhibitions: Exhibited widely in over forty group, award and survey shows in Australia and overseas

Collections: Represented in over twenty-five public and private collections in Australia and overseas, including all major state and regional public collections in Australia

JANINE BOYD
Adelaide, South Australia
Born: Melbourne, 1965
Studied: Underdale Collage of Advanced Education, (now the University of South Australia), B.Ed. Art Teaching, (Fibre/Textile Major)
Related Experience: Teaching art and fibre to Senior Students 1986–90; Specialising in art and fibre to Junior School Students, 1990– present; Continued to develop own style of free machine embroidery since graduating; Attended Surface Design Symposium in Columbus, Ohio, USA, 1991; Worked with Richard Daehnert
Awards: Highly commended, 1993, 1995; First Prize for 'Quilt for Helen', 1995
Exhibitions: National Embroidery Exhibition: Dame Nancy Buttfield 1991, 1993, 1995

CHERY BRIDGART
Adelaide, South Australia
Born: Adelaide, 1956
Studied: Adelaide College of Arts and Education; South Australian School of Art; Torrens College of Advanced Education
Related Experience: Taught Secondary Art for a number of years including Adult Education, specialising in Fibre and Textiles; Full–time Artist from 1988
Awards: Winner of Dreamtime '96, National Billy Can Art Competition
Exhibitions: (Selected Solo) Stafford Studio of Fine Art, Perth, 1991; Textile Gallery, Aldgate, SA, 1988; (Selected Mixed) 'Art to Wear', Sydney, 1995 and 1994; 'Noah's Art', Adelaide, 1995 and 1993; 'Surrealism', Art Gallery of SA, (Satellite Shop with Crafts Council of SA), 1993; Dame Nancy Buttfield Embroidery Prize, 1993 and 1991; CSA Gallery, Christchurch, NZ, 1990
Collections: Himeji, Japan; Plescher & Palmer Inc, USA; Elna Australia

ROGER BUDDLE
Victor Harbor, South Australia
Born: Adelaide, 1940
Studied: University of South Australia, Bachelor of Design, (Ceramics and Glass)
Related Experience: Part-time Flat Glass Design, 1982–89; Full-time Flat Glass Design, 1989–91; Full-time study, University of SA, Bachelor of Design, 1991–94; Working from own studio, 1995
Awards: Professional Encouragement Award, Design Institute of Australia, 1995; Certificate of Achievement, University of SA, Alumni Association
Exhibitions: (Selected) 'Gerry King & Graduates', Brisbane, Sydney, Wagga Wagga, 1996; 'Fragments of a Journey', Bethany Art Gallery, Angaston, SA; 'Compositions', Studio 20, Adelaide, 1995; Ausglass Selected Members Exhibition, Jam Factory Craft and Design Centre, Adelaide; Helpmann Academy Exhibition, Adelaide; 'Not Just One of a Kind', Glass Artist's Gallery, Sydney; Graduate Exhibition, Adelaide Central Gallery, 1994; 'Serves You Right', Studio 20, Adelaide; 'Designing Ways', Studio 20, Adelaide, 1993; Ausglass Student Exhibition, Canberra

PIERRE CAVALAN
Sydney, New South Wales
Born: Paris, France, 1954; arrived Australia, 1974
Studied: National Jewellery School, Paris
Related Experience: Worked for Sydney Jeweller Russel McColough
Exhibitions: (Selected Solo) Tin Sheds Gallery, Sydney, 1991; Blaxland Gallery, Sydney, 1992; Jam Factory Craft and Design Centre, Adelaide, 1994; Helen Drutt Gallery, Philadelphia, USA, 1995; (Selected Group Exhibitions) Artists for Peace, Mori Gallery, Sydney, 1985; Adelaide Festival Centre, 1990; Art of the Metropolis, NGA, 1991; First Australian Contemporary Jewellery Biennale; Contemporary Jewellery 1964–93, Arkansas Art Museum, USA, 1993; Schumuckszene '93; Munich, Germany; 'SOFA' '94 Chicago, USA, 1994; Jakarta National Museum, Indonesia
Awards: '91 Australia Council Project Grant; West Australian Neckworks Award, 1992; Australia Council Residency Grant, Los Angeles, 1994; National Contemporary Jewellery Award, Griffith
Collections: National Gallery of Art, Canberra; Powerhouse

Museum, Sydney; Art Gallery of South Australia, Adelaide; Northern Territory Museum of Arts and Sciences, Darwin; Griffith Regional Art Gallery; Wollongong City Gallery; Toowoomba Regional Art Gallery; Craft Council of the Northern Territory; Alice Springs Collection; Art Bank, Sydney

HEJA CHONG
Cottlesbridge, Victoria
Born: Japan, 1950; in Australia from 1975
Studied: BA (Ceramic Design), Monash University Caulfield Campus; Studied Bizen pottery under Master Yu Fujiwara for one year, 1982; Project Grant, Craft Board Australia Council; Wood firing in the Bizen style for ten years
Awards: Sydney Meyer Ceramic Acquisition Award, 1992; Shepparton Regional Art Gallery, Acquisition Joint Winner, 1992; Stanthorpe Arts Gallery, NSW, Heritage Arts Festival Acquisition Award
Exhibitions: Ten solo and over eighteen group exhibitions
Collections: Represented in public institutions and many private collections in Australia and overseas

RICHARD CLEMENTS
Tasmania
Born: London, 1950; in Australia from 1971
Studied: Apprenticed in glass, 1966–71
Awards: First Prize, Craft Awards, Canberra, 1979; First Prize, Craft Awards, Adelaide, 1980
Selected Exhibitions: Various solo and group exhibitions in Australia and overseas
Collections: Represented in various collections including: Queen Victoria Museum and Art Gallery, Launceston; Tasmanian Museum and Art Gallery, Hobart; Art Gallery of South Australia, Adelaide; National Gallery of Victoria, Melbourne; Powerhouse Museum, Sydney; National Art Glass Collection, Wagga Wagga

GREG COLLINS
Margaret River, Western Australia
Born: Perth, 1952
Studied: Self-taught
Related Experience: Churchill Fellowship, Design Study Tour in USA and Canada, 1990
Awards: Fellow of the Crafts Council of WA, 1994; City of Perth Award, 1990
Selected Exhibitions: Various solo and group exhibitions
Collections: Art Bank, Canberra; Art Gallery of Western Australia, Perth; Bank of Zurich, London; Parliament House, ACT; Edith Cowan University

DEBORAH COCKS
Brays Creek, New South Wales
Born: Sydney, 1958
Studied: Australian National University, Sydney College of the Arts
Related Experience: Pilchuck Glass School, Seattle, USA, Hot Glass, 1987; Engraving 1988
Awards: ACI Glass Award, 1993; RFC Prize, 1995
Exhibitions: (Solo) Glass Artist's Gallery, 1987, 1989 and 1994; Blaxland Gallery, 1992; Origins and Originality, ANG Drill Hall, 1993; Australian Contemporary Glass Show, Japan, 1994; Glass Artist's Gallery at 'SOFA' Chicago; (Solo) Distelfink, 1995; Vic Health National Craft Award, National Gallery of Victoria
Collections: Corning Museum of Glass; Art Gallery of Western Australia, Perth; Museum of Applied Arts and Sciences; Queensland Art Gallery, Brisbane; Wagga Wagga City Art Gallery; Tweed River Regional Art Gallery

SUSAN COHN
Melbourne, Victoria
Born: Sydney, 1952
Studied: RMIT, Graduate Diploma of Fine Art, Gold and Silversmithing, 1986; Diploma of Art, Gold and Silversmithing, 1980
Related Experience: Enrolled in Doctor of Philosophy, University of NSW, 1996; Founding Director of Workshop 3000, 1980–95; Craft Victoria Board Member, 1993–95; President, 1995
Awards: Fellowship Grant, VACB Australia Council, 1994–95
Exhibitions: (Selected Solo) 'Reflections', Anna Schwartz Gallery, Melbourne, 1995; 'Way Past Real', 1994; 'Cosmetic Manipulations', 1992; (Selected Group Exhibitions) 'Symmetry', National Tour, 1994–95; 'Australia Gold', Asia Tour, 1994–93
Collections: Represented in all major Australian public gallery collections

PETER COOMBS
Adelaide, South Australia
Born: Adelaide, 1965
Studied: South Australian College of Advanced Education, Underdale, Bachelor of Design (Jewellery and Metalsmithing), 1986
Awards: International Spectacle Design Awards, Japan, 1993; Grand Prix Winner, Proposal Design; Special Jury Award Winner, Completed Design; CLIO International Awards and Expo Silver Award Winner Tucker Design, 1995
Exhibitions: (Solo) 'Eyes on It', Spectacles and Jewellery, Makers Mark Gallery, Melbourne, 1990; With Stephen Moore, Makers Mark Gallery, Melbourne and Sydney and Jam Factory Craft and Design Centre, Adelaide, 1995; 'Face It' and 'Framed' Group Spectacle, Los Angeles, 1988; 'Eyeworks', LA; Eve France Gallery, Houston, USA; 'The Eyes Have It — History of Eyewear', Pine Lobby Gallery, San Francisco, USA, 1989; 'International Spectacle Awards Exhibition', Tokyo, Japan, 1993
Collections: Eyeworks, Los Angeles, USA; Powerhouse Museum, Sydney; Megane Kaikan, Fukui, Japan

MARTIN CORBIN
Adelaide, South Australia
Born: England, 1949; in Australia from 1973
Studied: York University, UK, BA (Biology), 1970; Travelled widely, 1970–80; Started Woodcarving in New Zealand, 1979; Self-taught
Awards: Project Grants from SA Department of the Arts, 1995, 1992; Professional Development Grant VACB, 1991
Exhibitions: (Solo) Legge Gallery, Redfern, NSW, 1995; Distelfink Gallery, Hawthorn, Victoria; Bungendore Woodworks Gallery, Bungendore, NSW; Distelfink Gallery, Von Bertouch Gallery, Newcastle, 1992; Beaver Galleries, Canberra, 1990; Jam Factory Festival Exhibition, Adelaide plus eight others since 1983; (Group Exhibitions) Over sixty including: 'SOFA', Miami and Chicago, 1995; Symmetry, touring four states, Melbourne, 1994
Collections: Queensland Art Gallery, Brisbane; Powerhouse Museum, Sydney; Alice Craft Acquisition, Art Bank; Art Gallery of South Australia, Adelaide; National Gallery of Victoria, Melbourne; University of Canberra; Museum and Art Gallery of Northern Territory, Darwin

PAUL COUNSEL
Mount Hawthorn, Western Australia
Born: Tasmania, 1953
Studied: Monash University College Gippsland, Graduate Diploma (Visual Arts), 1985; University of Tasmania, Master of Fine Art, 1987; Wollongong University, Doctor of Creative Arts, 1990
Awards: Special Projects Grant, Department for the Arts, WA, 1994; AMP Artist of the Year, WA, 1994; Edith Cowan University Research Development Award, 1994; Fellow of the Craft Council of Western Australia, 1995
Exhibitions: 'Possessed', Festival of Perth, WA, 1993; 'Remembrancing', Festival of Perth, WA, 1994; Sydney Myer Fund, Australia Day Invitational Ceramic Award, Shepparton, Victoria, 1994; Fourth Australian Contemporary Art Fair, Melbourne, 1994
Collections: Shepparton Art Gallery; Art Bank; Holmes a Court Collection; Ian Bernardt Collection; Max Watters Collection; University of Tasmania Collection; University of Wollongong Collection

JANE COWIE
Adelaide, South Australia
Born: Wollongong, 1962
Studied: Degree in Visual Arts (Glass and Sculpture), Sydney College of Arts, 1981–83; Glass Workshops, New Zealand and Melbourne, 1990; Pilchuck Glass School, Seattle, USA, 1993, 1994 and 1995
Related Experience: Assisted Maureen Cahill with kiln-formed glass, 1982; Travelled in UK, 1984–89; Assisted Glass Artist Ursula Huth, 1987; Assisted Itestyn Davies, 1988–89; Trainee, Jam Factory Craft and Design Centre, Adelaide, 1989–90; Self-employed glassblower, Jam Factory Craft and Design Centre, Adelaide, 1990; Travelled in Japan, 1991; Established own glass studio, 1992–95; Studio tenant, Jam Factory Craft and Design Centre, Adelaide tenant, 1995–96
Awards: ANZ Glass Prize, Highly Recommended, 1981; Hot Glass Achievement Award, Sydney; Department of Arts, SA Grant, 1995
Exhibitions: Various group and solo exhibitions in Australia and overseas
Collections: Marcel Heider Collection, Switzerland; Diamond Valley Art Acquisition, Victoria; Alice Springs Crafts Acquisition

SARAH CROWEST
Adelaide, South Australia
Born: Kent, England, 1957; in Australia from 1985
Studied: Medway College of Design, Kent, and Middlesex Polytechnic, London
Related Experience: Freelance textile design; Established design and print studios in London (Con-tex), Sydney (Alchemy), Adelaide (Jam Factory Craft and Design Centre, Adelaide and Hackle and Cackle Design Studio)
Awards: Australia Council Professional Development Grant, 1994; Department for the Arts and Cultural Development, SA Grants, 1989 and 1992
Exhibitions: (Solo Exhibitions) 'Love, Sex and Death', Craft Victoria Gallery, Melbourne, 1994–95; Jam Factory Craft and Design Centre, Adelaide; SA Touring Exhibition; Media Com, Okayama, Japan, 1993; Works on Cloth, Jam Factory Craft and Design Centre, Adelaide; (Selected Group Exhibitions) Numerous between 1983 and 1995
Collections: Ararat Gallery; Queensland Art Gallery, Brisbane; Alice Craft Acquisition Collection; Stanthorpe Art Gallery, Queensland; Powerhouse Museum, Sydney; Diamond Valley Art Collection, Victoria ; Northern Territory Museum of Arts and Sciences; Art Bank, Sydney

CINDY SOUTH CZABANIA
Adelaide, South Australia
Born: Adelaide, 1961
Studied: Kensington Park College of TAFE, SA, Commercial Art, 1977; Associate Diploma in Art, North Adelaide School of Art, 1988
Related Experience: Studio at Jam Factory Workshops, St Peters, SA; Art Circus, Norwood, SA, 1991–94; Joseph Krofta, Puppetry Workshop, Adelaide, 1995
Awards: SA Department for the Arts and Cultural Development, Project Grant, 1995
Exhibitions: (Solo) 'Puppets', Adelaide Festival Centre, 1995; 'Scatterlings', Old Bakery Gallery, Lane Cove, Sydney; Miss Mabel's Cottage, Burra, SA, 1992; (Group Exhibitions) Stangate House, Aldgate, SA, 1995; Studio 20, Blackwood, SA; 'Come Out', Adelaide, 1993; Blue Expressions Gallery, Semaphore, 1992; 'Artisans, Actors, Minstrels and Fools', Bullring Gallery, Jam Factory Craft and Design Centre, Adelaide, 1988

PAT DAVIDSON
Eleebana, New South Wales
Born: Sale, 1950
Studied: Newcastle Art School; Initially produced sculptural off-loom pieces, gradually moving through loom work to other creative textile techniques and dyeing. Currently using cyanotype, appliqué and creative machine embroidery
Related Experience: Selected workshops with Jutta Fedderson, Annemieke Mein, Mary Beeston; Studies in dyeing, handweaving and airbrushing
Exhibitions: (Selected) 'Experiments', Auswool Gallery, Newcastle, 1988; Lake Macquarie City Council Foyer, 1992; Dame Nancy Buttfield Embroidery Prize Exhibition, 1993 and 1995; Creative Embroiderers Twentieth Birthday Exhibition, Woolloomooloo Gallery, 1993
Collections: The Elinor Wroebel Collection; Lake Macquary City Council

RICHARD DOHENY
Melbourne, Victoria
Born: United Kingdom, 1966
Studied: University of South Australia, BA Design (Ceramics), 1990
Awards: EVA, SA, 1995; TTG, SA, 1993; Walker Ceramic Award, Victoria, 1990; Inglewood Ceramic Award, SA; Jam Factory Craft and Design Centre, Adelaide, 1991
Exhibitions: Various group and solo exhibitions in Melbourne, Sydney and Adelaide

MARK DOUGLASS
Melbourne, Victoria
Born: Ballarat, 1964
Studied: Monash University, Victoria, (formerly Chisholm Institute), BA Hons (Ceramic Design), Hot Glass Major, 1986
Related Experience: Worked as part-time Art Technician at Wesley College, Prahran, 1987; Established Whitehall Enterprizes with five other artists, specialising in hot glass and forged steel objects and furniture, 1988; Relocated work space to 91 Moreland Street, Footscray to set up extensive production facilities for glass and steel, 1990
Exhibitions: (Selected) 'La Boutique Fantastic', Adelaide Festival,

1990; Group Exhibition, Tasmania, 1991; Ipswich Council Commissioned Works Exhibition, Queensland, 1992; (Solo) Mark Douglass Design, 1993; Mock Baroque Exhibition, Contemporary Art Services Tasmania (CAST), 1994; Dual Exhibition, Mark Douglass Design Showroom, Various Art Glass Pieces in conjunction with painter Peter Walsh, 1994; (Solo Exhibition) Recent Works, Art House Gallery, NSW, 1995; Recent Works, Mark Douglass Design Gallery, Victoria, 1995; Numerous commissions and interiors
Collections: Footscray Council Glass Collection; St Kilda Council; Caulfield Council; BP Collection

CHARLOTTE DRAKE-BROCKMAN
Murrurundi, New South Wales
Born: UK, 1933; in Australia from 1964
Studied: Farnham School of Art, UK, University of Newcastle, Newcastle upon Tyne
Related Experience: Tutored basketry summer schools in Australia and overseas; Member of the board of Textile Fibre Forum; Artist-in-residence, Canberra School of Art
Awards: Projects grant, VACB, 1987
Exhibitions: Numerous
Collections: Powerhouse Museum, Sydney; Max Watters Collection, Muswellbrook; Sergeant Gallery, Wanganui, New Zealand

PIPPIN DRYSDALE
Perth, Western Australia
Born: Melbourne, 1943
Studied: Anderson Ranch, Colorado, USA; Curtin University, WA, BA Arts
Related Experience: Designer, Deruta Grazia Fabbrica, Perugia, Italy; Union Moscow Artists Invitation, Siberia; Lecture Tour, USA; Residency, Banff Center for the Arts, Calgary, Canada
Awards: Three creative development grants Visual Arts/Crafts Board since 1987
Exhibitions: (Selected) Eighteen solo throughout Australia and represented by Distelfink Galleries, Victoria, between 1986 and 1995; Narek Galleries, Canberra; Perth Galleries, WA; Manly City Art Gallery and Museum, NSW; Participated in selected exhibitions both nationally and internationally including CINAFE '93, Chicago; International Trade Fair in Surabaya, Indonesia; Singapore International Art Fair and the Fourth Australian Contemporary Art Fair in Melbourne; 'Delinquent Angel', Faenza, Italy, 1985–95
Collections: Represented in most major collections in Australia and overseas

ANNE DYBKA
Sydney, New South Wales
Born: England, 1921; in Australia from 1956
Studied: Drawing and painting under Martin Bloch; London Polytechnic, London, Fine Art
Related Experience: Artist and designer at Old Chelsea China and Glass which first stimulated her interest in glass; Established Bohemian Glass in Melbourne; Further life drawing and painting studies with Melbourne artist George Bell and the National Gallery Art School; Sydney Artist and Designer at Crown Corning, 1960s; Dybka Tichy Studios, 1970; Opened present studio, The Rocks, Sydney, 1973
Awards: Fellow of Guild of Glass Engravers in London; Australia Council Emeritus Award, 1995
Exhibitions: Numerous solo and group exhibitions in Australia and UK
Collections: State Gallery of Victoria, Melbourne; Powerhouse Museum, Sydney; State Gallery of Queensland, Brisbane; Wagga Wagga City Art Gallery; Ebeltoft Glass Museum, Denmark

TONY DYER
Moonie Ponds, Victoria
Born: Traralgon, Victoria, 1942
Studied: Melbourne Teachers College, 1961–63; RMIT, 1964–70
Related Experience: Workshops, lectures and exhibitions in Darwin, Tasmania and Malaysia; Participant, International Symposium in Canberra, 1988
Awards: Non-Functional Textiles, Mornington Peninsula Craft Event, 1992 and 1993
Exhibitions: Seventeen major and seventy group; (Solo) Art Works Gallery, Nungurner, Victoria, 1993; Saarkylien Koulu, Kangasala, Finland, 1991; (Group) 'Diversity', Studio Art Quilt Associates, Gatlinburg, Tennessee, USA, 1995; 'Directions — Contemporary Cloth', Crafts Council of the ACT, Canberra
Collections: (Selected Collections) Victorian State Craft Collection,

Melbourne; Queensland Art Gallery, Brisbane; Art Gallery of Western Australia, Perth; Art Bank; Powerhouse Museum, Sydney; Queen Victoria Museum and Art Gallery, Launceston; Museum and Art Gallery of Northern Territory, Darwin

BENJAMIN EDOLS
Sydney, New South Wales
Born: Sydney, 1967
Studied: Sydney College of Art, BA (Visual), 1991; Canberra School of Art, Post-graduate Diploma of Art, 1992
Related Experience: Teaching in Glass Workshop, Jam Factory Craft and Design Centre, Adelaide, 1995; Visit to Murano, Venice, 1994; Assistant to Richard Marquis and Dante Marioni, 1994, 1993; Assistant to Lino Tagliapietra; Practitioner, New York Experimental Glass Workshop, 1992; Numerous workshops in Pilchuck and elsewhere in USA
Awards: (Selected) Australia Council grants, 1995, 1994; Pilchuck Glass School Scholarship, 1995, 1990; Fellowship, Creative Glass Center of America, 1993
Exhibitions: (Selected) Pilchuck Glass Exhibition, Tacoma, 1995; 'Latitudes', The Bullseye Connection, Portland, USA; Glass Weekend, '95, Habatat Gallery; Creative Glass Center of America; 'SOFA', Chicago; Tenth Capitol Invitational, Glass Artist's Gallery, Chicago, 1994; Sixth Australian Glass Triennial, Wagga Wagga; Ben Edols and Kathy Elliott, de Vera Gallery, San Francisco, USA, 1993
Collections: National Art Gallery of Australia, Canberra; Queensland Art Gallery, Brisbane; American Glass Museum, Milville, USA; National Art Glass Collection, Wagga Wagga City Art Gallery; Art Gallery of South Australia, Adelaide

KATHY ELLIOTT
Sydney, New South Wales
Born: Sydney, 1964
Studied: 1991, Canberra School of Art, BA (Visual), 1991
Related Experience: Visiting Artist, Canberra School of Art, Glass Workshop, 1994; Technical Work, Cold Shop, New York Experimental Glass Workshop, 1993; Practitioner, New York Experimental Glass Workshop, 1992; Workshops in Pilchuck and New York Experimental Glass Workshop, 1992, 1994, 1995; Practitioner, Studio Access, Corning, New York, 1992
Awards: (Selected) Australia Council grants, 1995, 1994; 1995, Pilchuck Glass School Scholarship; Fellowship, Creative Glass Center of America, 1993; First Prize, 'Glass: Challenging the Medium', Competitive Exhibition
Exhibitions: (Selected) 'Latitudes', ACT, Crafts Council, 1996; Pilchuck Glass Exhibition, Tacoma, 1995; 'Latitudes', The Bullseye Connection, Portland, USA; Glass Weekend, '95, Habatat Gallery, Creative Glass Center of America; 'SOFA', Chicago; Resource Finance Corporation Prize, Finalist, Glass Artist's Gallery, Sydney; Tenth Capitol Invitational, Glass Artist's Gallery Chicago, 1994; Sixth Australian Glass Triennial, Wagga Wagga; Ben Edols and Kathy Elliott, de Vera Gallery, San Francisco, USA, 1993
Collections: National Gallery of Australia, Canberra; Corning Museum of Glass, New York; Queensland Art Gallery Brisbane; American Glass Museum, Milville, USA; National Art Glass Collection, Wagga Wagga City Art Gallery; Art Gallery of South Australia, Adelaide

BRIGITTE ENDERS
Canberra, Australian Capital Territory
Born: Offenbach, Germany, 1949; in Australia from 1985
Studied: Canberra School of Art, Graduate Diploma of Art, 1994; Canberra University, Industrial Design, 1988; Academy of Fine Arts, Hamburg, Degree in Industrial Design, 1980; School for Ceramic Design, Hoehr-Grennzenhausen, Germany, 1971–72; Academy of Fine Arts, Germany, 1969–70
Collections: Sammlunggen Der Veste, Coburg; Keramion Frechen; Westerwald Museum, Hoehr-Grennzenhausen, Germany; Emsland Museum; Kulturgeschichtkiches Museum; Museum Fuer Moderne Keramik; Sammlung Dr Hans Thiemann, Hamburg; Art Gallery of Western Australia, Perth

LANCE FEENEY
Leichhardt, New South Wales
Born: Sydney, 1948
Education: West Glamorgan Institute of Higher Education, Swansea, UK, Diploma of Art, 1979
Related Experience: Member Royal Society Architectural and Individual Designers; Royal Guild Examinations; Paddy Robinson, NSW, 1974–76 and David Saunders, NSW, 1980–81; Second International Architectural Design Workshop with Jocham Poensgen, Germany, 1986; Patrick Reyntiens, USA, 1991;

Architectural Glass Design Workshop, Ausglass and other positions, 1991
Awards: VACB Grant, 1989; Finalist for Howard Martin design Award, 1980
Collections: Numerous private and public commissions

DONALD FORTESCUE
Adelaide, South Australia
Born: Sydney, 1957
Studied: University of Wollongong, Master of Creative Arts (Sculpture), 1993–95; Canberra School of Art, Associate Diploma Visual Arts (Design in Wood), 1986–87; University of New South Wales, Sydney, B.Sc. (Hons in Botany), 1975–79
Related Experience: Head of Furniture Design, Jam Factory Craft and Design Centre, Adelaide, 1994; Established the Decorative Arts Workshop furniture studio with Antoon Meerman and Diane Smith, 1990; Self-employed furniture designer-maker, 1988–94; Nineteen months travelling and working in Japan, 1982–83
Awards: Australia Council Residency, New York, 1995–96; Churchill Fellowship, Japan and UK, 1991; Craft Training Grant, VACB, 1988
Exhibitions: (Solo) Contemporary Art Space, Wollongong City Gallery; Distelfink Gallery, Melbourne, 1990; 'Full Circle', Narek Galleries, Cuppacumbalong, ACT, 1989; (Selected Group Shows) 'SOFA', Chicago, USA, 1994, 1995; Art of the Object, Craft Australia Touring South America; The Light Fantastic, Canberra, 1991–92
Collections: Wollongong City Gallery, NSW; Powerhouse Museum, Sydney; Library, AGSM, University of NSW, Sydney

ROBERT FOSTER
Canberra, Australian Capital Territory
Born: Kyneton, Victoria, 1962
Studied: Canberra Institute of the Arts, BA Gold and Silversmithing, 1980–84; Canberra Institute of the Arts Post-graduate Diploma, 1985
Related Experience: Established FINK! Design with Anthony King, 1994
Exhibitions: (Selected Solo) Studio Noko Sydney, 1991; The Bougainvillea Festival Exhibition Framed, The Darwin Gallery, Darwin, 1994; Victorian Health National Craft Award Exhibition, National Gallery of Victoria, 1992; 'The Eloquent Vessel' Foster, Bunke, Rowe; Museum Für Angewandte Kunst, Cologne, Germany, 1992; 'Christmas Exhibition', Museum Für Kunst und Gewerbe, Hamburg, 1992; Contemporary Hollow-ware, Hamilton Art Gallery, Hamilton, Victoria and Australia and International Tour, 1991–92; 'Splitting Heads', National Design Triennial, Tasmanian School of Art, 1991; 'Vessels', Remo, Sydney, 1990
Collections: Victorian State Craft Collection, Melbourne; National Gallery of Australia, Canberra; National Gallery of Victoria, Melbourne; Art Gallery of Western Australia, Perth; Art Gallery of South Australia, Adelaide; Powerhouse Museum, Sydney

MARI FUNAKI
Melbourne
Born: Matsue, Japan, 1950; in Australia from 1983
Studied: Kobe-Gakuin University, B.Sc. (Law), 1973; RMIT, BA (Painting), 1984; RMIT, BA Hons Gold and Silversmithing, 1993
Related Experience: Director, Gallery Funaki
Awards: (Selected) L Puzsar Award, RMIT, 1989, 1990; Innovative Design Award, Castlemaine, 1990; Mornington Peninsular Craft Event Award, 1990; Graduate Medal, JMGA, WA, 1992; Young Achievers Award, JMGA, Melbourne, 1995
Exhibitions: (Selected) Three solo and fifteen group shows since 1990, 'Featuring Women', New Collectables Gallery; Australian Contemporary Art Fair, Melbourne, 1994; City of Perth Invitational, 1994; Artists of WA, San Francisco, USA, 1990
Collections: National Gallery of Australia, Canberra; RMIT, Victoria

BEVERLEY GALLOP
Perth, Western Australia
Born: Perth, 1951
Studied: University of Western Australia, BA, 1971; University of Western Australia, Dip. Ed., 1972; Perth Technical College, Diploma Studio Ceramics, 1984–86
Awards: York Craft Award, 1995; City of Perth Craft Award, 1995; City of Wanneroo Craft Award, 1995; City of Perth Craft Award, 1992
Exhibitions: (Selected) 'Featuring Women', New Collectables Gallery, 1995; Australian Contemporary Art Fair, Melbourne, 1994; City of Perth Invitational, 1994; Artists of WA, San Francisco, USA, 1990

Collections: Art Gallery Western Australia, Perth; Edith Cowen University

MARION GAEMERS
Townsville, Queensland
Born: Sydney, 1958
Studied: BA (Visual); James Cook University, Graduate Diploma Material Anthropology
Exhibitions: (Various group and solo shows including): 'Nature/Nurture', Umbrella Studio, Townsville, 1996; 'Baskets and Beyond', North Queensland Potters Gallery, 1994

MICHAEL GILL
Evatt, Australian Capital Territory
Born: Sydney, 1953
Studied: East Sydney Technical College, Fine Art/Graphic Design
Related Experience: Director/Tutor, Red Cedar Workshops, Sydney, 1984–89; Visiting Lecturer and Artist-in-residence, Wood workshop, Canberra School of Art, 1988–93; Director of 'Happiest Boy in the World School', Teaching and demonstrating throughout Australia, 1995–96
Collections: New Parliament House, Canberra; Powerhouse Museum, Sydney; Dubbo Regional Art Gallery

ANDREW GITTOES
Goulburn, New South Wales
Born: Goulburn, New South Wales, 1959
Studied: Private and at Sturt Craft Workshop, Mittagong, 1982
Related Experience: Teaching and demonstrating throughout Australia since 1989 and in England in 1992; (Judge) Canberra Wood Guild Annual Exhibition, 1994; Bega Wood Group Annual Exhibition, 1993, 1994
Exhibitions: (Selected) World Woodturning Conference, France, 1995; Solo exhibition, Goulburn Regional Art Gallery, 1995; 'Vase of Flowers', Goulburn Regional Art Gallery, 1994; (Solo) Bungendore Woodworks, Bungendore, 1992; Teachers Exhibition, Sturt Craft Workshop, Mittagong, 1993

AGNIESZKA GOLDA
Adelaide, South Australia
Born: Krakow, Poland, 1969; in Australia from 1982
Studied: North Adelaide School of Art, Certificate in Art (Fabric Design), 1988 and Associate Diploma in Art (Fabric Design), 1989–90; RMIT, BA (Textile Design), 1991–93
Related Experience: Lecturer at the Fabric Design Department, North Adelaide School of Art; Established 'Threaded Limbs Studio' with Martin Johnson; Numerous commissions
Exhibitions: (Solo) Jam Factory Craft and Design Centre, Adelaide, 1996; BMGART Gallery, Adelaide 1995; North Adelaide School of Art, 1994; (Group): Adelaide Festival Centre, 'Home Is Where The Art Is II', 1994; Dozynki POL–ART Festival, Adelaide, 1994; South Gate Boulevard, Melbourne, 1993; David Jones Gallery, Melbourne; 1992, Malthouse Gallery, Melbourne, 1992; Adelaide Festival Centre, 'The Shirt Show', 1991; Chapel Hill Winery Gallery, Adelaide, 1990

ROWENA GOUGH
Sydney, New South Wales
Born: Maryborough, Victoria, 1958
Studied: RMIT, Diploma Art (Design), Gold and Silversmithing, 1978; Sydney College of the Arts, MA (Visual), 1988
Exhibitions: (Selected Solo) Rowena Gough, Fingers Gallery, Auckland, New Zealand, 1990; Fluxus Gallery, Dunedin, New Zealand; 'From the Heart', Contemporary Jewellery Gallery, Sydney, 1988; (Group): 'The Art of the Object. Contemporary Craft from Australia, Uruguay, Brazil, Chile', 1994–95; Subjects, International Jewellery, Helsinki, Finland, 1993; 'Four Australian Jewellers', National Gallery of Victoria, Melbourne, 1987
Awards: Fellowship, Visual Arts/Craft Board of the Australia Council, 1993
Collections: National Gallery of Australia, Canberra; Art Gallery of South Australia, Adelaide; Art Gallery of Western Australia, Perth; National Gallery of Victoria, Melbourne; Powerhouse Museum, Sydney

MIES GRYBAITIS
Melbourne, Victoria
Born: Australia, 1968
Studied: Canberra Institute of the Arts, BA Hons (Visual Arts), Major in Glass, Sub-major in Painting, 1990–93
Awards: ANU, EASS Collection Purchases Award, 1993; Scholarship, Technical Assistant to German artist Franz Hoeller
Exhibitions: (Selected) Glass in Australia, Meat Market Craft

Centre, Melbourne, 1995; Australian Glass — A Recent Review, Glass Artist Gallery; 'Out of Canberra', Jam Factory Craft and Design Centre, Adelaide, 1994; Interval, Graduate Exhibition, Canberra, 1993
Collections: Lyons Collection

WAYNE GUEST
Melbourne, Victoria
Born: Melbourne, 1956
Studied: RMIT, Diploma of Gold and Silversmithing, 1974–77
Related Experience: Design assistant with John Truscott, Victorian Arts Centre
Awards: Rusden Foundation Award in Silver Design and Craftsmanship, 1994
Exhibitions: Makers Mark Gallery, Melbourne, 1979, 1986, 1993; Over fifteen group shows
Collections: National Gallery of Australia, Canberra; Sale Regional Gallery, NSW; Art Gallery of Western Australia, Perth; Launceston Art Gallery, Tasmania

ALVENA HALL
Adelaide, South Australia
Born: Adelaide, 1941
Studied: South Australia School of Art, Flinders University, MA (Visual)
Related Experience: Full-time freelance textile artist since 1975; Community Arts; Artist-in-residence, Dame Nancy Buttfield Youth Awards, 1991, 1994; Regular columnist for *Textile* magazine
Exhibitions: (Numerous but include) 'Gentle Genes', 1982; 'The Babbage Textiles', 1994; 'Regeneration Series', 1984; 'Antikythera Instrument', 1986; 'Chaos Series', 1990; 'The Fragile Zone', Lake Eyre, 1992; 'Crossing Borders', touring USA, 1994–95; The Littoral Zone, 1995
Collections: University of South Australia, Adelaide, (Levels); Queen Victoria Museum, Launceston; CSIRO, Adelaide; Royal Adelaide Hospital

PATRICK HALL
Hobart, Tasmania
Born: Germany 1962 (of British parents); in Australia from 1970
Studied: Centre for the Arts, University of Tasmania, BA (Fine Arts), Design and Printmaking, 1983–86
Related Experience: Board of Directors, Designer-Makers Tasmania, Cooperative, 1985–91; Established, Phish Designs, 1988; Board Member, Visual Arts and Design Panel, Tasmania, 1994
Awards: TAAB, Art in Public Places, 1995, 1991, 1990
Exhibitions: Seven solo and over twenty-five group shows including Vic Health National Craft Awards, 1995
Collections: Powerhouse Museum, Sydney; Tasmanian Museum and Art Gallery

GEOFFREY HANNAH
Lismore, New South Wales
Born: Australia, 1948
Studied: Apprenticed as a cabinetmaker, 1963
Related Experience: Furniture study tour overseas, 1980; Tutor in restoration and marquetry
Awards: Churchill Fellowship, 1984; Traditional Section, First Prize, National Woodwork Exhibition
Exhibitions: Various shows
Collections: The Australiana Fund (residence of Australian Governor General)

TONY HANNING
Yinnar, Victoria
Born: Traralgon, Victoria, 1950
Studied: Monash University, Diploma Visual Arts, 1971–72; Studied UK and Europe, 1976; Studied glass in Seattle, USA with Paul Marioni, 1984; Currently doing MA
Related Experience: Director, La Trobe Valley Arts Centre, 1972–81; Partnership with Budgeree Glass, 1981; Teaching glass, Pilchuck Glass School, Seattle, USA, 1987
Awards: Australia Council Grant for overseas study, 1984
Exhibitions: Over fifteen solo and over twenty group shows
Collections: All major state art galleries and most regional galleries in Australia; Pilchuck Collection, USA; Powerhouse Museum, Sydney; Tasmanian Museum and Art Gallery

MATTHEW HARDING
O'Conner, Australian Capital Territory
Born: Sydney, 1964
Studied: CSA, Fourth year Hons, BA (Visual Arts), 1995; Hamilton TAFE, Art Certificate Course, Hons, 1984–85; Gold Licence Carpenter

and Joiner, 1984; Apprenticeship, Tighes Hill College TAFE
Related Experience: Research of 'Shona' Sculpture, Zimbabwe; Workshops, 1994
Awards: (Recent Selected) Bega Woodcraft Awards, First Prize, 1994; Australia Wood Design Awards; Timber and Working with Wood Show, First Prize, 1993
Exhibitions: Various solo and group shows; Numerous commissions
Collections: Art Bank, Sydney; University of Newcastle; Chinese Embassy; Vanuatu Parliament; Sydney International Airport

BETH HATTON
Sydney, New South Wales
Born: Canada, 1943; in Australia from 1976
Studied: College of Fine Arts, Sydney, Diploma in Professional Art Studies, 1982
Related Experience: Employed at *Craft Australia* working as researcher and writer since 1976 (with one four year break); President of the Australian Forum for the Textile Arts, 1992–94; Has written about craft for various Australian journals since 1976
Awards: Canada Council Explorations Grant, 1974; CCNSW Merit Award, 1979; Australia Council Grant, 1994; Australian Stockmen's Hall of Fame Outback Craft Award, Second Prize, Weaving, 1995
Exhibitions: One solo and numerous group shows in Australia, most recently 'Below the Surface' which is touring SA, Tas, Qld and NSW to September 1998; Has also exhibited in Japan and the USA
Collections: Art Gallery of Western Australia, Perth; Goulburn Regional Art Gallery; Museums and Galleries of the Northern Territory, Darwin; Powerhouse Museum, Sydney; Queensland Art Gallery, Brisbane

GAY HAWKES
Dunalley, Tasmania
Born: Tasmania, 1942
Studied: Tasmania, BA, 1960–62; Associate Diploma in Art and Craft, 1979–80
Related Experience: Assistant to National Woodworking School, 1981; Student, National Woodworking School, 1982; Studio work, 1982–83, 1989, 1990–94
Awards: Queen Elizabeth Arts Council Distinguished Visitor; Special Development Grant, VACB, 1988; Professional Development Grant VACB, 1982
Exhibitions: Numerous group and solo shows; Selected to represent Australia in International Sculpture Show, Norway, 1988
Collections: Represented in all major state art galleries in Australia; Kundindustrmusem, Norway

GREG HEALEY
Adelaide, South Australia
Born: Washington, 1963; Arrived Australia, 1964
Studied: Sydney College of the Arts, BA, and Post-graduate Diploma, 1984–87; Traineeship with Ray Norman, Sturt Metal, Mittagong, NSW, 1982–83
Related Experience: Private studio, Sydney, 1987–91; Part-time teaching jewellery and sculpture, Sydney College of the Arts
Awards: Project Grant, VACB, Australia Council, 1995; Workshop Development Grant, Australia Council, 1987; Trainee Grants, Australia Council, 1982–83
Exhibitions: 'SOFA', Chicago, USA, 1995; 'Design '95 — New Directions', Aptos Cruz Galleries, SA, 1995; 'SOFA', Chicago, USA, 1994; 'Furniture '94', Melbourne, Victoria, 1993; 'Love(ly) Things', First Draft West, Sydney, NSW and EAF, Adelaide, 1992; 'Jugend Gestalted', Munich, 1991; Numerous commissions, 1989–95
Collections: Art Gallery of Western Australia, Perth; Orange Regional Gallery, NSW; Sturt Collection, NSW

COLIN HEANEY
Byron Bay, New South Wales
Born: Vancouver, Canada, 1948; in Australia from 1967
Studied: Self-taught
Exhibitions: (Numerous shows including): 'SOFA', Chicago, USA, 1995; Distelfink Gallery, Melbourne; Myer Pacific Fair, Gold Coast, Queensland
Collections: Tweed River Regional Gallery; Queensland Art Gallery; Glass Museum, Majorca, Spain; Wagga Wagga City Art Gallery; EbeltoftGlasmuseum, Denmark; Corning Museum of Glass, New York

PATSY HELY
Lismore, New South Wales
Born: Sydney, 1946
Studied: East Sydney Technical College and Southern Cross University

Awards: Thirteenth National Gold Coast Ceramic Art Award, 1993
Exhibitions: 'Being with Objects', with Susan Ostling and Toni Warburton, curated by Helen Stephens, 1995; 'The Bowl', Savode Gallery, Brisbane; Newcastle Ceramic Purchase Award, Newcastle Region Art Gallery
Collections: Victoria and Albert Museum, London (small tapestry); Powerhouse Museum, Sydney; Parliament House Collection, Canberra; Art Gallery of Western Australia, Perth; Art Gallery of South Australia, Adelaide; Victorian State Craft Collection, Melbourne; Shepparton Art Gallery; Manly City Art Gallery and Museum, Sydney; Gold Coast City Art Gallery; Perc Tucker Art Museum; Rockhampton Regional Art Gallery; Bathurst Regional Art Gallery

BRIAN HIRST
Annandale, New South Wales
Born: Gippsland, Victoria, 1956
Studied: Gippsland Institute of Advanced Education, Diploma of Arts (Visual Arts),
Awards: (Selected) Grand Prize, Hokkaido Museum of Modern Art Prize, 'World Glass Now '94', Hokkaido Museum of Modern Art, Japan; Ausglass Award 'Appreciating the Medium', Glass Artist's Gallery, Sydney, 1991; 'Glass Australia '88', Conceptual Award, Meat Market Craft Centre, Melbourne
Exhibitions: (Selected Solo) Glass Now 17, Tokyo, Japan, 1995; Glass by Brian Hirst, Gippsland Regional Art Centre, 1994; Blaxland Gallery, Sydney; (International Selected) CGCA Whateon Village with The Glass Gallery, 1995; 'SOFA', '94, USA, 1994; World Glass Now '94, Hokkaido Museum of Modern Art, Japan; The Glass Gallery, Bethesda, USA, 1990
Collections: National Gallery of Australia, Canberra; Victorian State Craft Collection, Melbourne; Queensland Art Gallery, Brisbane; Powerhouse Museum, Sydney; Corning Museum of Glass, USA; Museum of Modern Art, Japan; Ebeltoft Glasmuseum, Denmark; Kunstmuseum, Dusseldorf

FIONA HISCOCK
Melbourne, Victoria
Born: Australia, 1965
Studied: Melbourne University, BA, 1984–86; BA in Fine Arts (Ceramics), 1987–91; RMIT, Post-graduate, Fine Arts (Ceramics), 1992–93
Awards: Walker Ceramics prize for Excellence, RMIT, 1991; National Gallery Society of Victoria Award, 1991
Exhibitions: Fifteen group exhibitions, 1990–95

STEPHEN HUGHES
Aspendale Gardens, Victoria
Born: Melbourne, 1958
Studied: Melbourne State College; B.Ed. Arts and Crafts, 1977–80
Related Experience: Full-time secondary teacher of art and design subjects, Victoria, 1981–95
Awards: Acquisition Award, Shire of Eltham, Victoria, 1988; Acquisition, Northern Territory Craft Awards, Darwin, 1991; Excellence in Craftsmanship, Warburton Winterfest Woodwork Exhibition, 1995
Exhibitions: (Selected Solo) 'Extremities', The Blackwood Street Gallery, Melbourne, 1990; (Group) Selected Australian Works, A-Z Gallery, Studio 29, Tokyo, Japan, 1991; 'Turners Challenge III', Craft Alliance, Philadelphia USA, 1989; 'Enchanted Wood' Bendigo Regional Art Gallery, Victoria, 1993
Collections: Shire of Eltham, Victoria; The Woodturning Center, Philadelphia, USA; The Northern Territory Museum of Fine Arts, Darwin; The Reserve Bank of Australia Art Collection, Melbourne

INGA HUNTER
Leura, New South Wales
Born: England, 1938 (Afro-Australian); in Australia from 1947
Studied: Sydney University, BA Anthropology
Related Experience: Lecturer, Sydney College for the Arts, 1981
Awards: Indonesia House Award; CAC Award, 1982
Selected Exhibitions: Fourteen solo exhibitions in Australia and overseas
Collections: National Gallery of Australia, Canberra; Victorian National Craft Authority; Queensland Art Gallery, Brisbane; Powerhouse Museum, Sydney; American Craft Museum; Darwin Museum and Art Gallery, Darwin; Numerous regional Australian galleries

ANDREA HYLANDS
Melbourne, Victoria
Born: UK, 1952; in Australia from 1994
Studied: La Trobe University, Victoria, BA Ceramics, 1984; Monash

University, MA, 1986
Related Experience: Established Hillgrove Pottery, 1984
Awards: Grand prize winner, XIIIth Bienniale Internationale de Ceramique d'Art, Vallauris, 1992; Honourable Mention (Ceramic Arts), Third International Ceramics Competition, Mino, Japan, 1992 and 1995
Exhibitions: Numerous exhibitions in Australia and overseas, including Contemporary Porcelain, Keramique-Galerie, 1995
Collections: Represented in all major state public collections in Australia and overseas, as well as in private collections, including the International Museum of Ceramic Arts, Vallauris, France

GEORGE INGHAM
Braidwood, New South Wales
Born: UK, 1940; in Australia from 1982
Studied: Leeds College of Art, Final National Diploma of Design (Furniture), 1959–60; Designer of the Royal College of Art, Royal College of Art, London, 1961–64
Related Experience: Extensive travel to Europe; Partner in workshop, 1971–75; Chief Designer, Whiteleaf Furniture, England. 1975–77; Foundation Head and Senior Lecturer, Wood Workshop, Canberra School of Art, 1982–92
Awards: Royal Scholar for RCA, 1962; Finnish Government, Scholarship; RCA Scholarship
Exhibitions: Numerous solo and group exhibitions in Australia and overseas
Collections: Warwick Arts Trust Collection, London; Southern Arts Association Collection, UK; Victorian Craft Collection, Melbourne; Powerhouse Museum, Sydney

JAN IRVINE
Gulgong, New South Wales
Born: South Australia, 1950
Studied: South Australia School of Art
Related Experience: Exhibition Design, Festival Centre Gallery; Arts administration; Numerous workshops
Awards: Professional Development Grant, Australia Council
Exhibitions: (Selected) 'Virtue or Obsession', Jam Factory Craft and Design Centre, Adelaide, 1994; Beaver Galleries, Canberra, 1991, 1985; (Group) 'Australia Dreaming', Sydney and Japan, 1995; 'Crossing Borders', USA tour, 1995–97; 'Discerning Textiles', Goulburn Regional Gallery Tour
Collections: Powerhouse Museum, Sydney; Queen Victoria Museum and Art Gallery, Tasmania; Tamworth National Fibre Collection; Ararat Regional Art Gallery

DANIEL JENKINS
Melbourne, Victoria
Born: Wichita, Kansas, USA, 1947; in Australia from 1981
Studied: Georgia Southern University, USA, BS Visual Arts (Jewellery); Centre for the Preservation of Historic Buildings, San Servolo, Venice, Italy (Decorative Iron Forging and Repoussé in Steel); RMIT, Blacksmithing and Materials Technology Certificate of Trade Qualification
Related Experience: Director of Marshall Jenkins Studios, since 1981; Employed full-time as Lecturer-in-Charge, Three-dimensional Metalsmithing, School of Studies in Creative Arts, Victorian College of the Arts, Melbourne University
Awards: Palladio Foundation Fellowship to study repoussé in Italy, 1992
Exhibitions: Exhibits regularly through Makers Mark Gallery, Melbourne, showing only in solo exhibitions; Gasworks Sculpture Park (Invitational) Sculpture Exhibition, Melbourne, 1995; 'Poles Apart', Melbourne International Sculpture Triennial, 1993
Collections: National Gallery of Australia, Canberra; Queen Victoria Museum and Art Gallery, Launceston; Jewish Museum of Australia, Melbourne; Art Gallery of the Northern Territory, Darwin

LORRAINE JENYNS
Hobart, Tasmania
Born: Melbourne, Australia, 1945
Studied: Caulfield and RMIT, 1963–65; Melbourne Teachers' College; Currently Senior Lecturer in Sculpture, University of Tasmania, Hobart
Awards: (Recent) Australia Council Fellowship, 1992; Sydney Myer Foundation Ceramic Award, 1994
Exhibitions: (Selected Solo) 'Beyond Paradise Garden — Lorraine Jenyns — A Retrospective: 25 years', Toured three states, 1992; 'Dislocation', Recent Sculpture, Darren Knight Gallery, Melbourne, 1994; 'Double Dislocation', Recent Sculpture, Watters Gallery, Sydney, 1995; (International) Vessel as Subject, Tasmanian Studio Ceramics to Indonesia, Touring, 1995; 'Delinquent Angel:

Australian Historical, Aboriginal and Contemporary Ceramics', Italy
Collections: Most public state, national, numerous regional galleries and university collections in Australia

MARTIN JOHNSON
Adelaide, South Australia
Born: Adelaide, 1970
Studied: Central School of Art, Drawing and Design, 1987; North Adelaide School of Art, Certificate of Photography, 1988; North Adelaide School of Art, Associate Diploma of Photography, 1989–90; RMIT, BA Photography, 1991
Related Experience: Established Threaded Limbs Studio with Agnieszka Golda for production of hand-dyed and screen-printed textiles and furniture
Exhibitions: (Selected) Jam Factory Craft and Design Centre, Adelaide (Threaded Limbs), 1996; BMGART Gallery, Adelaide, 1995; North Adelaide School of Art Gallery, 1994

PETER JOHNSON
Adelaide, South Australia
Born: Pinaroo, South Australia, 1952
Studied: University of South Australia, Bachelor of Design (Ceramics)
Related Experience: Workshops: Artists in Schools Program, Paralowie School, SA 1989; Tutor (Ceramics) Worker's Education Association, Part-time, 1995; Ceramics Technician, Underdale Campus, University of South Australia, 1991–92; Establishment of Jamboree Clay Workshop, SA, 1990– to date; Jam Factory Craft and Design Centre, Adelaide, 1988–90; Artist-in-residence, University of South Australia, 1988
Awards: Australia Council for the Arts — Overseas Residency, Barcelona, 1993; Department of the Arts and Cultural Heritage, 1991; SA Department for the Arts, Project Grant, 1990
Exhibitions: 'Flights of Fancy', Adelaide Central Gallery; 'National Craft Award', Museum and Art Gallery of the Northern Territory, Darwin; 'Home is where the Art is', Adelaide; '1.2.3.', Jamboree Clay Workshop; 'The China Cabinet', Jamboree; 'All Boxed Up', Jam Factory Craft and Design Centre, Adelaide; 'Bela Domestica', Jamboree
Collections: Queensland University of Technology; The Gallery, School of Art, University of South Australia; University of Southern Queensland

SUSAN JORGENSEN
Melbourne, Victoria
Born: Mooroopna, Victoria, 1951
Studied: University of NSW, BA, 1972–74; University of Wollongong, Diploma of Education, 1976; Vrije Academie Psychopolis, Den Haag, Holland, Study of Ceramics, Full-time, 1979–81; East Sydney Technical College, Certificate of Ceramics, 1983–85; University of Wollongong, Master of Creative Arts (Ceramics), 1990
Related Experience: Conducted many workshops for various ceramic organisations; Taught ceramics part-time at East Sydney, Liverpool, Brookvale and Randwick TAFEs for seven years
Awards: Port Hacking Potters' Competition, Certificate of Merit, 1994
Exhibitions: (Selected) Delmar Trinity Gallery, Summer Hill; Gleneon Craft Expo; Porters Gallery, Kenthurst; Back to Back Gallery, Newcastle; Tea House Gallery, Canberra; Manly City Art Gallery and Museum, Sydney; Mura Clay Gallery, Newtown; (Solo) Craftspace Crafts Council, The Rocks, Sydney; Commonwealth Bank National Ceramics Award, Canberra School of Arts; Port Hacking Potters' Competition

VIRGINIA KAISER
Sydney
Born: Sydney, 1945
Studied: TAFE, South Australia, Weaving and Design; School of Colour and Design, Sydney
Related Experience: Numerous workshops in fibre in Australia and USA; Studied with visiting American artist Douglas Fuchs
Awards: Artists Development Grant VACB, 1991
Exhibitions: Various solo and group shows in Australia and overseas
Collections: Powerhouse Museum, Sydney; Ararat Gallery; Permanent Textile Collection, Victoria; Art Gallery of South Australia, Adelaide

ELIZABETH KELLY
Sydney, New South Wales
Born: Adelaide, 1960
Studied: Australian National University, Institute of the Arts,

Commenced MA, BA (Visual Arts), Glass, 1995; North Adelaide School of Art, South Australia, Certificate in Art, 1988; Glass Workshop Trainee, Jam Factory Workshops, 1985–87
Related Experience: Part-time Lecturer and Demonstrator, Glass Studio, Sydney College of the Arts, Sydney University, 1994–1995; Lecturer, Glass Studio, Sydney College of the Arts, Research Assistant, Hot Glass Workshop, Glass Studio, Sydney College of the Arts, 1993; Demonstrator, Glass Studio, Sydney College of the Arts; Studio Assistant, 1992
Exhibitions: (Selected) Earth Exchange Museum, Glass Artist's Gallery, Sydney, 1995; Latitudes: Portland/Canberra, Portland Art Museum, Oregon, USA; Craftspace, The Rocks, Sydney; Australian Contemporary Studio Glass Exhibition, Glass Artist's Gallery, Sydney; Ausglass, Selected Members Exhibition, Jam Factory Craft and Design Centre, Adelaide; The Great Goblet Show, Glass Artist's Gallery, Sydney, 1994
Collections: Australian National University Glass Collection, 1991

ELSJE KING
Subiaco, Western Australia
Born: Netherlands, 1947; in Australia from 1952
Studied: Curtin University, Associate in Art Teaching, 1972; University of London, Graduate Diploma in Art and Design, 1972
Related Experience: Consultancy; Curator for various exhibitions; Lecturer in textiles; Workshops
Awards: Edith Cowan University Research Grant, 1994 and 1991; Teaching Fellowship, Edith Cowan University, 1992; Development Grant, Australia Council, 1991
Exhibitions: Over twenty solo and over thirty group shows
Collections: Most major state and regional art galleries

ROBERT KNOTTENBELT
Wesburn, Victoria
Born: Amsterdam, Netherlands, 1947
Studied: University of Auckland, New Zealand, BA, 1971; South Australia School of Art, 1973–74; Jam Factory Workshops, Adelaide, 1975–77
Related Experience: SAW & 211 Inc, Artists' Co-operatives, Adelaide, 1978–82; Private Studio, Britannia Creek Glass, Wesburn, Victoria, 1984; Artist-in-residence ATEC, Regency College of TAFE, SA, 1990
Awards: Australia Council Grants: 1977, 1980, 1986, 1988; Australia Council Fellowship, 1991–92
Exhibitions: (Selected) 'World Glass Now', Hokkaido Museum of Modern Art, Sapporo, Japan, 1985, 1988, 1994; Ausglass, Jam Factory Craft and Design Centre, Adelaide, 1979; 'Australia, Canada, USA and Japan', Kyoto and Tokyo Museums of Modern Art, Japan, 1981; 'Contemporary Australian and New Zealand Glass', Germany, France and Switzerland, 1984; 'First Australian International Crafts Triennial', Art Gallery of Western Australia, Perth, 1989; 'Design Visions', Second International Crafts Triennial, Art Gallery of Western Australia, Perth, 1992; 'Sculptures de Verre Contemporaines', Musée des Arts de la Ville, Lausanne, Switzerland, 1992
Collections: Kunstmuseum, Dusseldorf, Germany; Musée des Arts Decoratifs, Lausanne, Switzerland; Art Gallery of Western Australia, Perth; Art Gallery of Queensland, Brisbane; Art Gallery of the Northern Territory, Darwin; Museum of Applied Arts and Sciences, NSW; New Parliament House, Canberra; Victorian State Craft Collection, Melbourne; La Trobe Valley Art Centre

WARREN LANGELY
Sydney, New South Wales
Born: Sydney, 1950
Studied: University of Sydney, B.Sc. Hons, 1972
Related Experience: Glass Studies in Australia, UK and USA
Awards: Silver Prize, International Exhibition of Glass Art, Kanazawa, Japan, 1988; Emerging Artist Award, Pilchuck Glass School, Seattle, USA, 1984
Exhibitions: Over forty-five solo and group exhibitions in Australia and overseas since 1976
Collections: Represented in over twenty-five public collections in Australia and overseas including all major state and regional public collections in Australia

MARIE LARKIN
Dubbo, New South Wales
Born: NSW, 1958
Studied: Alexander Mackie CAE, B.Ed. Art, 1970
Related Experience: Teaching Art in high schools in Australia, from 1980; Part-time TAFE teacher, 1994–95
Awards: First Prize, Contemporary Needlework, Esanda Open Championship Acquisitive Award, 1995; First Prize, Traditional

Needlework, Dubbo Arts and Crafts Exhibition, 1993; Winner Dame Nancy Buttfield Embroidery Prize, Adelaide, 1993
Exhibitions: Naomi Valley Cotton Fibre Exhibition, 1995; Creative Embroiderer's Group Annual Exhibition, Newcastle; Fifteenth National Craft Acquisition, Darwin; 'Wishful Thinking', Molong, 1994, 1993, 1992; Fibre '92, Tamworth, 1992

HELGE LARSEN
Sydney, New South Wales
Born: Copenhagen, Denmark, 1929; in Australia from 1961
Studied: Four years apprenticeship in Jewellery; College of Craft and Design, Copenhagen, National Diploma; Exchange Student Trainee, University of Colorado, USA, 1953–55
Related Experience: Set up workshop/studio in Copenhagen, 1955; Senior Instructor, University of New South Wales, 1962–74; Moya Dyring Studio, Cité Internationale des Arts, Paris, 1972; Visiting Professor, Sommer Akademie Bildende Kunst, Salzburg, Austria, 1975; Head of Jewellery and Silversmithing Department, Sydney College of the Arts, 1977; Principal Lecturer, Sydney College of the Arts, 1986; Deputy Director, Sydney College of the Arts, 1988; Acting Director, Sydney College of the Arts, 1990; Associate Professor, University of Sydney, 1990; Guest Professor, Nara Junior College of Art, Japan, 1990; Curator and Selector for Contemporary Jewellery in Australia and Japan, Kyoto, Japan, 1991; Head of School, School of Visual Arts, Sydney College of the Arts, University of Sydney, 1991–94
*For awards and exhibitions, see Lewers

KAY LAWRENCE
Adelaide, South Australia
Born: Canberra, 1947
Studied: Post-graduate Studies in Woven Tapestry as a Special Student at Edinburgh College of Art, Scotland, 1977–78; South Australian School of Art, Diploma Art Teaching, 1965–68
Related Experience: Initiated and involved in the development of Community Tapestry movement in Australia; Participated in five projects from 1981–94; Initiated organisation of symposium, 'Distant Lives/Shared Voices' on woven tapestry, Poland, 1992 and tapestry seminar, 'Texts from the Edge' on curating and writing, 1995
Awards: (Selected) Awarded a Member of the Order of Australia, 1989; Project Grant, Department of the Arts of South Australia, 1994
Exhibitions: 'Identities, Art from Australia', shown in Taipeh, Taiwan and Wollongong in 1993–94; 'Crossing Borders, Contemporary Australian Textile Art', touring USA, 1995–96; 'Texts from the Edge, Tapestry and Identity in Australia', touring Australia 1994–95
Collections: Represented in many public and private collections in Australia and overseas including Art Gallery of South Australia, Adelaide; Queensland Art Gallery, Brisbane; Art Gallery of Western Australia, Perth

GREGORY KWOK–KEUNG LEONG
Launceston, Tasmania
Born: Hong Kong, 1946; in Australia from 1981
Studied: University of Tasmania at Launceston, Graduate Diploma (Fine Art), 1991; University of Tasmania at Launceston, Bachelor (Fine Art), 1990; Polytechnic of Central London, Grad. Dip. Arts Administration, 1976; Hong Kong University, M. Phil, 1974; Hong Kong University, BA, 1968
Related Experience: Launceston Festival, Artist in the Community, 1994; Public Art Commission, Dodges Ferr School, Tasmania, 1993; Tasdance, fabric/costume/set design, 1989–92; Tasmanian Symphony Chamber Players Commission, 1990; Sydney Philharmonia Commission, 1989
Exhibitions: (Selected) Mutlicultural Art Award, Swing Bridge Art Galleries, Tasmania, 1996; 'Horizons', Contemporary Art Services Tasmania (CAST) Touring Exhibition, Hobart and other Tasmanian venues, 1996; 'Homocraft', CCNSW, National Touring Exhibition, 1995–96; 'Pins and Needles', University Gallery, Launceston and Bangkok, 1994–95; 'Adornments', CAST, National Touring Exhibition, 1993–94; Tamworth National Textile Touring Biennial, 1992–93
Collections: National Gallery of Australia, Canberra; Tasmanian Museum and Art Gallery

DARANI LEWERS
Sydney, New South Wales
Born: Sydney, 1936
Studied: East Sydney Technical College, Jewellery Apprenticeship Course, 1957; Trainee to Nina Ratsep, 'Anina Pty Ltd', Sydney, 1958; Trainee to Helge Larsen 'Solvform', Copenhagen, 1959

Related Experience: Partnership with Helge Larsen, Sydney, 1961; Moya Dyring Studio, Cité Internationale des Arts, Paris, 1972; Member of Sydney College of the Arts Council, 1976–80; Chairperson, Crafts Board; Joint curator with Helge Larsen, Australian Jewellery to Europe; Jointly coordinated and participated in 'Worn Issues', Touring Exhibition, 1983–86
Awards: Apprenticeship Silver Medal Award, Denmark (Helge Larsen), 1951; Guldsmedefagets Faellesraad, Denmark (Helge Larsen), 1955; Guldsmedefagets Faellesraad, Denmark (Helge Larsen and Darani Lewers), 1968; Salomonsen Award, Denmark (Helge Larsen and Darani Lewers), 1974; Darani Lewers awarded Fellowship, Visual Arts/Crafts Board, Australia Council, 1994
Exhibitions: (Both Larsen and Lewers) Over thirty solo exhibitions in Australia since 1961; Museum of Decorative Arts, Copenhagen, since and including 1973; Galerie Galtung, Oslo, Norway, 1973; Helge Larsen and Darani Lewers, 'A Retrospective, Jewellery, Hollow-ware and Sculpture', European tour, Schmuckmuseum Pforzheim, Germany, 1988
Collections: (Larsen and Lewers) All National Art Galleries and many regional galleries in Australia; (International) Museum of Decorative Arts, Vienna, Austria; Museum of Decorative Arts, Prague, Czechoslovakia; Museum of Decorative Arts, Copenhagen, Denmark; Jewellery Museum Pforzheim, Germany; Australian Embassy, Tokyo, Japan; Wuppertaler Uhren Museum, Germany

SARA LINDSAY
North Hobart, Tasmania
Born: 1951, UK, 1951; arrived in Australia, 1966
Studied: Kawashima Textile School, Kyoto, Japan, six months study of Kasuri Weaving, 1981; Melbourne State College, Diploma of Education, 1975; RMIT, Diploma of Art, 1974
Related Experience: Curator of Craft, Tasmanian Museum and Art Gallery, 1994–96; Lecturer in Charge of Textiles, Tasmanian School of Art, 1991–94; Manager, Victorian Tapestry Workshop, 1989–91; Weaver, Victorian Tapestry Workshop, 1976–88
Awards: Australia Council Fellowship, 1995; Arts Tasmania, Professional Development Grant, 1994; Crafts Board of the Australia Council Study Grant, 1981; Australia/Japan Foundation Travel Grant, 1980
Exhibitions: Has participated in over fifty selected exhibitions
Collections: Ruyton Girls School, Melbourne; Victorian State Craft Collection, Melbourne; National Gallery of Australia, Canberra; Melbourne University; Aichi Prefecture Collection, Japan; Tasmanian Museum and Art Gallery; University of Tasmania; Department of the Premier and Cabinet, Victoria

SANDY LOCKWOOD
Balmoral Village, New South Wales
Born: London, 1953; Australia from 1979
Studied: East Sydney Technical College, 1979–80
Related Experience: Teaching part-time in TAFE Colleges; Travel to Thailand, Japan, Canada and USA to survey ceramics and lecture
Awards: Craft Board Workshop Development Grant, 1985; Campbelltown City Art Gallery Ceramics Competition, Winner, 1992; National Gold Coast Ceramics Award, Commended, 1993; Australia Council VACB Professional Development Grant, 1995
Exhibitions: Potters Gallery, Sydney, 1986; Terrapotta, Gallery, Sydney, 1990; Sturt Gallery, Mittagong, 1993; National Gold Coast, Ceramics Art Award, 1993; National Museum of Indonesia, 1995; Distelfink Gallery, Melbourne, 1990–95; Newcastle Ceramic Art Award, 1995; Fusions Gallery, Brisbane, 1995
Collections: Jan Feder Collection, Monash University; Campbelltown City Art Gallery; Stanthorpe Art Gallery; Private Collections

SUE LORRAINE
Adelaide, South Australia
Born: Melbourne, 1955
Studied: Diploma of Fine Art and Design, 1979–80
Exhibitions: (Selected) 'Turning Ten', Dowse Art Museum, Wellington, New Zealand, 1995; (Solo) 'em/body', Adelaide, Artspace, Festival Centre; National Touring Exhibition, 'First Australian Contemporary Jewellery Biennial', 1991–92; Kyoto, Japan, 'Contemporary Jewellery in Australia and Japan'; Touring Exhibition, Pacific, Department of Foreign Affairs and Trade, 1991; Munich, 'Schmuckszene '88', 1988
Collections: National Gallery of Victoria, Melbourne; Art Gallery of Western Australia, Perth; Robert Holmes a Court Collection; Queen Victoria Museum and Art Gallery, Launceston; Art Gallery of South Australia, Adelaide

CORAL LOWRY
Perth, Western Australia
Born: Western Australia, 1951
Studied: Curtin University, WA, BA (Visual Arts), 1987–90
Awards: 'Third National Dame Mary Durack Outback Hall of Fame Craft Awards', Improvisation Award, 1992; City of Perth Craft Awards, Student Award, 1990
Exhibitions: (Selected) WA Week Citifest Inaugural Wesfarmers Biennial Regional Craft Award, 1995; 'Fourth Australian Contemporary Art Fair', Melbourne, 1994; 'Absence of Evidence', Fremantle; 'Footage', Crafts Council of WA; 'Advantage of Isolation', Sydney, 1993; 'The Three Australians — An Intimate Journey', HELP Institute, Kuala Lumper, Malaysia, 1992
Public Art Commissions: Art Project, Fremantle Dalwallinu Bandstand Design in collaboration with Peter Barrett, Donaldson Smith and Hooke Architects, 1995; City of Fremantle Kings Square Chess Table Project; Armadale Crest Project, 1994; Parkfield Primary School for Art Project, WA, 1993
Collections: Curtin University of Western Australia

CARLIER MAKIGAWA
Melbourne, Victoria
Born: Perth, 1952
Studied: RMIT, Master of Art
Related Experience: Lecturer, RMIT, 1985–96; Conducted numerous jewellery workshops in Australia and overseas; National Chair for Jewellers and Metalsmiths Group of Australia, 1993–95
Awards: Australia Council Fellowship, 1992
Exhibitions: Nineteen solo shows in Australia and overseas including: Inax Gallery, Tokyo; Helen Drutt Gallery, USA; Galerie Ra, Netherlands; Over thirty-five group shows in Australia and overseas
Collections: (Numerous public including): Kyoto National Museum of Art, Japan; National Gallery of Victoria, Melbourne; National Gallery of Australia, Canberra; Art Gallery of Western Australia, Perth; Queensland Art Gallery, Brisbane; Powerhouse Museum, Sydney; Cooper Hewitt Museum, USA

JANET MANSFIELD
Sydney, New South Wales
Born: Sydney, 1934
Studied: National Art School; East Sydney Technical College, Training in Ceramics, 1964 and 1965
Related Experience: Author of a number of books on ceramics, and editor and publisher of the international journals: *Ceramics: Art and Perception*; *Ceramics TECHNICAL*
Awards: Member of the International Academy of Ceramics since 1982; Award of the Australian Ceramic Society, 1986; Order of Australia Medal, 1987; Emeritus Award of the Australia Council, 1990; Her ceramics have won awards in regional competitions since 1972
Exhibitions: During the past thirty years has exhibited widely in Australia and overseas with over thirty solo exhibitions throughout Australia, Japan and New Zealand; Participated in selected group exhibitions and travelling international exhibitions
Collections: Represented in major public collections in Australia

ONDREJ MARES
Macclesfield, South Australia
Born: Prague, Czechoslovakia, 1949; in Australia from 1969
Studied: Diploma Art and Craft, 1979; Self-taught craftsman (toolmaker); Independent workshop, Macclesfield, 1975–90; Formative Study Travel in Europe and Asia, 1973–74
Related Experience: Designed and built own gallery, Macclesfield, SA, 1992–93; Numerous commissions; Collaborative interior furnishings with Aptos Cruz Galleries for private residence, Macclesfield, SA; Collaboration with Architect on interior design and furniture for private house, Finniss, SA, 1989
Awards: SA Arts Grant for Exhibition, 1987
Exhibitions: (Solo) One Off Gallery, Gulas Festival Exhibition, 1996; DiLux Gallery Adelaide, iCzech Connectioni, 1995; One Off Gallery, Macclesfield, Festival Exhibition, 1994; Foyer Exhibition, Crafts Council of SA Aptos Cruz Galleries, Stirling, SA, 1991; Foyer Exhibition, Crafts Council of SA, 1990; LiUnique Gallery, Adelaide, SA, 1988; Elmswood Gallery, Adelaide, SA, 1986

MARION MARSHALL
Melbourne, Victoria
Born: Melbourne, 1948
Studied: Swinburne Institute of Technology, Graphic Design; Melbourne State College, Secondary Art Teaching; Staatliche Zeichen Akademie, Hanau, Germany, Master of Gold and Silversmithing

Related Experience: Director, Marshall Jenkins Studios since 1976; Lectures part-time, RMIT in Gold and Silversmithing
Awards: Australia Council Fellowship
Exhibitions: (Invitational) 'Art of Adornment', Contemporary Australian Jewellery, Korea, Indonesia and Japan, 1994, 1995; 'Australian Contemporary Design in Jewish Ceremony', 1992, 1993; 'My Dear Blue Planet', Kyoto, Japan
Selected Exhibitions: Duo-Exhibition, Beaver Galleries, Canberra; Duo-Exhibition, Touring Exhibition, Queen Victoria Museum and Art Gallery, Launceston
Collections: Jewish Museum of Australia, Melbourne; Queen Victoria Museum and Art Gallery, Launceston; Melbourne University Art Collection; Museum and Art Gallery of Northern Territory, Darwin; Elwood Talmud Torah Synagogue

TERRY JOHN MARTIN
Bardon, Queensland
Born: Melbourne, 1947
Studied: University of South Australia and University of New England, Multicultural Studies
Awards: Writer's grant from VACB, 1995
Exhibitions: (Selected) 'Recontres Europèennes de la Tournerie', Exhibition of World Woodturning in Lons-le-Saunier, France, 1995; 'Yuukari no Kuni' (the Land of the Eucalypt), City Gallery, Nagoya, Japan, 1995; 'In Rapport', Tea House Gallery, Canberra, 1994; 'Sculptured Wood', Crafts Council of Queensland Gallery, 1994; 'Bowls to Behold', Distelfink Gallery, Melbourne, 1993; Exhibitor in Asahi Contemporary Craft Exhibition in Japan, Osaka and Tokyo, 1992, 1993

PHILL MASON
Glebe, Tasmania
Born: Sydney, 1950
Studied: Power Institute at Sydney University, Fine Arts, early 1970s; Self-taught in jewellery techniques, early 1980s
Related Experience: Taught jewellery fabrication at Hobart TAFE, late 1980s
Awards: (Selected) Finalist, 'Art '95' International Art Competition, New York, 1995; Acceptance into Twenty-sixth German Award for Jewellery and Precious Stones, Idar-Oberstein; Recipient of Inaugural Biennial 'Contemporary Wearables' Award, Toowoomba Regional Gallery, 1989 (and runner-up, 1991); National Craft Acquisition Award, Darwin, 1991, 1993; Overall Winner, Tasmanian Jewellery Design Award, AJA, Hobart, 1987
Exhibitions: (Selected) 'The Art of Adornment', Queen Victoria Museum and Art Gallery, Launceston, Japan, South Korea, Indonesia, 1993, 1994; CINAFE & 'SOFA', Chicago, 1992–95, and Miami 1995; 'Signaturen', Pforzheim, Hannover, Hanau, Vienna, Padua, 1991; 'Artcraft', Bicentennial National Invitational Exhibition, Melbourne; 'Biennial Australian Craft Survey Exhibition', Meat Market Craft Centre, Melbourne
Collections: Tasmanian Museum and Art Gallery; Museum and Art Gallery of Northern Territory, Darwin; Griffith Regional Gallery; Araluen Art Centre, Alice Springs

WILLIAM MATTHYSEN
Warrandyte, Victoria
Born: Australia, 1954
Studied: University of Witwatersrand, Johannesburg, B.Arch., 1974–77; Architectural Association, London, Diploma, 1979–82; RMIT, Master of Design 1990–92; RMIT, Clock and Watchmaking, 1993
Related Experience: Architect, London, Hong Kong, Melbourne, 1982–89; Established Wood Workshop, Melbourne, 1989; Teaching Experience, Architecture and Design, Part-time, RMIT, Melbourne, 1989–93; Architecture and Design, Part-time, Melbourne University, 1993–94
Awards and Exhibitions: (Prizewinner) Sculpture/Carving, Timber and 'Working with Wood', Exhibition Buildings, Melbourne, 1991; First Prize, 'Sculpture/Carving', Victorian Woodworkers Association, Exhibition, Melbourne, 1991; First Prize, Sculpture/Carving, 'Timber and Working with Wood', Melbourne, 1992; 'Times Change. About Time', Makers Mark Gallery, Melbourne, 1993; 'Best Overall Piece', Warburton Winterfest, 1993

TORI DE MESTRE
Sydney, New South Wales
Born: Wollongong, 1951
Studies: University of Wollongong, Master of Creative Arts/Textiles, 1991–92; Melbourne State College, Diploma, Art (Craft), 1976–78; National Art School, Sydney, Fine Arts, 1970–71
Related Experience: Numerous workshops, seminars and conferences

Awards: Visual Arts Crafts Board, Artist-in-residence, Northern Territory, 1991; Visual Arts Crafts Board, Overseas Study Tour, 1987
Exhibitions: Numerous solo and group shows
Collections: Ararat Gallery; Art Bank, Sydney; Victoria College; University of Wollongong; Australian Embassy, Washington

JEFF MINCHAM
Adelaide, South Australia
Born: Milang, SA, 1950
Education: South Australia School of Art, 1970–73; Tasmanian School of Art, 1974
Awards: Winner of numerous awards and prizes in Australia and overseas: Fletcher Challenge Award, 1985 and 1989; Mayfair Ceramics Award, 1982 and 1984; Australia Council Fellowship, 1991; Winner, Alice Springs Craft Award, 1992; Winner, Eleventh National Gold Coast Ceramic Award; Winner, Nillumbik Art Award, 1995
Exhibitions: Forty-five one-man exhibitions since 1976 in Australia and USA; Participated in over one hundred group shows, survey and touring exhibitions in Australia and overseas
Collections: Represented in over fifty public and private collections in Australia and overseas including all major state and regional public collections in Australia

MASCHA MOJE
Canberra, Australian Capital Territory
Born: Hamburg, Germany, 1964; arrived in Australia, 1985
Studied: Undergraduate Diploma, Gold and Silversmithing, 1985–87; ANU, Canberra School of Arts, Post-graduate Diploma, Gold and Silversmithing, 1988
Related Experience: Work experience in several Gold and Silversmithing Workshops, Germany; Lecturer, Part-time, Gold and Silversmithing, ANU Canberra School of Arts, and other institutions
Exhibitions: (Solo) Gallery IBO, Klagenfurt, Austria, 1995; Various Exhibitions in England, Germany and Holland, 1992; Triennial of Perth, 1992; Jewellery Biennial, Australia, 1991; Post-graduate Exhibition, 1989; Canberra School of Arts, Australia; Twelve Gold and Silversmiths, Solander Gallery, Canberra, 1988

PHILIP MONAGHAN
Crafers, South Australia
Born: London, 1960; in Australia from 1992
Studied: Kingston Polytechnic, UK, 1978–81
Related Experience: Furniture Design Link Project, Jam Factory Craft and Design Centre, Adelaide, 1995–96; Teaching, Indus Valley School of Art; Sculpture Studio, Karachi, Pakistan, 1994; Teaching, Carclew Youth Arts Centre, Craft Workshop, 1993; Development Project for British Aid Programme, Nigeria, 1991–92; Community Artist, London, 1988–90
Exhibitions: (Solo) Queen Street Fine Art Gallery, Sydney, 1996; Bungendore Woodworks Gallery, NSW, 1995; (Group): Jam Factory Craft and Design Centre, Adelaide Gallery, 1995; Craft Council of SA, 1995; Greenhill Gallery, Adelaide, 1994; Various group exhibitions in Australia and UK
Commissions: St John's Anglican Church, Adelaide, 1994; Various Commissions, UK and Australia

STUART MONTAGUE
Peakhurst, New South Wales
Born: Sydney, 1962
Studied: TAFE, Sydney, Cabinetmaker's Trade Course, 1978–80; TAFE, Sydney, Advanced Cabinetmaking Course; TAFE, Sydney, Drawing and Art Theory, 1984; University of Tasmania, BA (Fine Arts), 'Design in Wood', 1989–91
Related Experience: Cressy Furniture, Apprentice Cabinetmaker, 1978–80; Apprentice Cabinetmaker, 1980–85; Carpenter, joiner, 1989–91; Montague Furniture, 1992– present
Exhibitions: Numerous solo and group shows in Australia and overseas

MILTON MOON
Adelaide, South Australia
Born: Melbourne, 1926
Studies: Central Technical College Brisbane, Painting, 1949–50; Private Painting Classes, Margaret Cilento, Brisbane, early 1950s; Pottery training, no formal studies; Learned Wheel Throwing from Mervyn Feeney, Queensland Pioneer Potter, 1950
Related Experience: Worked with Harry Memmott in the 1950s; Own studio from the mid-1950s and began exhibiting in 1959; Since that time has had approximately seventy exhibitions in Australia, and in travelling exhibitions overseas

Awards: Foundation Churchill Fellowship for Study in the USA, Mexico, Europe, including Scandinavia, UK, Greece, Iran, 1966; Myer Foundation, Geijutsu Fellowship for one year's study in Japan, 1974; Winner, Mayfair Award, 1978; Awarded Member of the Order of Australia, 1984; Advance Australia Foundation Award, 1992; Australian Government Creative Artists Fellowship 1994–98, 1993
Exhibitions: Over fifty one-man, and numerous group shows in Australia and overseas
Collections: Represented in all major state public collections in Australia and overseas, as well as in many private collections

TOM MOORE
Canberra, Australian Capital Territory
Born: Canberra, 1971
Studies: BA (Visual), First Class Hons in Glass, 1994
Awards: Emerging Artists Support Scheme, 1994; Hot Glass, 1993
Exhibitions: Canberra School of Art Graduates, 1994; Numerous Solo and Group Shows; 'Out of Canberra', Jam Factory Craft and Design Centre, Adelaide, 1994; Ausglass National Students Exhibition, 1993

RICHARD MORRELL
Coburg, Victoria
Born: UK, 1926; in Australia from 1979
Studies: West Sussex College of Design, 1975–76; Stourbridge School of Art, 1976–79
Related Experience: Tutor in Glass Studies, CIT, Melbourne, 1979–81
Awards: Prizewinner, 'Gas and Fuel' Show, Melbourne, 1985; Development Awards, Australia Council, 1987 and 1991; First Prize, Ausglass Exhibition, Sydney, 1991
Exhibitions: (Various one-man and group shows in Australia and overseas, including): Galerie L, Hamburg, Germany, 1992 and 1994
Collections: Glasmuseum, Ebeltoft, Denmark; Hamburg Museum of Art, Germany; Toho Corporation Collection, Japan; National Gallery of Victoria, Melbourne; Powerhouse Museum, Sydney, and various regional art museums in Australia

NICK MOUNT
Adelaide, South Australia
Born: Adelaide, 1952
Studied: Pilchuck Glass School, Seattle, USA, 1995; Head of Glass Workshop, Jam Factory Craft and Design Centre, Adelaide, from 1994; Teaching Assistant, Pilchuck Glass School, Seattle, USA, 1993, 1992; Teaching, University of South Australia, 1992; Glass Studio, Adelaide, 1991; Director of Budgeree Glass, 1988; Teaching Assistant at Pilchuck Glass School, Seattle, USA, 1985 and 1987
Exhibitions: Numerous group shows including: 'Workers in Glass', Lyall Burton Gallery, Melbourne, 1996; 'Ausglass in Adelaide 1995', Adelaide, 1995; Ausglass, Glasmuseum, Ebeltoft, Denmark, 1995; 'SOFA', Miami, USA, 1994 and 1995
Collections: National Gallery of Victoria, Melbourne; National Gallery of Australia, Canberra; State Gallery of South Australia; State Gallery of Queensland; Victorian Ministry for the Arts; Wagga Wagga City Art Gallery; Powerhouse Museum, Sydney; New Parliament House, Canberra; Ararat Regional Art Gallery; The Gordon Institute Collection; Museum of Applied Arts and Sciences; Sale Regional Art Gallery; Latrobe Valley Schools Art Foundation; Latrobe Valley Arts Centre; State Gallery of Western Australia; Art Bank, Sydney

ANDREW MUNN
Normanville, South Australia
Born: South Australia, 1947
Studied: South Australia School of Art, Sculpture and Drawing, 1963–64
Related Experience: Fashion designer, antique dealer, 1967–69; Studio workshop established at Normanville, 1990– present
Exhibitions: (Group) Greenhill Galleries, 1991; (Solo) 'Andrew Munn', Outdoors on Parade, 1994; 'Beachcomber', Outdoors on Parade, 1996

FIONA MURPHY
Boronia, Victoria
Born: Melbourne, 1958
Education: PIT, Graduate Diploma of Fine Art, 1985; Victoria College, Diploma of Art and Design, 1980
Awards: Bathurst Gallery Art Purchase, 1987 and 1995; Shepparton Australia Day Meyer Ceramic Award, 1992 and 1993
Exhibitions: Fifteen solo exhibitions in Melbourne, Sydney and Shepparton, 1981–95; (Various Group Shows include): New Art Forms, Chicago, USA, 1992; 'Australia a Faenza', Italy, 1995
Collections: Sixteen major Australian public galleries

SHAELENE MURRAY
Sydney, Australia
Born: Australia, 1960
Studies: Various Certificates in Ceramics, 1979–88; Randwick TAFE, Creative Jewellery, 1990–91; Sydney College of the Arts, Commenced BA (Visual), 1992
Related Experience: Part-time Ceramics Teacher, 1989–94; 1993–1994, Technical Assistant, Extension Course, Glass Department, Sydney College of the Arts, 1993–94; Glass Workshops, 1993–94
Awards: William Dobell Foundation Scholarship, 1994
Exhibitions: Numerous ceramics exhibitions throughout Australia, New Zealand and Japan; 'Wearable Glass', Glass Artist's Gallery, Sydney, and Asa Gallery, Japan, 1992; 'Small Works', Glass Artist's Gallery, Sydney, 1993; Ausglass Selected Members Show, Jam Factory Craft and Design Centre, Adelaide, 1995; 'Void of a Kind', Glass Artist's Gallery, Sydney; 'Domestic Icons', Zitlip Gallery, Sydney
Collections: East Sydney Technical College; Manly City Art Gallery and Museum, Sydney

ANNE NEIL
Fremantle, Western Australia
Born: Cairns, 1951
Studies: Curtin University of Technology, Perth, 1981–85; Institute of the Arts, ANU, Canberra, 1991–92
Awards: Basel, Switzerland Residency/Exchange with Steve Tepper, 1994–95
Exhibitions: (Recent) Solo Installation, Basel, Switzerland, 1995; Reveal and Conceal Exhibition, Adelaide Female Writers' Week, 1994; 'Schmuckszene '93', International, Munich, 1993; Glass Jewellery, Canberra School of Art
Collections: Queen Victoria Museum and Art Gallery, Launceston; Art Gallery of Western Australia, Perth; Powerhouse Museum, Sydney

JENNY ORCHARD
Sydney, New South Wales
Born: Turkey, 1951, (raised in Zimbabwe); in Australia from 1976
Studied: Alexander Mackie School of Art, Sydney
Related Experience: Part-time teaching in various institutions, including Sydney University, Sydney College of the Arts, 1989–95
Exhibitions: Numerous exhibitions in Australia, London, Los Angeles and Japan
Collections: All major state art galleries, and in many regional galleries in Australia

ADELE OUTTERIDGE
Kenmore, Queensland
Born: Melbourne, 1946
Studied: University of Melbourne, B.Sc., 1967; School of Colour and Design, Sydney, 1984–88
Related Experience: CSIRO, Experimental Scientist; Tutor, La Trobe University, 1975–79; Tutor, School of Colour and Design, Sydney, 1987–89
Exhibitions: (Selected Group) Queensland Museum, 1995; Toowoomba Galleries; Crafts Council of Queensland; Vision Gallery, 1994

CHRIS PANTANO
Nambour, Queensland
Born: Sydney, 1948
Studied: Self-taught Artist/Craftsman
Awards: Caloundra Arts Festival Glass Award, 1985, 1986 and 1987; Australian Woolshed/Sheraton Craft of Excellence Award, 1988, 1990 and 1993; Maroochy Bicentennial Award, 1990
Exhibitions: Numerous throughout Australia, New Zealand, Japan and the USA
Collections: New Parliament House, Canberra; Art Gallery of Queensland, Brisbane; Art Gallery of the Northern Territory, Darwin; Wagga Wagga City Art Gallery, and numerous private collections throughout the world

SYLVIA PARR
Hobart, Tasmania
Born: Tasmania, 1937
Studied: Hobart Technical College, Diploma of Commercial Art, 1959; Hobart Technical College, Certificate of Weaving, 1980
Related Experience: Adult Education Tutor in Weaving, 1995; Lecturer in Textile School of Art, University of Tasmania, 1986–95; Extensive Workshop Participation, 1973–93; AVL Computer Systems and Software Experience, USA, 1988
Awards: Research Grant, University of Tasmania, 1992

Exhibitions: Over thirty group exhibitions
Collection: Tasmanian Museum and Arts Gallery; Crafts Council, NSW

MARC PASCAL
Melbourne, Victoria
Born: Melbourne, 1959
Studied: Victorian College of the Arts, Painting and Printmaking, Melbourne, 1981; RMIT, Bachelor of Industrial Design, 1991
Related Experience: Product Designer for Sciavello; Domus Academy Winter School, RMIT; Established own studio, M2 Products, 1994; Lecturer, Monash University, Design Department, Gold and Silversmithing and Visualisation, 1995
Awards: Fringe Furniture Show, First Prize, 1992; Australia Council Development Grant, 1991
Exhibitions: (Group) Fringe Furniture Shows, 1995, 1994, 1992; (Solo) Designer Products, Gallery 101, 1994; Artists and Industry, Furniture '95, Melbourne
Collection: Queensland Institute of Technology

ALAN PEASCOD
Bulli, New South Wales
Born: England, 1943; in Australia from 1952
Studied: East Sydney, 1964–65; Awarded Doctor of Creative Arts, University of Wollongong, 1994; Artist and teacher since 1965
Related Experience: Extensive experience in early Islamic lustre and alkaline technology since 1972 — specialising in the study of the philosophical relationships developed in historic and contemporary Persian culture and their application to contemporary Western art; Artistic experience in ceramics, drawing, photography and contemporary philosophical discourse
Awards: Various prizes, most recent being Newcastle City Art Gallery Ceramics Purchase Award
Exhibitions: Seventy solo exhibitions since 1968; Work in all state and national collections as well as represented in major public and private collections overseas
Collections: Represented in over thirty public major state and regional public collections in Australia, as well as in five overseas collections

KEVIN PERKINS
Launceston, Tasmania
Born: Launceston, 1945
Studied: Carpentry, Industrial Arts and Sculpture
Related Experience: Lecturer in Furniture Design, University of Tasmania; Churchill Fellow, Study Tour
Awards: Churchill Fellow, 1982; Cultural Exchange Visit, China, 1982; Tasmanian Wood design Collection, Prize Winner
Exhibitions: (Numerous group and solo exhibitions include) 'Pieces of Importance', Craft Council ACT, 1995
Collections: Queen Victoria Museum and Art Gallery, Launceston; National Gallery of Australia, Canberra; Powerhouse Museum, Sydney; Tasmanian Wood Collection

NORMAN PETERSON
Cambrai, South Australia
Born: Schleswig, Germany, 1946; in Australia from 1950
Studied: Self-taught in carpentry and turning
Exhibitions: Various group and solo exhibitions
Collections: Araluen Art Centre, Alice Springs; Himaji City Town Hall; Hagen City Collection, Germany

GWYN HANSSEN PIGOTT
Netherdale, Queensland
Born: Ballarat, Victoria, 1935
Studied: University of Melbourne, BA (Fine Arts), 1954; Trained with Ivan McMeekin, Sturt Pottery, and worked with Bernard Leach and Michael Cardew, UK, 1955–60
Related Experience: Elected Fellow, Society of Designer Craftsmen, UK, 1963; Established pottery at Acheres, France, 1966–73; Established Workshop, Tasmania, 1975–80; Established Pottery at Netherdale, Queensland, 1989
Awards: (Selected) Mayfair Ceramic Award, Victoria, 1976; Gold Coast Ceramic Award, 1992; South Australia Ceramics Inglewood Award, 1992; Eugene Kusch Ceramic Award, Victoria, 1995; Australia Council Emeritus Award, 1996
Exhibitions: (Selected) Sydney Meyer Australia Day Invitational, Shepparton, 1996; Garth Clark Gallery, New York, 1995; Sydney Meyer Australia Day Invitational, 1995; Fletcher Challenge Ceramic Award Exhibition, NZ, 1995; Delinquent Angel, Australian Ceramics, Faenza, Italy, 1995; Art of the Object, Travelling Exhibition, South America, 1994
Collections: Represented in numerous public and private

collections in Australia and overseas including: Victoria and Albert Museum, London; Henry Rothschild Collection, UK; Museum of Contemporary Art, Shigaraki, Japan

DAVID POTTER
Melbourne, Victoria
Born: Melbourne, 1955
Studied: Caulfield Institute of Technology, Ceramics, 1976–79; RMIT, Diploma in Fine Arts, Ceramics, 1980; RMIT Graduate Diploma, 1981; RMIT, MA, 1993–95
Awards: Several
Exhibitions: Numerous solo and group shows
Collections: Widely represented in all major collections and galleries in Australia, USA and Europe

CEDAR PREST
Adelaide, South Australia
Born: Melbourne, 1940
Education: Melbourne, BA Dip.Ed., 1961; Hornsey College of Art, London, Post Diploma, Stained Glass
Related Experience: Patrick Reynties and Lawrence Lee, England, 1971
Awards: Order of Australia Medal for Services to Stained Glass, 1987; Chancellor's Medal, Flinders University, 1994; Crafts Board Grant for Study of Modern German Designers, 1973; Crafts Board Grant for Second Session Glass Blowing Engraving and Technology, Brierly Hill, England, 1977; Community Arts Board Grant for First Community Glass Project, Parks Community Centre, Adelaide, 1979; Elected British Society Master Glass Painters, 1968; Foundation and Life Member of Crafts Council of SA; Chairperson of Crafts Board Australia Council, 1980–83.
Collections: Queensland Art Gallery, Brisbane; Art Gallery of South Australia, Adelaide; Meat Market Craft Centre, Melbourne; Crafts Council of South Australia Collection; Numerous commissions

DAVID RALPH
Richmond, Tasmania
Born: Sydney, 1946
Studied: Mining engineer, self-taught in woodworking
Related Experience: Full-time craftsman in wood since 1975
Collections: National Gallery of Australia, Canberra

GERRY REILLY
Margaret River, Western Australia
Born: Gippsland, Victoria, 1958
Studied: Gippsland Institute and University of Tasmania, Glass and Ceramics
Related Experience: Worked in various studios in Tasmania and in Jam Factory Craft Workshops, Adelaide, 1980s
Awards: Winner, Glass Section, South-West Survey Exhibition, Bunbury Art Galleries, 1992 and 1994; Winner, Leonora Art Prize, 1994; Winner, Studio 77 Award, The York Society Art and Crafts Awards, 1994
Exhibitions: Numerous group shows around Australia
Collections: Holmes a Court Collection; University of South Australia; Tasmanian University School of Art Collection

CHRISTOPHER ROBERTSON
South Fremantle, Western Australia
Born: Norseman, Western Australia, 1957
Studied: Curtin University, WA, BA, Craft, Distinction, 1983; Royal College of Art, London, MA, Furniture Design, 1986
Awards: 'City of Perth Craft Award', Prizes for Excellence 1983, 1990, 1991; Grand Prize, International Cutlery Design Competition, Sakai, Japan, 1992
Exhibitions: (Selected) 'Cross Currents', International Collection of Jewellery Touring Australia, 1985–86; 'Design Visions', Australian International Craft Triennial, Perth, 1992; 'Directions — Cutlery 1992', High Court of Australia, Canberra; RMIT Gallery, Melbourne; Jam Factory Craft and Design Centre, Adelaide; 'Victoria Health National Craft Award', National Gallery of Victoria, Melbourne, 1995
Collections: Art Gallery of Western Australia, Perth; Museum of Applied Arts and Sciences; National Gallery of Australia, Canberra

JENNIFER ROBERTSON
South Fremantle, Western Australia
Born: Weston-super-Mare, England, 1962; in Australia from 1986
Studied: West Surrey College of Art and Design, BA Hons (Woven Textiles), 1984; Royal College of Art, Post-graduate (Woven Textiles), 1985
Related Experience: Lecturer in woven textiles

Exhibitions: (Selected) Seven Dials Gallery, London, 1984; International Textile Competition, Kyoto, Japan, 1994; Victoria Health National Craft Award, Melbourne, 1995; Contemporary Cloth, Crafts Council of the ACT, 1995
Awards: Commendation, Royal Society of Arts, London, 1983; City of Perth Craft Award, Prizes for Excellence, 1991; York Craftsman of the Year Award, 1993
Collections: National Gallery of Australia, Canberra

SUE ROSENTHAL
Woodside, South Australia
Born: South Australia, 1950
Studied: Handarbetets Vanner, Stockholm, Sweden, Diploma in Weaving, 1975
Related Experience: Diploma in Teaching, South Australia School of Art, 1967–69; B.Ed., SACAE, 1982–83; Initiated partnership in architectural commissions
Awards: Project Grant, South Australia Department for Arts and Cultural Heritage, 1993.
Exhibitions: (Various group shows around Australia, including): 'Below the Surface', Goulburn Regional Art Gallery, 1995–96; 'Second Look', Textile Biennial, Prospect Gallery, Adelaide, 1996; Symmetry, AETA, National Touring Exhibition, 1994–95; Beaver Gallery, Canberra, 1990
Collections: Ararat Regional Art Gallery; Goulburn Regional Art Gallery; New Parliament House, Canberra; Glen Murcutt and Associates, Sydney

PETER RUSHFORTH
Blackheath, New South Wales
Born: Manly, 1920
Education: RMIT, 1946–48; National Art School, Sydney, 1950–51
Related Experience: Former Head, National Art School; Churchill Fellow, working in Japan, UK, USA, Denmark, 1967
Awards: Churchill Fellow, 1967; Order of Australia, 1985; Visual Arts/Crafts Board Emeritus Fellow, 1993
Exhibitions: Twenty-five one-man, and numerous group exhibitions in Australia and overseas
Collections: All state and a number of regional galleries, including: National Gallery of Australia, Canberra; New Parliament House, Canberra; Represented in many private collections, and in Australian Embassies

OWEN RYE
Gippsland, Victoria
Born: Cooma, NSW, 1944
Studied: University of NSW, B.Sc., 1961–65; University of NSW, Ph.D, 1966–70; Studied Ceramics with Ivan McMeekin
Related Experience: Archaeologist with Smithsonian Institute, USA and ANU, Canberra, USA, Israel, Pakistan and Papua New Guinea, 1970s; Part-time Lecturer in Ceramics, Canberra School of Art, 1980–84; Monash University, Gippsland Campus, Senior Lecturer and Head of Ceramics, 1985–present
Awards: Diamond Valley Award, 1992; Gold Coast Award, 1989; Ampol Arts Award, 1965
Exhibitions: (Solo) Distelfink Gallery, Melbourne, 1995; (Group) 'Delinquent Angels, Contemporary Australian Ceramics', Faenza, Italy, 1995; Colin and Cecily Rigg Award, National Gallery of Victoria, Melbourne, 1994; Minokamo Festival, Japan, with Chester Nealie and Janet Mansfield, 1994; Woodfire, Ceramic Art Gallery, Sydney, NSW, 1993
Collections: International Arrowmont Permanent Collection, Tennessee, USA; Tajimi City Collection, Mino, Japan; Art Gallery of Western Australia, Perth; Queensland Art Gallery, Brisbane; Numerous regional galleries

LEON SADUBIN
Thornleigh, New South Wales
Born: Mt Carmel, Israel, 1948; arrived in Australia, 1958
Studied: University of NSW, BA, 1969; University of NSW, Dip. Ed., 1970; University of NSW, Department of Industrial Arts, Craft and Design, 1969
Related Experience: Full-time Furniture Designer-Maker, 1977; Churchill Fellow, Furniture Study Tour, Denmark, Norway and Bavaria, 1982
Exhibitions: Numerous exhibitions; Member of Winslow Group, Exhibiting nationally at Kirribilli
Awards: Churchill Fellow, 1982
Collections: Powerhouse Museum, Sydney; New Parliament House, Canberra; Numerous commissions

BEATRICE SCHLABOWSKY
Melbourne, Victoria
Born: Lunen, West Germany, 1958; in Australia from 1960
Studied: RMIT, BA (Fine Art), Gold and Silversmithing, 1986; Adelaide College of Arts and Education, B.Ed. (Design), 1979
Related Experience: Master of Research, Gold and Silversmithing, RMIT, 1995; Founding Member of EGS, a contemporary metal production team, 1992
Awards: Personal Development Grant, 1993; Puszar Award for Excellence in Jewellery Design, 1985
Exhibitions: More than fifteen group shows
Collections: Powerhouse Museum, Sydney; Victoria State Collection; NSW State Craft Collection, Melbourne; RMIT

NALDA SEARLES
Midland, Western Australia
Born: Kalgoorlie, Western Australia, 1945
Studied: Curtin University of Technology, WA, Visual Arts, Painting as Major, 1991
Related Experience: Self-taught in fibre arts
Exhibitions: (Selected) 'Language of the Land: Learning Ngaanyatjarra', 1995; Longitudinal Project, Minya Kutjarra with Mary McClean, 1995; 'High Fibre Diet', 1994; 'Language of Form', 1993; 'Sticks and Stones' with Eileen Keys, 1989
Collections: Art Gallery of Western Australia, Perth; Edith Cowan University; Curtin University

KEIKO AMENOMORI SCHMEISSER
Canberra, Australian Capital Territory
Born: Japan, 1949; arrived in Australia, 1979
Studied: Degree in Industrial Design, Textiles, Academy for Fine Art Hamburg, Germany, 1979
Related Experience: (Commissions) Work Experience and Research in Textile Companies in Frankfurt, Marburg and Munich, 1977–78; Part-time Lecturer in Open Art Workshop, Australian National University, Canberra School of Art, 1985; New Parliament House, Canberra, Commission Work for The Members' and Guests' Dining Room and Reception Hall, 1988; Australian High Commissioner's Residence, Vanuatu, 1994; University of Canberra, Rug Design Commission for the Council Room, 1994
Awards: The Canberra Critics Circle Award, 1994
Exhibitions: (Selected Solo) Perc Tucker Regional Gallery Townsville, 1992; The Craft Council of Queensland Gallery, Brisbane, 1994; Toowoomba Regional Art Gallery, 1995; Goulburn Regional Art Gallery, 'Below the Surface', Touring Exhibition, 1996
Collections: Museum of Fine and Applied Art Hamburg, Germany, 1979; University of Southern Queensland, 1995

MITSUO SHOJI
Sydney, New South Wales
Born: Osaka, Japan, 1946; in Australia from 1977
Studied: Kyoto City University of Fine Arts, Kyoto, Japan, BA (Fine Art); MA (Fine Art)
Related Experience: Senior Lecturer, Sydney College of the Arts, University of Sydney
Awards: Purchasing Award, Faenza International Ceramics Exhibition, Faenza, Italy, 1982; Second National Ceramics Award, Premier, Award, ACT, 1988; Fletcher Challenge Ceramics Award, Premier, Award, Auckland, New Zealand, 1994; Member of International Academy of Ceramics
Exhibitions: More than thirty group shows and over forty solo shows
Collections: Faenza International Ceramics Museum, Faenza, Italy; International Ceramics Museum, Shigaraki, Japan; Museum of Decorative Arts, Prague, Czech Republic; Major Australian galleries

STEPHEN SKILLITZI
Adelaide, South Australia
Born: London, UK, 1947; in Australia from 1950
Studied: National Art School, Sydney, Ceramics Certificate; University of Massachusetts, USA, MA (Fine Art), 1970
Related Experience: First student of Dale Chihuly, USA, 1968; Established Glass Studio in USA, 1968–82; Considerable activity in glass art in Australia, Pioneer Glass Blower, 1969–75; Established Cosmos Glass with Karin Rumpf for tableware production, 1995
Awards: Craft Board Grants, 1971, 1974, 1975; Silver Award, Kristallnacht Project, USA, 1992
Exhibitions: Over twenty solo and over thirty group shows in Australia and overseas
Collections: Most state and regional Art Galleries in Australia; Glasmuseum, Ebeltoft, Denmark; USA art museums

PAMELA STADUS
Melbourne, Victoria
Born: Melbourne, 1953
Studied: Melbourne University, Painting and Design; Monash University, MA (Glass)
Related Experience: Lecturer in Glass at Monash University; Own studio and furnace; Fellowship at Creative Glass Center of America, New Jersey '93; Scholarships to Pilchuck Glass School, Seattle, USA, 1990, 1993
Exhibitions: (Selected) RFC Award, Sydney 1995; (Solo) Glass Artist's Gallery, Sydney, 1993
Collections: Monash University; Wagga Wagga City Art Gallery; Creative Glass Center of America, USA; Diamond Valley; City of Hamilton

RAY TAYLOR
Melbourne, Victoria
Born: Melbourne, 1944
Studied: Chisolm Institute of Technology, Graduate Diploma, Ceramic Design, 1982; Phillip Institute of Technology, Diploma of Fine Art, 1975
Awards: Royal Adelaide Show Craft Award; Award of Merit in Fletcher Brownbuilt Award, New Zealand; Eugene Kupsch Memorial Award for Ceramics, Victoria; Capricorn Open Competition and Exhibition Prize, Queensland; Box Hill Invitation Prize; Costain Coal Ceramic Award; Honorary Degree, Third World Triennial of Small Ceramics, Yugoslavia
Exhibitions: Twenty-nine one-man exhibitions, as well as a number of group shows in Australia and overseas since 1982
Collections: Represented in over forty-one public and private collections in Australia and Japan

THANCOUPIE
Weipa, North Queensland
Born: Weipa, North Queensland
Studied: East Sydney Technical College, Ceramics with Peter Rushforth
Exhibitions: Numerous solo and group shows since 1972 including: 'Delinquent Angels, Contemporary Australian Ceramics', Faenza, Italy, since 1972
Collections: Represented in all major art galleries in Australia; Numerous commissions

MARLENE THIELE
Adelaide, South Australia
Born: Adelaide, 1936
Studied: Certificate of Further Education, Art and Craft
Related Experience: Maori basket techniques with Tina Wirihana and Eddie Maxwell; WEA natural basketry course; Work in drawing, design, jewellery and sculpture; Experienced enameller
Awards: Dame Mary Durak Outback Award, 1990; National Crafts Acquisition Award, NT, 1990 and 1992
Exhibitions: Various group exhibitions throughout Australia

BLANCHE TILDEN
Hackett, Australian Capital Territory
Born: Kiama, NSW, 1968
Studied: Canberra School of Art, Australian National University, Graduate Diploma, Gold and Silversmithing, 1995; Sydney College of the Arts, BA (Visual), Glass, 1992; BA (Visual), two years completed, Glass and Jewellery, 1988–89
Awards: ACT Government Grant for Studio Equipment, 1994
Exhibitions: RFC Glass Prize Exhibition, Glass Artist's Gallery, Sydney, 1995; Directions — Jewellery, Crafts Council of the ACT and touring; Talentbörse, Handwerksmesse, Munich, Germany, 1993; Australian Wearable Glass, Asa Gallery, Tokyo, 1992; Glass Jewellery, Goldschmiedehaus, Hanau, Germany
Collections: National Gallery of Australia, Canberra; Wagga Wagga City Art Gallery

CATHERINE TRUMAN
Adelaide, South Australia
Born: Adelaide, 1957
Studied: Secondary Fine Art (SACAE), Diploma, B.Ed., 1975–78; School of Design, Ass. Dip. Jewellery/Metalsmithing, 1981–85
Related Experience: Working at Grey Street Workshops, 1985–95; Studied Netsuke Carving, Japan, 1990
Awards: Australia Council Multi–year Fellowship, 1995; Japan/South Australia Cultural Exchange, 1990
Exhibitions: (Selected Solo) 'Lifeboat', Craftspace, Sydney, 1992–94; Craftwest, Perth; Okayama, Japan; San Francisco, USA; Jam Factory Craft and Design Centre, Adelaide; 'Fish Carvings', Contemporary Jewellery Gallery, 1987; (Group) Vic Health

National Craft Award, National Gallery of Victoria, 1995; 'Family: Tradition and Diversity', National Museum, Jakarta, Indonesia, 1994; 'Australian Fashion: The Contemporary Art', Victoria and Albert Museum, London, Powerhouse Museum, Sydney, Tokyo, Japan, 1989–90
Collections: National Gallery of Australia, Canberra; Powerhouse Museum, Sydney; Art Gallery of South Australia, Adelaide

ELIZABETH TULIP
Sydney, New South Wales
Born: Australia, 1966
Studied: Accepted as a Licentiate of the British Society of Designer Craftsmen, 1994; Hereford College of Art and Design, England, HND, Blacksmithing and Design, 1993–94; Hereford College of Technology, England, Metalwork and Restoration Crafts Course, 1992–93; Sydney College of the Arts, BA (Visual), Sculpture Major, 1986–88
Exhibitions: (Solo) 'My Cup', Sydney, 1991; 'Fill', Gallery 228, Sydney, 1991; 'Nocturnes', Zitlip Gallery, Sydney, 1995; (Group) 'Graduate Diploma "Show"', Hereford College of Art and Design, England, 1994; 'A Constructivist Garden', Chelsea Flower Show, London, 1994; 'Fresh From the Forge', Hereford City Gallery, Hereford, 1993–94; 'Arousal', Alternative Arts Space, Central London, 1993; 'Real and Forged', Jam Factory Craft and Design Centre, Adelaide, 1992

PRUE VENABLES
Melbourne, Victoria
Born: Newcastle upon Tyne, England, 1954
Studied: Harrow College of Higher Education, Studio Pottery, London, 1981–83; RMIT, MA (Fine Art), Ceramics, 1991–95
Related Experience: Studio Assistant, London, 1977–86; Mouldmaking, Jigger/Jolley Courses, UK
Awards: (Selected) Windsor and Newton Art Prize, 1981–86; Crafts Council UK, Studio Grant; (Honourable Mentions) International Ceramics Competition, Mino, Japan, 1994–95; Second Prize, Austceram, Sydney; Australia Council, Project Grant; Premier Award, Fletcher Challenge Ceramics Award
Exhibitions: (Selected) Distelfink Gallery, Melbourne; Contemporary Applied Arts, London, 1984–95; Oriel 31 Gallery, Powys; Nottingham Castle Museum; 'Creative Eye', Crafts Council; 'The Harrow Connection'; 'Aspects', RMIT, Melbourne; Shepparton Art Gallery; Fletcher Challenge Ceramics Award; Fifteenth National Craft Acquisition Award, NT
Collections: Bathurst Art Gallery; Deakin University; Fletcher Challenge Collection; Nillumbik Shire Council; RMIT; Shepparton Art Gallery; Tasmanian Museum and Art Gallery

BETTINA VISENTIN
Sydney, New South Wales
Born: Adelaide, 1965
Studied: University of South Australia, BA (Visual Arts)
Related Experience: Summer Course, Pilchuck Glass School, Seattle, USA, 1995; Study at Haystack Mountain School of Crafts, Maine, USA with Lino Tagliapietra and Dan Daily, 1995; Traineeship at the Jam Factory Craft and Design Centre, Adelaide, 1988–89; Worked for two years at Sunbeam Glassworks, Pty Ltd, Auckland, New Zealand
Awards: Mary B Bishop/Francis S Merritt Scholarship Fund, Maine, USA
Exhibitions: (Selected) 'Not Just One of a Kind', Glass Artist Gallery, Sydney, 1995; 'Something Simply Stunning', Beaver Gallery, Canberra, 1994; 'Recent Works by Bettina', North Shore Fine Art, Sydney; 'Dancing with Fire', The Vault Design Gallery, Auckland, 1993; Group Exhibition, Masterworks Gallery, Auckland, 1991; Sculpture and Glass, Italian Festival, Adelaide, 1990

DAVID WALKER
Perth, Western Australia
Born: Manchester, UK, 1941; in Australia from 1964
Studied: Manchester Regional College of Art, 1958–63; Currently Associate Professor, Jewellery and Three-dimensional Design, Coordinator of Graduate Studies, School of Art, Curtin University of Technology, WA
Related Experience: Asialink Artist-in-residence, Silapakorn University, Thailand, 1995–96; Jeweller, Writer, Designer; Editor of LEMEL, journal of the Jewellers and Metalsmiths Group of Australia; Chair, Editorial Advisory Committee for Craftwest, journal of Crafts Council of Western Australia, (CCWA)
Awards: Life Member of CCWA, 1994; Honorary Fellow of the CCWA, 1994; Visiting International Professor, School of Art, San Diego State University, California, USA, 1994; Artist-in-residence in

the Australia Council's Overseas Studio, Besozzo, Italy, 1992–93
Exhibitions: Exhibited widely in solo and group exhibitions throughout Australia and internationally, most recently in USA, Europe, Japan, Korea and Indonesia
Collections: Represented in national collections throughout Australia; Museum of Art, Montreal, Canada; The Helen Drutt International Collection, USA

GERRY WEDD
Adelaide, South Australia
Born: Adelaide, 1957
Studied: Kingston TAFE College, Certificate Course, Jewellery, 1976–79; SACAE, Bachelor of Design, (Ceramics), 1984–86
Related Experience: Study trip to Italy, 1995; Travel/study through Europe and Mexico, 1994; Founder of Jamboree Clay Workshop, 1991; Artist-in-residence, SACAE Ceramics Department
Awards: Inglewood Ceramics Award, 1990; Potters Guild Student Award, 1986; Walkers Award (Fourth Place)
Exhibitions: (Selected) 'Art Irritates Life', Mambo Exhibition, Melbourne, 1995; The South Australian Ceramics Award Exhibition, SA, 1994; 'The Emperors New Clothes', Ray Hughes Gallery, NSW, 1993; 'Lie of the Land (Fabric)', Powerhouse Museum, Sydney, 1991; 'An Australian Willow Pattern', Jam Factory Craft and Design Centre, Adelaide; 'Australian Fashion: The Contemporary Art', Victoria and Albert Museum, London, Powerhouse Museum, Sydney, Japan and Korea, 1989
Collections: Queensland University Gallery; Craft Council of Alice Springs; Powerhouse Museum, Sydney

STEVE WEIS
Toowoomba, Queensland
Born: Toowoomba, 1952
Studied: Darling Downs Institute of Advanced Education, Creative Arts, Sculpture, 1974–75
Related Experience: Adult Education Classes and private tuition with Bill Spencer at 'The Smithy', Montville, Queensland, 1979; Foreman to Schappi Metalcraft, Sydney, 1985; Churchill Fellowship Study Tour, various studios in USA, including California, New York, and in Western Australia, 1987; Director, Crafts Council of Australia, 1990–91
Awards: (Selected) Finalist, NZI Small Business Award, 1994; High Commendation, Society of Manufacturing Engineers, Small Business Awards, 1993
Exhibitions: Various solo and group shows
Collections: Numerous commissions

PENNY CAREY WELLS
Kingston Beach, Tasmania
Born: Hobart, Tasmania, 1950
Studied: Tasmanian School of Art, University of Tasmania, 1970
Related Experience: Currently employed as Part-time Lecturer and Technician in Papermaking, School of Art, University of Tasmania; Working with handmade paper as an art material, since 1980; Studied and lectured in America, UK, Japan, The Philippines and Europe; Head of Organising Committee of First National Papermaking Conference, Hobart, 1987
Grants: Received from Arts Tasmania, Craft Australia, Japan/Australia Foundation
Exhibitions: Participated in various solo and group shows within Australia and overseas
Collections: University of Tasmania; TAFE College Toowoomba, Queensland; Central Washington University, USA

MARGARET WEST
Sydney, New South Wales
Born: Melbourne, 1936
Studied: MSC, Diploma of Education, 1977; RMIT, Graduate Diploma of Art, 1976; Diploma of Art, 1975; Certificate of Art, 1954–55
Related Experience: Various visiting lectureships
Exhibitions: Ten solo and over twenty-five group shows, including Vic Health National Craft Award; National Gallery of Victoria, Melbourne, 1995
Collections: Represented in all major state art galleries

KEVIN WHITE
Melbourne, Victoria
Born: Reading, England, 1954
Studied: Leeds Polytechnic BA Hons, 1974–77; Kyoto City University of Fine Arts, Japan, 1979–80; Royal College of Art, London, 1983–85
Related Experience: Freelance work in studio of Satoshi Sato, Kyoto, Japan, 1980–83; Currently Course Coordinator, Department

of Fine Arts, Ceramics, RMIT
Awards: (Selected) Fifteenth National Craft Acquisition Award, Art Gallery Northern Territory, 1995; Newcastle Art Gallery, Ceramic Purchase Award, 1995; Colin and Cecily Rigg Craft Award, National Gallery of Victoria; Fletcher Challenge Ceramics Award, NZ, 1993
Exhibitions: (Selected Solo) Macquarie Galleries, Sydney, 1989 and 1991; Craft Victoria, Melbourne, 1994; Beaver Galleries, Canberra, 1995
Collections: Powerhouse Museum, Sydney; Shepparton Art Gallery, Victoria; Gifu Prefectural Ceramic Museum, Japan

MAUREEN WILLIAMS
Melbourne, Victoria
Born: Port Pirie, South Australia, 1952
Studied: Chisholm Institute of Technology
Related Experience: Teaching Assistant, Pilchuck Glass School, Seattle, USA, 1987
Awards: Mornington Peninsula Craft Event, Glass Award
Exhibitions: 'SOFA', Miami, USA, 1995; 'Symmetry, Crafts Meet Kindred Trades and Professions', Ian Potter Gallery, Melbourne, Touring Exhibition, 1994–95; 'Australia Revisited — Celebrating 20 Years of Studio Glass', Meat Market Craft Centre, Melbourne, 1994; 'Studio Glass Design', Wagga Wagga City Art Gallery, 1992–93; Jahresmesse Kunsthandwerk, Museum Für Kunst and Gewerbe, Hamburg, Germany, 1992; Tenth Australian Glass Triennial, Wagga Wagga City Art Gallery, 1991; 'Australian Crafts, 1990', Meat Market Craft Centre, Melbourne, 1990
Collections: Art Gallery of Queensland, Diamond Valley; Art Bank, Sydney

LIZ WILLIAMSON
Sydney, New South Wales
Born: Victoria, 1949
Studied: RMIT, BA (Textile Design), 1981–83
Related Experience: Weave Design Studio, NSW, 1985–94; Lecturer, Woven Textile Design, Sydney College of the Arts, 1986–87; Designer, Arkitex Fabrics, Sydney, 1988–89; Lecturer, Woven Textile Design, Strathfield College of TAFE, Sydney, 1989; Design Consultant, Living Fabrics, Sydney, 1991–92; Lecturer, Textiles Workshop, Canberra School of Art, 1991–95; Acting Head of Workshop 1992–95; Lecturer, University of NSW, 1995; Lecturer, Art Theory Workshop, CSA, 1995; Visiting Lecturer at various tertiary institutions, 1989–95; Conducted numerous workshops in woven textiles
Awards: Hoechst National Textile Award, 1984; Norwellan Upholstery Designer Award, 1988; Visual Arts and Crafts Board, Creative Development Project Grant, 1993–94; Curator, 'Directions — Contemporary Cloth', Crafts Council of the ACT, Canberra, 1995; VACB Quick Response Grant to attend opening and artist seminars in association with the Eighth Triennial of Tapestry, Lodz, Poland, 1995; VACB grants in 1985, 1987, 1993–94, 1995
Exhibitions: (Numerous solo and group shows including): 'Crossing Borders', Touring USA, 1994–95 ; 'The Art of the Object', Contemporary Craft from Australia touring South America; 'Interior', National Museum of Indonesia, Jakarta, Indonesia; 'Eleventh Tamworth Fibre/Textile Biennial Exhibition', Tamworth City Art Gallery, NSW; Eighth International Triennial of Tapestry, Central Museum of Textiles, Lodz, Poland, 1995; Vic Health National Craft Award, National Gallery of Victoria, Melbourne
Collections: In all major state art galleries as well as in regional art galleries in Australia

WENDY WOOD
Darwin, Northern Territory
Born: Cairns, Queensland, 1970
Studied: Canberra School of Art, Australian National University, BA (Visual), 1993
Related Experience: Part-time tutor, Ceramics Workshop, NTU, Darwin, 1996; Artist-in-residence, Ceramics Workshop, NTU, Darwin, 1995–96; Tutor in ceramics, Crafts Council of NT, 1994–95; Artist-in-residence, Canberra Church of England Girls Grammar School, 1994
Awards: (Selected) Canberra School of Art, Emerging Artist Support Scheme, 1993; Joy Carrodus Prize for Art, 1988
Exhibitions: Four solo and seven group shows in Australia
Collections: Museum and Art Gallery of Northern Territory, Darwin; EASS Loan Collection

DAVID WRIGHT
Melbourne, Victoria
Born: Melbourne, 1948
Studied: University of Melbourne, B.Arch., 1972

Related Experience: From 1960s worked in glass as commissioned artist and on work for exhibition; Taught Master Classes at Pilchuck Glass School, Seattle, USA
Exhibitions: Over twenty solo and group shows in Australia and overseas, including: 'World Glass Now', Hokkaido Museum of Modern Art, Japan, 1994
Collections: (Selected) Over twenty-eight major commissions including New Parliament House, Canberra; Victorian Contemporary Craft Collection, Melbourne; Meat Market Craft Centre, Melbourne; National Gallery of Australia, Canberra; Powerhouse Museum, Sydney

ROBERT WYNNE
Manly, New South Wales
Born: Yarram, Victoria, 1959
Studied: Monash University, Australian Diploma of Visual Arts, 1977–79; Graduate Diploma of Visual Arts, 1981; California State University, California, MA, 1982–83,
Related Experience: Employment in Budgeree Glass, 1979–81; Jody Fine Glass Studio, California, 1982
Awards: (Selected) California State Fair, Hon Mentions, 1982 and 1983; Sydney Royal Agricultural Show, First Prize, 1988; Glass Australia '88, Meat Market Craft Centre, Melbourne, Highly Commended
Exhibitions: Over thirty-four solo and group shows in Australia and overseas.
Collections: (Selected) Victorian State Craft Collection, Melbourne; Meat Market Craft Centre, Melbourne; La Trobe Regional Arts Centre, Victoria; Queensland National Gallery, Brisbane; Wagga Wagga City Art Gallery; New Parliament House, Canberra; Glasmuseum, Ebeltoft, Denmark

KLAUS ZIMMER
Melbourne, Victoria
Born: Berlin, Germany, 1928
Studied: Monash University, MA, 1989; RMIT, 1961–71; Meisterschule Fuer Das Kunsthandwer, Berlin, Painting, Printmaking and Graphic Design, 1947–52;
Related Experience: Established glass studies in Chisholm (now Monash University), 1974; Studied glass design with Patrick Reyntiens, Ludwig Schaffrate in the studios of Dr H Oidtmann, England and Germany, 1975–79; Curated exhibition of forty-five Australian and New Zealand glass artists, 1984–86; Founded Australia Studios (1983) for twenty architectural commissions including New Parliament House, Canberra, 1987–88; St Michael's, Collins Street, Melbourne, 1988; Queen's College, University of Melbourne, 1989; Royal Melbourne Hospital, 1995
Awards: Fellow, British Society of Master Glass Painters, 1990
Exhibitions: From 1963 created two hundred and eight autonomous glass panels for more than seventy solo and group exhibitions in Australia and abroad
Collections: National Gallery of Victoria, Melbourne; Powerhouse Museum, Sydney; Landesmuseum, Darmstadt; Museum Für Kunst and Gewerbe, Hamburg; Museum for Contemporary Stained Glass, Langen, Germany; Museum for Contemporary International Glass Art, Ebeltoft, Denmark

SELECT BIBLIOGRAPHY

The following selected bibliography lists books published over the past decade or so in Australia and overseas for further reading on both the contemporary and historic crafts

Patricia Anderson, *Contemporary Jewellery — The Australian Experience, 1977–1987*, Millennium, Sydney, 1988

Tim Andrews, *Raku: A Review of Contemporary Works*, Craftsman House, Sydney, A & C Black, London, 1994

Michael Bogle and Peta Landman, *Modern Australian Furniture*, Craftsman House, Sydney, 1989

Garth Clark, *American Ceramics: 1876 to the Present*, Abbeville Press, New York, 1987

Grace Cochrane, *The Crafts Movement in Australia*, New South Wales University Press, Sydney, 1992

Peter Dormer, *The New Ceramics: Trends and Traditions*, Thames and Hudson, London, 1995

Peter Dormer, *The Art of the Maker*, Thames and Hudson, London, 1994

Peter Dormer and Ralph Turner, *The New Jewellery: Trends and Traditions*, Thames and Hudson, London, 1994

Helen Drutt English, *Jewellery of Our Time: Art, Ornament and Obsession*, Thames and Hudson, London, 1995

Susanne Frantz, *Contemporary Glass: A World Survey from the Corning Museum of Glass*, Harry Abrams, New York, 1989

Noris Ioannou, *Ceramics In South Australia 1836–1986: From Folk to Studio Pottery*, Adelaide, Wakefield Press, 1986

Noris Ioannou, *The Culture Brokers: Towards a Redefinition of Australian Contemporary Craft*, State Publishing, Adelaide, 1989

Noris Ioannou, *Craft in Society: An Anthology of Perspectives*, Fremantle Arts Centre Press, Perth, 1992

Noris Ioannou, *The Barossa Folk: Germanic Furniture and Craft Traditions in Australia*, Craftsman House, Sydney, 1995

Noris Ioannou, *Australian Studio Glass: The Movement, its Makers and their Art*, G+B Arts International, Craftsman House, Sydney, 1995

Jan Irvine, *Australian Quilts: The People and their Art*, Simon and Schuster, Sydney, 1989

Jennifer Isaacs, *The Gentle Arts: 200 years of Women's Domestic and Decorative Arts*, Landsdowne Press, Sydney, 1987

Dan Klein, *Glass: A Contemporary Art*, Collins, London, 1989

Peter Lane, *Contemporary Porcelain*, Craftsman House, Sydney, A & C Black, London, 1995

Janet Mansfield, *Saltglaze Ceramics: An International Perspective*, Craftsman House, Sydney, 1991

Janet Mansfield, *Contemporary Ceramic Art in Australia and New Zealand*, Craftsman House, Sydney, 1995

Martina Margetts, *International Crafts*, Thames and Hudson, London, 1991

Terry Martin, *Wood Dreaming: The Spirit of Australia Captured in Woodturning*, Angus & Robertson, Sydney, 1996

Christopher Menz, *Australian Decorative Arts 1820s–1990s: Art Gallery of South Australia*, Art Gallery of South Australia, 1996

Anne Schofield and Kevin Fahy, *Australian Jewellery: 19th and 20th Century*, David Ell Press, Sydney, 1990

Beverley Sherry, *Australia's Historic Stained Glass*, Murray Child, Sydney, 1991

Peter Timms, *Australian Studio Pottery and China Painting*, Oxford University Press, Melbourne, 1986

Jenny Zimmer, *Stained Glass in Australia*, Oxford University Press, Melbourne, 1984

INDEX